Jewish Belief and Practice
in Nineteenth Century America

Jewish Belief and Practice in Nineteenth Century America

*Seminal Essays by Outstanding
Pulpit Rabbis of the Era*

Edited by ELLIOT B. GERTEL

McFarland & Company, Inc., Publishers
Jefferson, North Carolina, and London

Library of Congress Cataloguing-in-Publication Data

Jewish belief and practice in nineteenth century America : seminal
essays by outstanding pulpit rabbis of the era / edited by Elliot B.
Gertel.

     p.   cm.
   Includes index.

   ISBN 0-7864-2524-5 (softcover : 50# alkaline paper)

   1. Judaism — Works to 1900.   2. God (Judaism)   3. Judaism
and science.   4. Bible, O.T.— Criticism, interpretation, etc.
I. Gertel, Elliot.
BM42.J46   2006
296.0973 — dc22   2006006089

British Library cataloguing data are available

Cover: Photo © 2006 Artville, Hebrew text © 2006 Photospin.

Manufactured in the United States of America

McFarland & Company, Inc., Publishers
  Box 611, Jefferson, North Carolina 28640
   www.mcfarlandpub.com

Acknowledgments

With the publication of this book, long delayed by other duties and projects, I recall with gratitude those who have encouraged me in my study of American Jewish history, particularly of the American rabbinate and the development of Jewish religious thought. I cherish recollections of conversations in the seminary library and cafeteria with Rabbi Isidore S. Meyer, a pioneer in these fields, a leader of the American Jewish Historical Society, and an editor of its journal. Rabbi Samuel H. Dresner, Dr. Shimon Bakon, Archie and Grace Savet, Dr. Meyer Ezrin, Rabbi Herman E. Snyder, Rabbi Jacob Freedman, Rabbi Israel H. Levinthal, Professor Seymour Siegel, Professor Fritz Rothschild, Dr. Alex Tobias, Mrs. Eugenie Gerstel, Rabbi William E. Kaufman, Rabbi Wolfe Kelman, Rabbi David W. Silverman and Rabbi Jerome Gurland encouraged me in my studies and writings on these themes in earliest years, as did Dr. Simon Greenberg, Dr. Max Kadushin, and Dr. Robert Goldy. Rabbi Gurland introduced me to his mentor, Rabbi William Braude, who was also a great inspiration and encouragement.

In more recent years, Drs. Jacob R. Marcus, Michael N. Dobkowski, Marc Lee Raphael, Rabbi Shamai Kanter, Pamela Nadell and Gary P. Zola have encouraged my interest in American Jewish history by soliciting articles in that field from me. I am also grateful to Kevin Proffitt, Fannie Zelcer, Gail Naron Chalew, and Dr. Abraham J. Peck for their help and encouragement. My involvement with the Jewish Historical Society of New Haven was an inspiration, and I especially thank Harvey N. Ladin, Barry E. Herman, Werner S. Hirsch, Judith A. Schiff, and Joel A. Wasserman for their encouragement.

In Chicago, Walter Roth, Burt Robin, Norman Schwartz, and Irving Cutler of the Chicago Jewish Historical Society have urged me to write and to speak about local history. Charles B. Bernstein, master genealogist, one of the twelve founders of the American Jewish Genealogical Society and a founder and first president of the Chicago

Jewish Historical Society, has been especially encouraging of my work in American Jewish history and most helpful with this book. Rabbis Ralph Simon, Arnold Wolf and Mordecai Simon have also been most encouraging in Chicago, as have Rabbi Laurence Edwards and Susan Boone. I have also benefited from Joseph Schiff's insights into the history of the New York Jewish community.

I shall always owe a debt of gratitude to Dr. Nathan A. Kaganoff, of blessed memory, associate editor, and Dr. Marc Lee Raphael, editor, of *American Jewish History*. In the early 1980s, they asked me to review several congregational histories for that organization's journal, thus making me a pioneer in the analysis of such literature and "professionalizing" my interest in American Jewish history.

I am grateful to the members and staff of Congregation Rodfei Zedek in Chicago and of Congregation Beth El-Keser Israel in New Haven who have encouraged my writings and research and my experimentation with programs, lectures and classes based on themes and personalities found in this volume. I am especially indebted to Harold Graham, of blessed memory, and to Donna Graham, for arranging for my use of the Regenstein Library at the University of Chicago, and to the Sterling Library of Yale University and the Yale Divinity Library for their generous open door policies regarding local clergy during my years in New Haven (1982–1988). I have also benefited from the kindness of the JKM Library at Lutheran School of Theology and McCormick Theological Seminary in Chicago. Over the past year or so, Eleanor Yadin of the New York Public Library's Dorot Jewish Division has been most helpful in checking and copying material for me.

I thank Rabbi Elliot Stevens of the Central Conference of American Rabbis for permission to reprint material in my introduction that I first published in the *C.C.A.R. Journal* (for a while called *The Journal of Reform Judaism*), and to Joellyn Rich Cattell, Lee Weingarten Goldsmith, Scott Kalisch and John Stowell for their gracious cooperation. Special accolades to Pamela Spitzner for her care and skill in the typing of the introduction and the various selections onto computer diskettes.

I am grateful for the encouragement and support of my parents, William and Sylvia Gertel, and of my brother and sister-in-law, Dr. Theodore and Joan Gertel. This book is dedicated to Ted and Joan, who are knowledgeable and dedicated American Jews, and to their children, Alex, Aaron, Jason and Diana, who are following in their parents' footsteps.

Contents

Preface

This anthology is an acknowledgment of the inspiration, instruction and initiation into theological reflection, preaching and religious polemics that I derived, since undergraduate and graduate school days at the Jewish Theological Seminary, from reading nineteenth century Jewish pulpit thinkers. I am indebted to these teachers to whom I was drawn for reasons I cannot explain, ever since I read, in high school, *The Beloved Rabbi*, a biography of Rabbi Henry Berkowitz I found on my maternal grandparents' shelves, and Moshe Davis's volume on *The Emergence of Conservative Judaism*. These books prodded me to ransack the library of the Jewish Theological Seminary, and then the libraries of Union Theological Seminary, Columbia University and the New York Public Library, for volumes on similar themes. It was in those days that I collected much of the material cited and reproduced here.

For over thirty years, the rabbis presented in this book have stimulated and impressed me, even, or especially, when I disagreed with them strongly. I have always been heartened by their thoughtfulness, sense of mission and nobility of purpose, and I know that new generations of readers will benefit from the same blessings in these writers.

In collecting and editing the essays anthologized here, I have been most careful to reproduce exactly the spellings and punctuations of the originally published versions. My own emendations or questions regarding wording, or footnotes added to the text, are found in brackets.

Several of the essays originally contained passages in the Hebrew alphabet. In those instances, I have transliterated the passages according to generally accepted contemporary usages, and have eliminated the lengthier Hebrew passages in favor of the exact English translations already provided by the authors or their original editors.

1

Notes to the introduction are numbered and appear at the end of the introduction. Notes on the text itself are signaled by asterisks and appear as footnotes. In the text, my own notes are in brackets. Notes not in brackets are original to the text edition being reproduced.

Introduction

The outstanding thinkers of nineteenth century American Jewry were all pulpit rabbis. There were, of course, no chairs of Judaica for them, and they all managed admirably to lead in the building of congregations that, in many instances, feel their influence until this very day.

It is necessary to define exactly what we mean by "American" and by "thinker." In the former category, I would include anyone in the United States whose best work was either delivered orally or written in English, or was translated into English within years or decades after it was composed — and within the nineteenth century. The German-American sermon is a genre unto itself, and does not belong to our investigation.[1] The individuals whom we would describe as "American" were, without exception, immigrants, but they sensed the need to make their best statements in English. In the case of Liebman Adler, those statements were translated posthumously. These individuals became proud citizens of the United States. They were also most sensitive to the meaning of American liberty and to the currents of American thought, and were honored as scholars and as spokesmen for the Jewish people in the learned circles of their general communities.

By "thinkers," I mean those individuals who dealt with theological issues such as God, providence, revelation, *halakhah* (Jewish Law), evolution, Biblical criticism, and science — in sum, with matters of belief and of practice. Some individuals, like Alexander Kohut, were devoted primarily to philology, to textual scholarship. I include Kohut here because he made significant theological statements. I do not, however, include men like Marcus Jastrow (1829–1903) and Benjamin Szold (1829–1902), who made significant contributions, respectively, in Talmudic and Biblical philology, but who, although outstanding rabbis and scholars, did not leave theological essays of the caliber of the others discussed here. Likewise, I have not included those who devoted their ener-

3

gies to the delineation of classical Jewish theology as they understood it. I refer specifically to Kaufmann Kohler (1843–1926), the outstanding Reform scholar, whose classic work, *Jewish Theology, Systematically and Historically Considered*,[2] is essentially a Reform commentary on classic Rabbinic thought, and represents the culmination of American Reform ideology of the nineteenth century. Reform and Orthodox ideology do not interest us here as much as individuals' encounters with challenges to religious faith. The documents that resulted reflect denominational stances, to be sure, but are, more importantly, intelligent *personal* statements which take cognizance of external trends of thought and yet demonstrate deep faith and courage of conviction.

Not all of the thinkers to be examined here were original. Some, like Joseph Krauskopf, summarize, digest and affirm certain central tenets of scientific inquiry of the time. The talented pulpit thinker can legitimately be a popularizer who presents difficult ideas in a manner that is engaging and even entertaining. As long as these ideas are synthesized and interpreted by an individual who affirms the Jewish tradition and is committed to his fellow Jews, we witness a legitimate mode of theological discourse.[3]

In the case of each of the thinkers to be discussed here, it turned out that there was *one* essay or discourse that embodied that individual's *Weltanschauung* and style. Indeed, it is almost uncanny the way one essay by each stood out above the others, and seemed to embody everything else that individual said. Perhaps this is the unique legacy of an age in which traditionalist and reformer alike felt that they had to be absolutely consistent in all that they said, and regarded every discourse as an opportunity to restate one's religious outlook. In a few instances, I have included other essays by individual thinkers because they enhance appreciation of the *Weltanschauung*, creativity and breadth of interests in an individual's life and work.

These essays are, for the most part, not statements of belief per se, but the declarations made about various theological and personal issues do mirror the soul of the individual. Though we shall glance at each individual's life and works, it is the representative essay that will concern us most. This introductory survey, like the sequence of the essays anthologized here, will follow the order in which the representative essays were first delivered orally or published. Where other essays by the same author are added, they will be in chronological order, to the extent that it could be determined.

Max Lilienthal

Rabbi Max Lilienthal[4] (b. 1815, Munich, Bavaria; d. 1882, Cincinnati, Ohio) was *the* pioneer of American Reform Judaism. In 1837, he received his Ph.D. from the University of Munich; he wrote on Alexandrian Jewish religious philosophy. He studied at the yeshiva in Furth, and received ordination from Rabbi Hirsch Aub of Munich, to whom he dedicated his doctoral dissertation. Lilienthal always wanted to be a rabbi, but when he was offered an ambassadorship by the government, he seriously considered taking it, since his family had lost many valuable items in a fire. He turned it down, however, when he learned that conversion to Christianity was a prerequisite.

Shortly after receiving his doctorate, Lilienthal was recommended to Russia by Rabbi Ludwig Philipson as an individual eminently qualified to reform its Jewish schools. (Since 1828, the czarist government had ordered that Jewish schools be organized along modern lines, and that, after 1833, all teachers be graduates of seminaries recognized by the government.) Needless to say, the pietists opposed such changes on the grounds that they might lead to assimilation. Lilienthal therefore had a terrible reputation among the orthodox Jews of Europe, which persists in certain quarters of America and Israel until this very day. His biographer, David Philipson, maintains that this bad reputation was undeserved, that if someone had to do the unpopular job in Russia, it is better that it was someone with Lilienthal's scholarship, dedication to Judaism, and love of the Jewish people. Philipson, a radical Reform rabbi, a disciple of Lilienthal, and Lilienthal's successor in a Cincinnati pulpit, had his biases as well, but makes a strong case for Lilienthal's good intentions.[5]

Lilienthal became superintendent of the school in Riga in 1840 and was a preacher in the local congregation. According to Philipson, he got along well with the older rabbinate and with the Russian *maskilim* (secular "enlighteners"). The czar presented Lilienthal with a diamond ring as a token of his admiration, but, Philipson declares, it became apparent to Lilienthal that the Russian government was deceiving him, and that Jews were either hounded to convert or were stricken with various edicts, such as the ghettoizing Pale of Settlement decree of 1843.

The full extent of Lilienthal's collusion with the Russian government has yet to be studied. In 1845, he decided to emigrate to the United

States, and was elected rabbi of Congregation Anshe Chesed,[6] Rodeph
Shalom and Shaarey Hashamayim in New York City.[7] In his early American career, he tended to side with modern orthodoxy, but became convinced that the "demands" of the American environment called for a
more reformed Judaism. He dedicated synagogues throughout the
Northeast. In October 1846, he established the first rabbinical organization in the United States. The following spring, he initiated the first
Jewish confirmation service in the United States.

In the 1850s, Lilienthal left his New York position in three congregations to found a day school in Cincinnati, the "Hebrew Union
School," which attracted boys from all over the country, including boys
from that city. The parents of the latter urged Lilienthal to become the
rabbi of the Bene Israel Congregation in Cincinnati. He accepted the
position in 1855 and remained there until his death. He introduced
minor reforms at first, and became more radical as the years progressed.
Angry traditionalist members left Bene Israel to form Shearith Israel
Congregation in the 1860s. In 1869, the famous Mound Street Temple[8]
of Cincinnati was built through his efforts.

Lilienthal participated in various efforts to arrange national rabbinical conferences representing all points of view in American
Judaism. He was particularly concerned that the Reform rabbinate show
unity. Hence, he helped Isaac Mayer Wise to found the Union of American Hebrew Congregations in 1873. In 1874, he established the *Sabbath Visitor*, the first journal for Jewish children in America. One of
the founders of the Hebrew Union College (established 1875) together
with Isaac Mayer Wise (see below), Lilienthal taught homiletics there
during the early years.

Isaac Mayer Wise attributed the decline of anti-Jewish prejudice
in Cincinnati to Dr. Lilienthal, who was always active in various civic
groups, including the Board of Education. Lilienthal's preaching and
writing were characterized by a strong Americanism. He advocated
total separation of church and state, especially in the face of various
movements in the 1870s to evangelize America. He was also a leader in
special action for the rights of Jews throughout the United States and
Europe.

The essay most characteristic of Lilienthal's work — the ideologi-
cal reform of Judaism — is, without doubt, "Rabbinical Codices, or the
Shulchan Aruch," which is part of his "Letters on Reform Judaism
Addressed to the Rev. I. Leeser," the leading partisan of traditionalist

Judaism in nineteenth-century America. This particular letter is dated "Cincinnati, Dec. 26, 1856."[9] It is what may now be regarded as a typical nineteenth-century Reform polemic, but at the time its arguments were fresh and not at all clichéd, and grew out of Lilienthal's own rich experience with classical Jewish learning and modern Jewish life.

Lilienthal states the widespread Reform premise of his day that the "spirit of the age" challenges the notion of "immediate trust in any authority whatever." Yet he also invokes the equally established Reform principle that evidence of historical development is to be found in the traditional authorities themselves. The authorities, Lilienthal points out, are also not universally accepted and not pristine. The *Shulchan Aruch* was not adopted "in toto" by "all the Jews throughout all centuries," and it was subject to "additions and accretions" that were "imported" from local "manners and customs" long after Talmudic law.

Lilienthal shows how the *Shulchan Aruch* "complicates" simple biblical and Rabbinic intents in matters of the divorce, the second day of Festivals, and the reading of the Torah. Interestingly, he concludes that attention to the "spirit of the age," which denies ancient authority, restores that very authority by enabling moderns to make decisions about religious practice. Since traditionally decisions in Jewish Law were left to the scholars of every generation who generally *added* to the Law, and since modern scholars, who wish to abolish later "accretions," believe that they should not be intimidated by past authorities, no matter how great, it follows that modern scholars have every right to make deletions, and are actually fulfilling their obligation to tradition by returning to the basics.

This ingenious argumentation became the battle cry of nineteenth-century American Reform Judaism. Lilienthal did not deal with the claims of the classical tradition that there were core legal categories for every generation and a continuity in legislative method that somehow united the Bible and Talmud and the *Shulchan Aruch*. This may be regarded as a failure to confront Jewish orthodoxy from within its own strictures, and, consequently, as a failure to legitimize Reform from within the classical tradition. Yet the "spirit of the age" was, to Lilienthal's generation, enough of a justification for reform, even though it had become, a century later, a rather nebulous and untrustworthy criterion for theologies of the role of Jewish Law within Reform Judaism itself.

JAMES K. GUTHEIM

Rabbi James Koppel Gutheim[10] (b. Westphalia, Germany, 1817, d. New Orleans, Louisiana, 1886) was an eloquent and moving preacher, and was therefore in much demand for the dedication of synagogues, funeral orations and other milestone events. Although largely self-educated, he did attend the Teachers Institute at Munster. In 1843, he came to the United States, and he made his living in private business until 1846, when he became the rabbi of B'nai Yeshurun Congregation in Cincinnati. In 1849, he assumed the spiritual leadership of Shaare Chesed Congregation in New Orleans, Louisiana. Six years later he became *hazzan* of the Sephardic congregation, Nefutzoth Yehudah, in the same city. During the Civil War, he was a staunch supporter of the Confederacy (a rarity among American rabbis). In 1862, he went to Montgomery, Alabama, and Columbus, Georgia, to flee the Union troops; he returned to New Orleans after the Civil War.

In 1868, Gutheim was called to Temple Emanu-El in New York, where he distinguished himself as an orator. In 1872 he returned to New Orleans to become the first rabbi of the newly founded Sinai Temple. He became a leader in American Reform and was a friend and supporter of Isaac Mayer Wise. He was also active in the civic affairs of New Orleans. Among his writings are most of the English hymns for the Merzbacher prayer book known as *The Temple Pulpit* (1872), and a translation of the fourth German volume of Graetz's *History of the Jews* (1873).

Most representative of Gutheim's personal approach to theology is the third of four lectures on "The Spirit of God in Man," delivered at Temple Emanu-El in New York on March 30, 1872.[11] The lecture reveals Gutheim's psychological approach to religion, reminiscent of the medieval pietistic tracts of Bachya ibn Pakudah and others, with their roots in the exhortations of biblical wisdom literature.[12] Gutheim's theory is that every human being is endowed with the spirit of God, which one must heed in order to overcome the "spirit of selfishness." Gutheim asserts that "only those deeds, which are devoid of selfish motives and ends are emanations of the spirit of God within us, are entitled to be characterized as good and noble." (Interestingly, this declaration seems somewhat closer to the Christian view that only Divine grace makes for good and noble deeds, than to the Rabbinic teaching that good and noble acts are in and of themselves meritorious even if one's intentions are not perfect.)

According to Gutheim, God's spirit is "active, though in limited degree and in isolated instances, at all times and in every place." Judaism, which opposes pessimism and original sin, believes in the "God-like character of the human soul." Because the human soul is "God-like," we are "justified in assuming, that the spirit of God is revealed and is manifested through man, just as much in our day, as at any previous period of history."

The real spirit of wisdom is benevolence, not merely "worldly prudence." Gutheim elaborates: "The prudent man may be just and moral, and yet far from being benevolent and religious." True justice is more than "petty honesty"; it is "*impartial, diffusive benevolence*" (italics in the original). It is precisely the self-interest through which the spirit of God is banished that is responsible for corruption of personal lives and of national institutions. "True religion," Gutheim concludes, "forbids us, to abuse any circumstance, which puts our neighbor in our power, or to extort his consent to injurious measures, or to reduce him to the necessity of sacrificing his property, by threatening him with evils, to which we are able to expose him. It recommends the weak and poor to our protection."

Though, by modern standards, Gutheim's psychology may seem naïve and simplistic, his religious sentiments remain noble, impressive and moving. Most noteworthy is that he restates guiding principles and assumptions of classical *halakhah* (Jewish Law), particularly property laws and the concept of *lifnim mi-shurat ha-din* (the obligation to go beyond the letter of the law), and attributes them to this "spirit of God in man" as a confirmation of the old Scriptures.

ISIDOR KALISCH

Rabbi Isidor Kalisch[13] (b. Krotoschin, Prussia, 1816, d. Newark, New Jersey, 1886) was a brilliant and versatile Reform thinker. He was also the most mobile, either because his personality did not allow him to settle down, or because of a strong sense of mission as religious reformer, or both.

In Europe, Kalisch studied at *yeshivot* and then at universities in Berlin, Breslau and Prague. In Germany, he was a journalist, a composer of patriotic hymns, and later, an insurgent. In 1848 he had to flee Germany after participating in the revolution of that year. Upon arriving in America, he was appointed rabbi of Anshe Chesed Congregation (now known as "Fairmount Temple"), Cleveland, Ohio, but his radical religious views divided the community. In 1850, his followers established a new congregation, Tifereth Israel (later to become known as "The Temple," and still later to be associated with Rabbi Abba Hillel Silver) after he was dismissed from Anshe Chesed. Though Kalisch's group had more liberal tendencies than those who stayed at Anshe Chesed, both congregations remained quite traditional, and veered toward Reform Judaism only several years later.[14]

In 1856, Kalisch, confident that he had established a viable institution in Cleveland, departed for Cincinnati, Ohio, where he became rabbi of Ahavat Achim Congregation. A year later, we find him taking the reins at Bene Jeshurun Congregation in Milwaukee, and uniting two other pioneering congregations under its banner. In Milwaukee, Kalisch was known for his establishment of the "True Sisters," a significant benevolent society, and for his correspondence with President James Buchanan, whom Kalisch took to task for using the expression "all the nations of Christendom," while greeting Queen Victoria in 1858. The president later apologized to Rabbi Kalisch: "For many of your persuasion I entertain the highest personal regard, and I should be the last man in the world, either in official document or in private letter, to use any expression derogatory to their character or calculated to wound their feelings." In 1860, economic depression forced Bene Jeshurun to let go of its distinguished rabbi, but not without accolades of affection and respect.[15]

In 1867, Kalisch brought his message to Indianapolis, Indiana. Previously, in 1864 he had been in Detroit, Michigan, and, in 1866, had voiced his plan to spread his views of historical Judaism as much as possible, and accepted a pulpit in Leavenworth, Kansas. While in Leavenworth, he translated Lessing's *Nathan the Wise* and observed in 1867 to a Young Men's Literary Association that "Christianity did not provide the Roman Empire with an *escape from* barbarism, but with a *lapse into* it." (Already in 1853 he had published, in German, a polemic against Christianity which was translated into English four years later as *A Guide for Rational Inquiries into the Biblical Writings, being an Examination of the Doctrinal Differences Between Judaism and Primitive Christianity, Based upon Historical Exposition of the Book of Matthew.*)

Kalisch went to New York in 1868 and opened, with funds from translations, lectures and sponsors, the Educational Institute (West 36th

Street). During this period, he wrote articles on the Talmud and other aspects of Jewish culture for Henry Ward Beecher's "Christian Union." He did intensive lecturing, and, in 1872, agreed to become the rabbi of Temple B'nai Abraham of Newark, New Jersey (now in Livingston, New Jersey). The same year, he delivered one of his most noted lectures, "Ancient and Modern Judaism," at Ohavay Shalom Temple, Nashville, Tennessee. In 1874–5, Kalisch delivered many significant lectures in Newark, including "Divine Providence," "The Origin of Language," "Jewish Ethics," and "The Life and Works of Moses Maimonides." Kalisch's remaining years were spent visiting congregations, helping out at B'nai Abraham, teaching children Hebrew and German, and writing essays on varied topics such as "Demons and Evil Spirits According to Judaism and Christianity," "Leeser's Translation of the Bible" (a critique of the widely used Orthodox Jewish Bible translation, from the standpoint of critical Biblical scholarship), "The Old Biblical Idea of God," "Christian Theologians on the Talmud," and "Attacks on the Talmud by Radical Reformers."[16]

Kalisch's most impressive and representative essay is "Divine Providence."[17] The year of this talk, 1874, is reflected in references to the "wild Indians on the plains." Here, he reviews the ancient Greek and Manichean views on providence, demonstrating his general erudition in order to provide perspective while analyzing the agonizing question of why evil seems to function so effectively in a world held to be governed by the Divine. Kalisch posed the question as follows: "Why does ... [God] allow, that this or that man perish in the fight for human right, justice and liberty?" As perplexing as the problem of human evil is, of course, that of natural disasters. Kalisch cites as an example the thunderstorms that destroy the labors of the hard-working farmer.

It is Kalisch's thesis that the world provides more welfare than suffering. A fellow may break his leg, but his calamity could prevent him from boarding a train fated for disaster. Kalisch introduces psychological considerations into the discussion of providence. Modern man must overcome his superstitions and fears, and become attuned to the positive aspects of existence. If he would but assume a proper psychological perspective, he might realize that "bad times" may later turn out to be one's best times, and that things we wanted but did not get could have proven detrimental. Likewise, in the case of natural disasters, the hurricane may ravage, but it purifies the atmosphere from unhealthy mephistis (an assumption of the time).

The key to perceiving God's providence is, according to Kalisch, the mastery of the laws of nature to whatever extent humanly possible, and the cultivation of an enlightened human attitude. The latter entails the realization that there is no gain without pain, that the vicious individual creates his own misery. Natural realities such as death are not in and of themselves horrible, he says, but unhealthy preoccupation with them is the problem.

Needless to say, Kalisch affirms typical nineteenth century meliorism (along with some dicta in classical Rabbinic theology) in citing human activity as the medium through which God works. The essay concludes with a celebration of the United States of America as the culmination of the best workings of human history, and as a sign of Providence amidst the rise and decay of civilizations. The final declaration is, of course, an adaptation of Hegelianism for American patriotic purposes, but Kalisch can hardly be faulted for his enthusiasm for the freedom he found in America.

FREDERICK DE SOLA MENDES

Rabbi Frederick de Sola Mendes[18] (b. Montego Bay, Jamaica, 1850; d. New York, N.Y., 1927) had one of the longest and most stable careers of his day. He was spiritual leader of Congregation Shaaray Tefilla in New York City from 1874 to 1920, when he was appointed Rabbi Emeritus. Born to a prominent Sephardic family, raised in England, he received a B.A. degree from London University, later attended the University of Breslau, and earned his Ph.D. from the University of Jena in 1871. He graduated from the Breslau Jewish Theological Seminary in 1873 and began his rabbinic career in England as a Sephardic rabbi. In 1873, Congregation Shaaray Tefilla invited him to become assistant to its distinguished rabbi, Samuel Myer Isaacs (1804–1878), who retired in 1877. The congregation remained traditional during Isaacs's career, but veered toward Reform under Mendes, who began to espouse a "Conservative Reform" Judaism. In order to provide a forum for his evolving views, de Sola Mendes founded in 1876 the short-lived *Independent Hebrew*, and was later instrumental in launching the *American Hebrew* (1879), and serving as its editor for the first six years of its long duration. De Sola Mendes translated the Book of Deuteronomy for the Jewish Publication Society *Holy Scriptures*, and penned *Defence*

Not Defiance: A Hebrew's Reply to the Missionaries (1876); *Outlines of Bible History* (1886), and various hymnals and children's books.

Though Mendes's career bridged the centuries, the work which best represents his thoughtful pulpit style is the pamphlet *Tyndallism and Judaism* (1874),[19] which reflects scientific discussions in the nineteenth century. Mendes reviews aspects of the atomistic theory of John Tyndall (1820–1893) in clear, concise terms. Mendes is not as worried about the materialistic aspects of Tyndall's thought as about the implications of the latter's charge that God is a man-made concept.

Mendes finds a possible openness to theological discussion in Tyndall's view that the atoms of which the world is composed somehow "cause Life," though "the cause of life is an unsolvable mystery, the development of some inherent tendency in the atoms to life." Mendes suggests that perhaps Tyndall and the theologian might come to agreement if a mature view of God were given. Indeed, Mendes sympathizes with Tyndall's distrust of a deity possessing "human organs of vision, or human sympathies."

Instead of elaborating on an alternative approach to the God-faith, however, Mendes chooses to wander into the argument that what we cannot conceive as true — namely, God — can in fact *be* true. The problem with this point, however, is that Tyndall's main argument — that the idea of God originates in the human mind — is ignored. Tactically and logically, then, Mendes concludes his sermonic essay poorly.

Yet Mendes's sermon is still effective because of its fine features which make it a paradigm for future polemics against various trends of thought that challenge Judaism. First, he summarizes Tyndall's thought in such a way as to show that Tyndall himself is aware that his challenge to religion is not new, that the Greeks had long before developed an atomistic theory. By arguing that Judaism faced similar challenges before, he cleverly suggests that such challenges were surmounted in the past. Secondly, Mendes argues that the atomistic theory can be accepted by "the most religious, nay the most bigoted," so suggesting that while Tyndall's scientific orientation may be correct, it still leaves room for a God-concept, given the proper theological arguments. Incorporating external challenges into Jewish theology has been a time-honored habit of Jewish thinkers since biblical and Talmudic times.

ISAAC MAYER WISE

Rabbi Isaac Mayer Wise (b. Steingrub, Bohemia, 1819; d. Cincinnati, Ohio, 1900) remains the most effective and far-reaching organizer that American Jewry has ever known. In addition to being the father of fourteen children of his own, he was the father of American Reform Judaism and of its various organizations. He was also the most prolific author in the nineteenth century American rabbinate. The most comprehensive biographical study of any nineteenth century rabbi has been written about Dr. Wise, and may be consulted for the myriad and noteworthy details of his life and works.[20]

Largely self-educated, Wise did attend various *yeshivot* at Prague and Vienna. By 1843, we find him acting as the rabbinical officiant at Radnitz, Bohemia. In 1846, he emigrated to the United States and became the rabbi of Temple Beth El, Albany, New York. In 1847, he helped to organize the first *bet din* (rabbinic court) in New York State. He originally contributed to *The Occident*, the journal of the leading traditionalist rabbi in America, Isaac Leeser (1806–1868), but his views became increasingly more radical. Due to Wise's Reform tendencies and to internal synagogue politics, there was an attempt to oust him from Beth El in 1850, which culminated in a brawl in the synagogue on Rosh Hashanah of that year. After this event, certainly one of the most dramatic in the annals of American Reform Judaism,[21] Wise and his followers founded Temple Anshe Emeth in Albany. (In time the two congregations reunited under the name Beth Emeth.)

In 1854, Wise accepted a call to the pulpit of Kehilla Kedosha B'nai Yeshurun in Cincinnati, Ohio, where he remained for the rest of his life. His congregation, together with Bene Israel, led by Rabbi Max Lilienthal, were the pillars that enabled Cincinnati to become the capital city of American Reform Judaism. In 1854, Wise began to publish two periodicals, *The Israelite* (which later became *The American Israelite*) and *Die Deborah* (an American Jewish weekly in German). He also worked at establishing Zion College, a short-lived precursor to the Hebrew Union College.

In 1855, Wise called for one of the first national synods of American rabbis, which occurred in Cleveland, Ohio. Interestingly, the more orthodox rabbis were satisfied with Wise's declarations that the Bible is divine, and that it "must be expounded and practiced according to the comments of the Talmud." Wise's vision was actually for an *Amer-*

ican Judaism along moderately Reform lines. Hence, in 1856, he published the *Minhag America* ("The American Rite"), a prayer book that he considered traditional and yet conducive to the nineteenth century American spirit.

In the years preceding the Civil War, Wise expressed his abhorrence of slavery, and yet his deepest concern was for the Union. He advocated an evolutionary abolition of slavery for the sake of the Union. He therefore supported the "Copperhead Democrats" and was nominated to the Ohio State Senate under that party, but was forced to withdraw his name because of the opposition of his congregation's board of directors.

While Wise's political career was cut short, his enduring contributions to American Jewish life were just beginning. In 1873, he founded the Union of American Hebrew Congregations. In 1875, he finally succeeded in establishing his rabbinical seminary, the first in America, which he named the Hebrew Union College. In 1889, he established the Central Conference of American Rabbis, the first American rabbinical organization, and served as its president until his death.

Wise had ten children with his first wife, Therese Bloch, whom he married in 1844, and four children with his second wife, Selma Bondi, whom he married in 1876 after becoming a widower. His youngest son, Jonah Bondi Wise, was a prominent Reform rabbi who served Central Synagogue in New York and founded the Radio Synagogue.

Wise's writings are vast and varied. The most important of these are *Judaism: Its Doctrines and Its Duties* (1872), *The Cosmic God* (1876), *Judaism and Christianity, Their Agreements and Disagreements* (1883), *A Defence of Judaism versus Proselytizing Christianity* (1889) and the posthumously published autobiographical *Reminiscences* (1901).

Of all of Wise's theological writings the lecture, "Nature's God," the decisive chapter in his volume *The Cosmic God*, is certainly the most representative and the most revealing. The chapters that comprise *The Cosmic God* were delivered as a series of lectures in 1874–5, and then published in 1876.[22] "Nature's God" and an accompanying essay titled "God in Nature" appeared together in Wise's book under the section heading "On Metaphysics." Both pieces are reproduced here.

Wise informs us that *The Cosmic God* was written after the untimely death of his first wife, and was "conceived in sorrow, composed in grief and constructed at the brink of despair," containing "my mind's best thoughts, and my soul's triumph over the powers of darkness." Wise found a balm for his pain and depression in reading and pondering philosophy, science, metaphysics and religion.

The villain of *The Cosmic God* is Darwinism, which Wise describes as "homo-brutalism." Wise dismisses Darwin by observing that if man were in fact descended from the ape, the latter would have to indicate more similarity to the human species. Man possesses a larynx to "utter articulate speech and human song," but the ape has no analogous organ.[23] Of course, Darwin would argue that humanity simply developed by natural selection what the ape did not have, but Wise dismisses this argumentation. Though "modern biologists succeed so well in discovering physiological and morphic semblances between parts of men and this and that animal ... they will never succeed in discovering the human organism in any animal." By "human organism," Wise appears to mean human thought-characteristics. In other words, Wise expects Darwin to point to a little man in every animal before he can accept Darwin's theories.

It would seem, therefore, that Wise does not argue against Darwinism on its own terms, but sets up standards for Darwin that are quite outside the context of the biologist's own theory. Wise is willing to concede, however, that nature may have employed combat for survival, natural selection, and other processes described by Darwin, but that "neither or all of these auxiliary means account for the origin of the whole organism."

Yet Wise's presentation of his own views of humanity and history is more compelling than his critique of Darwin, and very much in the spirit of nineteenth century thought.

Though Wise has much to say about nature, he begins *The Cosmic God* with a discussion of mind. Without causality, science is impossible, for "the main object of all science is to discover the laws of nature by the guiding compass of causality."[24] The human mind possesses "the innate ability to form words for objects, feelings, etc., and the necessity of representing them by sounds or signs."[25] Since children and deaf people can make words of their own, it must follow that "the mind makes words ... without having seen or heard them."[26] Language is "not the product of mechanical brain action," as there is "no freedom imaginable in connection with mechanical causes."[27] Language, rather, is the basic indication of mind, of a non-mechanical cause. History is the second such indication. "Mind-force has produced myriads of mental phenomena which, in their totality, are the history of the human race."[28] Materialism cannot be at the base of history or nature, for it does not account for "Mind." Wise elaborates:

> As this earth consists of its atoms by the inherent force of cohesion, so history consists of innumerable ideas coherent by their internal force of physical affinity, which we will call the Genius of History.[29]

The human "Genius of History" is not, according to Wise, without some external guidance. Wise observes that

> having admitted ... the law of causality, it must also be admitted that man can not make history by his will and intellect exclusively; he must be in harmony with the law which is superior to man's will and intellect, as the whole is superior to any of its parts.[30]

With typical nineteenth century confidence in the understandability of the workings of history, Wise proceeds to describe the operations of the superhuman will, which he dubs the "Logos of History." Citing events in Jewish and general history (from the point of view of Wise's own interpretations), Wise concludes that the Logos of History

> rights the wrongs, turns the course of events in favor of progression in spite of all the wickedness of rulers or nations, preserves the elements of truth, goodness and usefulness, to be shaped in new events, and neutralizes falsehoods, wickedness, all that is useless or nugatory.[31]

This kind of progressivistic faith persisted in Reform theology until the Nazi Holocaust of the 1940s.

Wise observes that the Logos of History operates "exactly as the extra-organic will and intellect works in the organic kingdoms."[32] He regards it as his burden of proof to show that the "superhuman life, freedom, will, intellect and justice"[33] embodied by the Logos of History reflect, in fact, Nature's God as well.

The chapter "Nature's God"[34] is Wise's attempt to prove that the Logos of History and the genius behind nature's laws are, in fact, one and the same God. What is significant about this chapter is that Wise employs contemporary scientific theory and biblical passages in order to reaffirm nineteenth century notions of nature and history and, more impressive still, to synthesize them. He believes that through such synthesis he can affirm a single cosmic God. The chapter also contains a significant, perhaps even the first, affirmation of the possible existence of extraterrestrials by a leading American rabbi.

The rest of his book goes on to explore metaphysical literature in the light of this affirmation. It was Wise's belief that there is but one substance: the Cosmic God. Matter is not substance because it is "passive." There is a psychical, divine force that acts upon matter, "the material substance is the resultant." [35]

An earlier, panoramic statement of Wise's thought can be found in his remarkable eighty-three page catechism, *Judaism: Its Doctrines and Duties*, issued in 1872 by Wise's newspaper, *The Israelite*. The book covers many aspects of Jewish beliefs and ethical teachings, with copious and direct use of biblical verses to make his points. Most of the book consists of statements of faith with scriptural illustrations.

Wise's thirty-eight addenda to this catechism qualify as creative and thoughtful theological statements. In these addenda, Wise makes his approach clear from the outset — namely, that "Judaism teaches no dogmas or mysteries, on the belief of which salvation exclusively depends. It maintains that everlasting bliss will be the reward of all those who, from pure motives, do that which is right, and shun that which is evil." Wise does not say that Judaism has no dogmas; he asserts that there are no dogmas that are the "exclusive" test of salvation. Thus, he can speak of Jewish "doctrines" regarding God, divine attributes, providence, the afterlife, and sin and atonement. Wise does warn, however, that while one can make observations about divine providence from history, "history" as we can know it "is but a meager record of the fate, experience, and transactions of the human family." One can, however, as the Bible teaches, count on providence's using even abuses of power for divine ends.

"Happiness and perfection," Wise observes, "can be acquired only through the path of wisdom and righteousness." He affirms human superiority to the animals. Like Maimonides, he suggests that human beings can attain prophecy by perfecting their intellectual capacities. The divinely created conscience in each person sets a "principle" of right and wrong that is bolstered by Scriptures and by knowledge. Love functions as "the force of attraction" in human beings, much as matter requires such forces. We know that we have an immortal soul, the "image of God" (Gen. 1:27; 9:6) because intellect is "indestructible." For "God being all-wise would not destroy the intellect he created; being all-good he would not disappoint the highest hope with which He impressed us; and being all-just He could not have commanded man only to subordinate his carnal inclinations to his spiritual welfare, if the soul was not destined to everlasting life."

In the addenda of *Judaism: Its Doctrines and Duties*, Wise strongly affirms the doctrine of divine reward and punishment. Most of his interpretation of this doctrine is psychological. He asserts that "the consciousness of guilt and wickedness is the torment of the wicked on this earth and his hell in the future state of existence." Wise emphasizes a doctrine of merit. "We have certainly no right to expect of an all-just God, in time or eternity, perfections not attained, blessings not deserved, or gifts which we are not prepared to enjoy." Yet he speaks of divine graciousness (p. 17), and leaves open the possibility that it may be granted even if undeserved; one must live in such a way, however, as not to count on such intervention. However, the final addendum offers a touching affirmation of the efficacy of prayer in the possible fulfillment of "wishes if they are not against ... [one's] own happiness."

In the addenda, Wise offers an unusual explanation of why God entered into a covenant with Abraham and his descendants (Gen. 17) after having engaged all humanity in a covenant with Noah (Gen. 9). The second, more intimate covenant was a divine response to urbanization, for "with the increase and closer contact of men, a better knowledge of the moral law became a necessity." Precisely because morality must be actualized through covenants in society, Wise dismisses monastic expressions of religion, for "if all men would lead such a life, civilization would come to a speedy end, and all must return to the solitary life of the savage.... To be good, one must do good to man." In a memorable passage, Wise points out that refusing to do what is good is tantamount to theft. "The law," he writes, "makes no provisions for beggars, and there should be none.... Every person has a right to live, hence also to the means of support. If one has more than he needs, he owes support to him who needs it. To refuse it is indirect robbery."

The theology presented by Isaac Mayer Wise, in both the addenda and in *The Cosmic God*, is very much in tune with nineteenth century religious thought and consonant with the writings of other discourses in this anthology. His listing of the "doctrines" of Judaism is, by and large, consistent with classical Jewish beliefs, *mutatis mutandis*, for he does depart from the tradition in such matters as his rejection of a personal messiah. Though his words reflect a genuine piety and an impressive creativity, he embarrasses himself with his feeble attempts to portray the Hebrew prophets as rejecting the intrinsic holiness of the Land of Israel and Jerusalem and the spiritual significance of "Israel's political restoration." After all, the prophets regarded the return of the

Jews to Zion as the *sine qua non* of the vision, well articulated by Wise himself, that the "habitable world must become one holy land, every city a Jerusalem, every house a temple, every table an altar, every person a priest of the Most High, his own prince, priest and prophet."

BERNHARD FELSENTHAL

Rabbi Bernhard Felsenthal[36] (b. 1822, Muchweiler, Bavaria; d. 1908, Chicago, Ill.) was the elder statesman of the nineteenth century American Reform scholarship. He attended the Polytechnic High School in Munich, and was a prodigious auto-didact in Jewish and secular subjects. He was proficient in mathematics, history and philosophy, and had a vast knowledge of German literature. From 1842 to 1854 he taught Jewish children in Germany and took an interest in the Reform rabbinical conferences of the 1840s. In 1854, he came to the United States with his father and sister, and he corresponded with the scholarly ideologues of American Reform, David Einhorn (1809–1879) and Samuel Adler (1809–1891), whom he later dubbed "the Luther and the Melanchthon of the Jewish Reform Movement."

Upon his arrival in the United States, Felsenthal taught in Lawrenceburg, Indiana, and Madison, Wisconsin. In April 1858, urged by friends and relatives, he went to Chicago, Illinois, where he worked as a bank clerk for his cousins, the Greenebaum Brothers, and sat and studied when business was slow. A year later, he wrote a Reform manifesto, *Kol Kore Bamidbar* ("A Voice Crieth in the Wilderness"[37]), a forty-page pamphlet describing Judaism as a religion of historical development. He formed the *Judische Reform Verein* ("The Jewish Reform Society"), which became Chicago Sinai Congregation in 1861. That same year, Rabbi Samuel Adler conferred upon Felsenthal the well-deserved title of *morenu harav* ("our teacher, the rabbi").

In 1861, Felsenthal acted as full-time rabbi of Sinai Congregation, at the urging of friends and relatives, but the congregation did not rehire him in 1864 because they did not find his oratory "exciting" enough. Yet his friends and followers wasted no time in forming, in another neighborhood, Zion Congregation, where Felsenthal served from 1864 until his retirement in 1887. Both congregations founded by Felsenthal flourished and became landmarks on the Chicago scene.[38] Due to shifts in Chicago Jewish demography, Zion Congregation merged with Temple B'nai Abraham in 1920. (The merged congregation, B'nai Abraham–Zion, is now known as the Oak Park Temple.)

During the early years of Zion Congregation, Felsenthal spoke out against slavery, and began to reconsider his views of Reform Judaism. As early as 1869, he observed in correspondence in the *Jewish Times*: "I am in favor of reforms within Israel but not of the abandonment of Israel. I do not wish Israel to be absorbed—not yet—by humanity as a whole. It is still one or two thousand years too early for that."

As a thinker, Felsenthal demonstrated by a consistent fascination with Jewish nationalism and by a concern for the responsible development of Reform Judaism. Unlike most of his colleagues who reduced Judaism to "pure Mosaiasm'" (see, below, my discussion of Adolph Moses), Felsenthal regarded the faith of Abraham as quintessential Judaism.[39] (The emphasis here is not only on Abraham's humanity, but on his role as a tribal chieftain.) Back in *Kol Kore Bamidbar*, Felsenthal observed that "Judaism is older than the Bible, Judaism originated at the moment when God breathed into the first man the breath of life."[40] By throwing the essence of Judaism back further than Moses, and by tracing the origins of pure Judaism to Abraham rather than Moses, Felsenthal foreshadowed the polarity in his thought between natural religion and Jewish nationalism, a polarity that he never successfully mediated in his writings.

Felsenthal's tendencies toward Jewish nationalism led him to become one of the first Zionist leaders in American Reform Judaism, along with Rabbi Gustav Gottheil (1827–1903) of Temple Emanu-El in New York City. By the end of his career, Felsenthal affirmed, in his Second Series of "Jewish Theses,"[41] that Jews were an unassimilable race. Yet Felsenthal's devotion to liberal Reform postulates regarding the historical development led to impatience with Orthodox Judaism, though he was noted for his kindness to immigrant East European Orthodox Jews. Abraham, symbol of brotherly love as well as of the enduring Jewish tribe, was fittingly the patron spirit of Felsenthal's complex, often contradictory, but noble soul.

The most significant expression of Felsenthal's scholarship and enlightened approach to religion is his essay on "Bible Interpretation: How and How Not" (1884).[42] This sophisticated polemic for objective Bible scholarship lay new ground rules for interfaith dialogue by rejecting medieval interpretations of biblical texts and the old battles they provoked. Felsenthal begins by observing that there is only one

Hebrew grammar, the key to the one true exegesis of the Hebrew Bible. Christians, Moslems and Jews *sin* in interpreting the Bible according to religious prejudices rather than to its inner rules. Indeed, Felsenthal demonstrates sophisticated methodology by rejecting allegorical approaches to Scripture, the reading of "hidden meanings" into simple Hebrew words. He urges that in the case of *Rashi* and other medieval Jewish commentators, as in the case of Jerome and Luther, "we take respectful and grateful notice [of their insights], but we do so in the same spirit and manner as historians take notice of the old documents of scientific views and systems."

Felsenthal eloquently urges that in order to understand the Bible, we must employ our scholarship to recover its original meaning. In studying Isaiah, for example, we must look at the historical situation. Whereas Christians have read into his words references to their messiah, we must realize that Isaiah could not have referred to a savior of Jews to come hundreds of years later, but to someone to deliver them from the onslaught of Assyrian armies.

ALEXANDER KOHUT

Rabbi Alexander Kohut[43] (b. 1842, Felegyhaze, Hungary; d. 1894, New York City) was a leading philologist of Talmudic language of the nineteenth century, and became known, as well, as an eloquent spokesman for traditional Judaism. His Hebrew studies were directed by Professor Heinrich Deutsch, the outstanding Hungarian-Jewish scholar. He was ordained by the Breslau Seminary in 1867, having earned his doctorate in Oriental languages from the University of Leipzig in 1864. From an early age, Kohut immersed himself in the task of issuing a comprehensive lexicon of Talmudic language. He began his monumental *Aruch Completum* while in Hungary, where he served exemplarily as rabbi, educator and statesman. He was elected to the Hungarian Parliament as a representative of the Jews.

Kohut's reputation spread across the Atlantic, and he was urged to emigrate to the United States by the historic Congregation Ahavath Chesed (later known as Central Synagogue) in New York City, which had evolved a moderate Reform ritual. Kohut arrived in the United States in 1885 with the hope of stemming the Reform tendencies in his and other congregations. He attacked the Reformers that same year in a series of lectures on the ancient Rabbinic ethical and dogmatic treatise, *Pirkei Avot* (literally, "Chapters of the Fathers"), a part of the *Mishnah* portion of the Talmud. These lectures, delivered in German, were translated into English the same year and published in volume form as *The Ethics of the Fathers*, after having been serialized in *The American Hebrew*. They provoked a major polemic with Dr. Kaufman Kohler, the Reform scholar who headed Temple Beth-El in New York City and was later to become the president of Hebrew Union College in Cincinnati, Ohio.[44]

There is little question that Kohut was the foremost ideological spokesman for the traditionalist party. No like-minded thinker dealt with theological issues as such. Isaac Leeser (1806–1868) had been the chief organizer of the traditionalist party in America; the dedicator of synagogues; the founder and editor of its journal, *The Occident*; and the spirit behind its short-lived academy, Maimonides College, which opened shortly before his death.[45] Yet his published discourses, which run into tome upon tome, are actually sermonic polemics, with little signs of sophisticated theological thinking. Another outstanding early spokesman for Orthodoxy in America, Rabbi Morris Raphall (1798–1868), who served Congregation B'nai Jeshurun in New York City from 1849 until his retirement, was an eloquent defender of traditionalist practices, but his best ideological statements, particularly a defense of the Sabbath in a book called *Festivals of the Lord* (1840), were written during his distinguished career in Great Britain, and epitomized the tradition of Anglo-Jewish polemics, having little to do with the intellectual climate of nineteenth century American Jewry. Raphall cut short his own career at his congregation by suggesting in a January 4, 1861, discourse on a National Fast that civil war could be averted if the South would adopt the more humane biblical view of slavery and if the North would accept that, at least for a time. Immediately after that sermon, Raphall was forced to retire.[46]

Kohut's discussion of "The Foundations of Judaism" in *The Ethics of the Fathers*[47] is his best statement and is remarkable for its defense of orthodox doctrines in Judaism by approximating certain motifs of Reform thinking and preaching. It is, in essence, a commentary on the Ten Commandments, utilizing as a point of departure the famous dictum in *Pirkei Avot* (1:2): "The ethical world of Judaism rests upon three things: upon the Torah, upon Divine Worship, and upon the Practice of Charity" (Kohut's translation).[48] Kohut affirms that the Sinai event, which marked the national birth of Israel, represented a transformation in the human consciousness. Before Sinai, there was only moral anarchy. After Revelation, the human spirit was never the same.

Significantly, Kohut illustrates his assertions with rabbinic, rather than biblical, passages. He attributes to rabbinic literature not only scriptural but theological authority. Hence, his chief argument for the God-faith — that to deny God is to doom creation to moral chaos — is supported by rabbinic dicta.

To Kohut, the first four commandments of the Decalogue form the "substance of our spiritual consciousness," prescribing our duty toward God. The rest of the Decalogue, which deals with man's duties toward his fellow man, is predicated upon the affirmation that God is truth (a motif of rabbinic thought) and that human relationships must be moral, both in regard to life and property and in respect to ethical conduct.

Kohut may be regarded as reflecting the Reform preoccupation with the Decalogue as the basis of religion, as purest Judaism, as it were. This seems dangerous when one considers that the Reformers often invoked the Ten Commandments as the only binding commandments. In view of the times, Kohut's presentation of the "foundation of Judaism" comes across as inordinately general, for it was obviously his intent to defend the need for the rest of the commandments. True, he devotes chapters in the same volume to arguing for the binding character of the Oral Law.[49] Yet one must conclude that, even among leading nineteenth century American traditionalists, the emphasis in theology was upon general principles rather than on theology inherent in the *halakhah* (Jewish religious law).

GUSTAV GOTTHEIL

Rabbi Gustav Gottheil[50] (b. 1837, Pinne, Posen; d. 1903, New York City) was an elder statesman of the American Reform rabbinate: its emissary in ecumenical activities, its patron of Jewish scholarship in the university, and its driving spirit in the Zionist cause. Gottheil began his career in 1847 as a teacher of Hebrew, the Bible, and Jewish history in a common school at Tierschtiegel, Posen, after graduating from *yeshivot* and from the religious high school in that city.

In 1855, Gottheil entered into a contract with the Reform

Gemeinde Trustees of Berlin to teach in their religious school and to serve as the number three minister and reader. In 1858, he earned his Ph.D. at the University of Jena. Two years later, he was called to the Manchester Synagogue of British Jews. Though Gottheil did not know any English when he arrived in Manchester, he learned the language after a few months, and developed into one of the most eloquent English-speaking rabbis of his time. He was known for his fine interfaith work in England, and even found time to play the violin.

In 1873, Gottheil was called to Congregation Emanu-El of the City of New York, then the leading synagogue in the United States and a congregation of four hundred member units. Gottheil was expected to assist Dr. Samuel Adler at Emanu-El until the latter's retirement. (Adler's son, Felix, was to have succeeded him, but he had shocked New York Jewry with his "Ethical Culture" philosophy. Gottheil was most offended by Felix Adler's assaults on Judaism and other "established" religions, and stated to the board at Emanu-El that he could never work with Felix, who founded his own Ethical Culture Society in 1876.) When Adler retired around 1876, Gottheil succeeded him as senior rabbi of Temple Emanu-El, with which he was associated for the rest of his life.

Gottheil was known in New York for his interfaith work. Within the Jewish community he was instrumental in founding a preparatory school for the rabbinate in 1877, which evolved into the Emanu-El Theological Seminary in 1881 or 1882, a short-lived experiment that petered out around 1885. In 1886–7, Gottheil published a hymnal after revising the Emanu-El ritual. One of Gottheil's hymns, "Come, O Sabbath Day," has enjoyed long popularity. In 1896, *Sun and Shield,* his anthology of spiritual readings, was published by Brentano's. It was very well-received in Jewish and general circles.

In 1887, Gottheil succeeded in convincing the directors of Temple Emanu-El to sponsor a professorship of Jewish studies at Columbia University. It was first occupied by his son and biographer, Richard James Horatio Gottheil, a philologist of Semitic language. Also in 1887, Gustav Gottheil organized the Emanu-El Sisterhood of Personal Service, a pioneering Jewish social service organization, which worked with immigrants. In the 1890s he became a champion of Zionism.

The essay which best demonstrates Gottheil's effectiveness as a polemicist and his clear and cogent thinking is "The Great Refusal, Being an Open Letter of Rev. S. Calthrop, and His Article Entitled

'Israel's Last Word,'" which appeared in the *Unitarian Review* of January 1887.[51] Apparently, Gottheil became upset when a Unitarian minister began to censure the Jews for not accepting Jesus in comparable fashion to more fundamentalist Christian pronouncements of the same kind. Gottheil responds to this cleric's assertion that in rejecting Jesus as a teacher, the Jews ignored the world's "grandest inspiration."

Gottheil begins his essay with a clever rhetorical question. Even if Jesus *were* the "grandest inspiration," are Jews, according to Christian strictures, to be blamed or pitied for not acknowledging this? (Gottheil cleverly points out that to all Christian denominations besides Unitarianism, Jesus' greatness consists in things that Unitarians deny — namely, the doctrine of the Trinity, the passion, the resurrection, etc. He therefore scores points by reminding the Unitarians that they are regarded as no less heretical than the Jews.) Gottheil notes that many Jews did in fact gather around Jesus. He was not rejected for his beliefs regarding God's fatherhood and man's brotherhood. Rather, the Jews refused to accept what Unitarians themselves reject — the Jesus of Christian orthodoxy.

Remarkably, Gottheil, who did in fact come to embrace Zionism not long after this essay was written, polemicizes against Christianity from the vantage point of Jewish nationalism. This is, of course, most unusual for a Reform rabbi of the period, since nineteenth-century Reform rejected the nationalistic aspects of the Jewish religion. Gottheil insists that Christians have no right to view ancient Judaism as a small group of teachers and believers who should have changed their allegiance "in the twinkling of an eye." Rather, Jewish society was part of a complex national religion that must have been offended by the claim of the early Christians that the Romans and other nationals who had made Jewish life miserable were suddenly to join in a new world faith.

Gottheil also invokes the findings of modern scholarship which should demonstrate to Christians that the Pharisees are unjustly depicted in the polemics of the New Testament. He brilliantly takes his Unitarian opponent to task for preaching religious liberalism in one breath and repeating the clichés of christological triumphalism in the next, failing to appreciate the dynamics of ancient Jewish life on its own terms as truly enlightened people should:

> Were the people to close the gates of the temple, cease the offering of sacrifices, disrobe the priests and Levites, scatter the rabbinical schools, for-

bid the observance of the traditional law, declare Moses superseded by a new prophet, and start a Protestant or Unitarian religion? Were they to abrogate their national feasts, their new moons and Sabbaths, embrace the heathen as brothers, eat, drink and make merry with them?

Gottheil goes on to observe that the ancient Jews are denounced by Christian theologians, fundamentalist and Unitarian, for not giving up their ancient religious constitution, whereas America honors precisely those who gave life and limb to honor *her* Constitution.

Gottheil invokes modern scholarship, as well, to observe that "every candid critic admits that it is exceedingly difficult, if not impossible, to lay hold of the actual, historical Jesus. A veil of legend, and, worse, of the dogmatical contentions ... of his followers, has been spread over the fair figure, and has become almost inseparable from it, like the bandages we find wound around Egyptian mummies." A powerful image indeed! Furthermore, Gottheil adds, Jesus is reconstructed "in the likeness of his followers." He shows that the Gospels themselves are divided as to whether Jesus was a new Moses, a new lawgiver, or a continuation of what was already given. If Christians can be so divided, Gottheil observes, is the Jew to be blamed for refusing to forsake his national heritage, is his martyrdom to be considered any less pious that that of Jesus himself, and are his latter-day sages and saints and philosophers to be regarded as without wisdom? Surely, the Jews should not be censured for their glorious history in the centuries following the death of Jesus!

Gottheil's polemic with a liberal Christian thinker remains insightful and fresh even after subsequent outstanding polemics with Christian belief and thought.[52] It shows that the nineteenth-century American rabbinate did not hesitate to employ, with the utmost effectiveness, the scholarly tools today taken for granted.

JOSEPH KRAUSKOPF

Rabbi Joseph Krauskopf[53] (b. 1858, Ostrowo, Posen; d. 1923, Philadelphia, Pennsylvania), a member of the first graduating class of the Hebrew Union College (1883), was considered the most charismatic orator of the nineteenth-century American rabbinate. In 1872, he had come to America with his older brother, and worked briefly as a clerk for a tea merchant in Fall River, Massachusetts. Three years later, he

entered the Hebrew Union College, which guided his high school studies and his education at the University of Cincinnati. Krauskopf is, in
fact, the only American-trained rabbi in our study.[54]

Upon graduation from the Hebrew Union College, Krauskopf
became rabbi of Temple B'nai Jehudah, Kansas City, Missouri, and
articulated in his inaugural sermon his commitment to "natural religion without supernaturalism." Yet Krauskopf was also committed to
Jewish education for the children of his congregation. He stressed the
study of the Hebrew language, and insisted on at least two days a week
of religious instruction. While in Kansas City, he dedicated a new temple, and filled it weekly with worshipers anxious to follow his famed
lecture series. In 1885–6 he delivered eighteen lectures on "The Jews
and Moors in Spain," and followed this series with another of sixteen
talks on "Evolution and Judaism."[55] In the fall of 1885, he distinguished
himself as one of the leading voices in the Pittsburgh Platform of American Reform Judaism, which rejected all "primitive" traditions, customs and beliefs "not in harmony with the views and habits of modern
civilization," as well as the idea of a restored Jewish State in Palestine,
proclaiming instead a mission of the Jews to improve society wherever
they live and to regard themselves as a religious example and not as a
nation.[56]

In 1887, Krauskopf was called to the pulpit of the historic Congregation Kenesseth Israel of Philadelphia, where he became renowned for
his Sunday morning lectures and dynamic religious leadership. American Jewry will always be indebted to him for being the prime mover
behind the Jewish Publication Society of America, which he founded
with various backers in 1887. In 1896, he founded the National Farm
School at Doylestown, Pennsylvania, for Jewish and other orphans.
Though originally a fierce opponent of Zionism, he later supported its
efforts for the relief of the Jewish people, and he represented Philadelphia Jewry at the first session of the American Jewish Congress in 1918.
In addition to several volumes of sermons, widely circulated by sub-
scription, he boldly published *A Rabbi's Impressions of the Oberammer-
gau Passion Play* (1901), in which he cited the anti–Semitism of that
notorious German tradition. Krauskopf headed Kenesseth Israel until
his death and was buried at his farm school.

While Krauskopf's originality has been called into question,[57] the
historian will readily forgive him for the popularizing of others' scholarship, for Krauskopf is to be regarded primarily as a gifted spokesman

for naturalistic religion of the late nineteenth century as enshrined and Judaized by Classical Reform Judaism. We are indebted to him for preserving for us the leading schools of scientific and theological inquiry in his era.[58]

The "Summary" of Krauskopf's published lectures on *Evolution and Judaism*,[59] delivered on sixteen successive Friday nights in the winter of 1886–1887, in the Kansas City Temple, is a fascinating document in its own right. After noting the unpleasant controversies surrounding the "Doctrine of Evolution," and after reviewing the various theories of creation and biology prevalent at the time, Krauskopf attempts to synthesize evolution with religious belief. His guiding proposition is that religion has been responsible for most human progress in history, and that evolution, which has been used to challenge religion, must be reconciled with it.

Evolution, Krauskopf notes, still does not account for "origins," and itself suggests an "evolver." The power behind matter and force is to be regarded as God. Man worships God more profoundly with the help of the instruments of science, which magnify or isolate the wonders of the universe. More important still, evolution reveals much about the nature and workings of God by pointing to the "supreme harmony" and "supreme design" of the universe. Krauskopf goes so far as to suggest that belief in the afterlife is a corollary of the theory of evolution.

Employing the rhetorical and exhortative skills for which he was widely known, Krauskopf describes the end of his talks on evolution as an "evening for rejoicing":

> Harassing doubts have been changed to comforting convictions. Instead of an abstract uthinkable God, we have a God who is in everything that exists [,] in everything that is highest and best within us, in everything that tends towards our happiness, our ennoblement, our intellectual and moral unfolding reveals Himself as our loving Father.

Krauskopf then attempts to refute those who charged that his religious standpoint was heretical. He cites an historical example of religious intolerance against one accused of atheism who was in fact opposed to atheism, and draws a parallel to his situation and to that of others who approach the Bible critically and insist upon "severing the eternal from the transitory ... the original from the borrowed, the rational from the untenable...." Indeed, Krauskopf makes a point of emphasizing again, toward the end of his talk, that he advocates a "pure and simple" Judaism which is closest in spirit to that of the Bible.

Not surprisingly, Krauskopf cites examples of scientists who were mocked and persecuted in their times but emerged triumphant in succeeding generations. He traces the history of Jewish emancipation, and then shares his view that the minister, service, and religions worthy of adherents in the future are those which quicken the intellectual search for God in the spirit of modern science.

While Krauskopf's thought is far from rigorous or original, the "Summary" of *Evolution and Judaism* is an important document, first and foremost, because it remains a yeoman Jewish acceptance of the theory of evolution. Secondly, it departs radically from the theology of Isaac Mayer Wise, which, as we have seen, was hostile to the theory of evolution or to "homo-brutalism," as Wise described it. Finally, although not without internal flaws,[60] it is a fine example of the liberal sermonic rhetoric that predominated in nineteenth-century American Judaism, a Judaism that was largely the arena of classical Reform.

LIEBMAN ADLER

Rabbi Liebman Adler[61] (b. 1812, Lengsfeld, Saxe-Weimar; d. 1892, Chicago, Illinois) was an early pioneer of the American rabbinate and one of its most pious and amiable spirits. Though his sermons influenced the thinking of many in the German-speaking Jewish community of nineteenth-century America, it was not until the end of the century that his work was translated into English, and that it became "American" in the sense of being available in the principal language of the United States.

Adler's father was a teacher, and he studied with him and with another local schoolmaster until his thirteenth year. Hebrew he learned from Rabbi Isaac Hess of Lengsfeld. Later, he studied Talmud and Rabbinics with Rabbi Kunreuther of Gelnhausen, and at the Jewish high school of Frankfort-am-Main with Rabbis Solomon Trier and Aaron Fuld. After two years at the Teachers Seminary of Weimar, he became the director of the congregational school in his native town of Lengsfeld. When, in 1849, the Jewish school was united with the public school, Adler became head of the newly amalgamated institution.

It was in 1854 that Adler emigrated to America and became rabbi of Temple Beth-El in Detroit, where he remained until 1861, when he accepted the call to Kehillath Anshe Maarav (sometimes spelled

"Mayriv"), the oldest congregation in Chicago. Adler remained there until the end of his life, touching generations with his teaching and pastoral skills. Before and during the Civil War, he preached against slavery, and he encouraged his son Dankmar to fight for the cause of the Union. In the theological sphere, Adler advocated moderate reforms, and Kehillath Anshe Maarav, soon known as "K.A.M. Temple," remained more traditional in its services than Chicago Sinai Congregation and Zion Temple in the same city. Adler contributed to popular and scholarly German-Jewish periodicals. Toward the end of his life, he collected various German sermons in a volume, *Tzena Ur'ena,* several of which were translated into English and posthumously published in a book called *Sabbath Hours.*[62]

In 1872, the congregation urged Adler to step down as preacher and to devote himself exclusively to the school and to chanting the services. It was decided that since Adler preached only in German, an English-speaking rabbi was needed. Dr. M. Machol of Leavenworth, Kansas, filled this need until he retired in 1876, when Adler resumed preaching until his retirement in 1883. Though Adler may well have been hurt by this course of events (the congregation's decision can in no way be regarded as a derogation of the content of his sermons which, judging from *Sabbath Hours,* was excellent), there is no evidence of any rancor, and the congregation more than compensated for any ruffled feelings by unanimously voting in November 1882 to pension Adler for the rest of his life.

Adler's son Dankmar became the foremost synagogue architect in Chicago, and was a partner in the famous Adler-Sullivan architectural firm in which Frank Lloyd Wright had his apprenticeship.[63] Besides the legacy of his children and of his rabbinate, Liebman Adler left a remarkable "Last Will." Part of it warrants citation here as an intimation of Adler's remarkable piety:

> If financial conditions permit, each of my married children should join a Jewish congregation, the fittest being the K.A.M.— Kehillath Anshe Maarabh, "Congregation of the Men of the West." ....
> Those children who do not live too distant should, if the weather permit, and if it can be done without disturbing their own domestic relations, gather every Friday evening around the mother.
> My children, hold together.... Every deed of love you do to one another would be balm to my soul....
> The small savings which I leave will come to you only after the death of the mother.... The heritage which is already yours is a good name and as good an education as I could afford to give.... [R]emain strictly honest, truthful,

industrious and frugal. Do not speculate. No blessing rests upon it even it if be successful. Throw your whole energy into the pursuance of the calling you have chosen. Serve the Lord and keep Him always before you; toward men be amiable, accommodating and modest, and you will fare well even without riches. My last word to you is: Honor your mother. Help her bear her dreary widowhood. Leave her undisturbed in the use of the small estate, and assist if there should be want.

Farewell, wife and children!

Another point, children. I know well you could not, if you would, practice Judaism according to my views and as I practiced it. But remain Jews and live as Jews in the best manner of your time, not only for yourself, but also where it is meet to the further whole.[64]

The sermons that comprise *Sabbath Hours* indicate that Adler was a highly sophisticated preacher, conversant with textual analysis, philosophy, and science, who was able to cushion his keen insights and strong beliefs in an engaging pedagogical rhetoric.

"The Story of the Creation,"[65] the first sermon — and one of the best — in *Sabbath Hours* is most learned indeed. Adler refers frequently to the Targumim, the Midrash and the details of the biblical text. The Bible begins with the "beginning," with *creatio-ex-nihilo*. This, according to Adler, is its great wisdom, since the Bible thereby avoids the gross mythologies of pagan literature, and touches all generations by commencing with the world as humanity knows it. "Strictly speaking," Adler observes, the Bible "contains no theology, no metaphysics, no mysticism, no heaven, no hell, no angels, no devils, nothing of another world. The Bible, according to its contents, may be divided into natural history, laws, and ethics."

Whereas science "deals with the creation only, regardless of the Creator," the Bible rises to eternal grandeur by directing humanity's eyes to the *wonder* of creation and to the presence of a creator. Unfortunately, Adler laments, people have become "*children* of the nineteenth century" (italics his); they have more "advanced" scientific instruments than were known in the days of the Bible, but they do not share the *inquistiveness* of the biblical writers, the eagerness of the ancients to explain every natural phenomenon. The masses mock the ancient explanations of the world-order, but are not conversant enough with natural science to offer more sophisticated answers of their own.

In other words, Adler holds up the Bible as a noble example of an attempt to investigate nature. The Bible thus becomes the model of a healthy wonder about the universe, neither offensive like pagan mythology nor technical like modern science. Rather than getting bogged down in any superficial religion versus science controversies, or in arguments about any specific statements in the Bible, Adler affirms that modern man should respect both the Bible *and* natural science as worthy efforts to awaken humanity to the wonders of the world, and hence to the glory of the creator. To Adler, then, the Bible is a manifesto of the centrality of wonder to human religiosity.

Adler also gives science its due. In another sermon, "Immortality," he cites the courage of intellectuals who risked all for knowledge. Adler admires intellect, but with reservations. He notes that the brightest people may not make the best parents, and that "rationalists" who deny the continuity of the soul are actually abetted by belief in immortality. The sermon is thought-provoking, if prone to generalization, but it fails to anticipate the argument that the "immortality" desired by at least some scientists is a professional one and not necessarily an affirmation of "soul."

Still, Liebman Adler demonstrates creditable rationalism and remarkable sophistication in his interpretation of biblical verses. The sermons "The First Verse of the Bible" and "The So-Called Fall of Man" testify to his modern methodology, which demonstrates reverence for, and appreciation of, the ancient Scriptures. His approach is reminiscent of the allegorical tact of Philo of Alexandria (20 B.C.E.–40 C.E.). Thus, in the very first verse, which speaks of God creating "the heaven and the earth," Adler finds a biblical mandate for people to explore the spiritual ("heaven") even as we "raise our eyes to the glorious azure." The so-called "fall of man," as described in the Bible, is interpreted by him — and not at all out of context — as an exhortation that work, human labor, is the best antidote to destructive thought. Though, given the times, Adler does echo stereotypes of women and "natives," he does pioneer in the use of child psychology to make his points effectively.

ADOLPH MOSES

Rabbi Adolph Moses[66] (b. 1840, Kletchevo, Poland; d. 1902, Louisville, Kentucky) was the only Reform leader of nineteenth-century America to designate his interpretation of Judaism (which was actually typical of the views of many of his colleagues) as an independent, universal religion, which he called "Yahvism" after the ancient pentateuchal name for God. After years of preaching this faith, Rabbi Moses published his manifesto, *The Religion of Moses.*[67]

Adolph Moses studied in Breslau, where he was close to Abraham Geiger (1810–1874), the father of German Reform Judaism, and to Hermann Cohen (1842–1918), the Jewish Kantian philosopher. He fought in various armed services for Polish and Italian liberty, and was looked upon as a quixotic character. Geiger and Cohen supported him in his activities, however, and guided him to the University of Vienna, where he studied with Adolf Jellinek (1821–1893), the famed scholar-preacher, and with Moritz Gudemann (1835–1918), the Judaica scholar. From 1868 to 1870 he worked as a teacher at Segitz, Bavaria, and then emigrated to Montgomery, Alabama, where he acted as rabbi. His brother, Rabbi Isaac S. Moses (1847–1926), had already emigrated to the States, and was one of the leaders of American Reform. Isaac ultimately became the molder of the 1895 edition of the *Union Prayer Book* for Reform congregations.

One gets the impression that Adolph Moses fell into the rabbinate by chance. His biographer, Rabbi Hyman G. Enelow (1877–1934), states that Moses preached extemporaneously and vaguely at first, not really rooted in any particular standpoint. From 1870 to 1881, Moses utilized his stay in Montgomery to perfect his English. His later passion for Reform seems to have come from his association with Isaac Mayer Wise, whom he met through his brother, Isaac. He assumed the pulpit of Temple Adath Israel, Louisville, Kentucky, in 1881, and remained there until his retirement.[68] Remarkably, Moses became a physician after completing the course at the Medical School in Louisville from 1887 to 1893, in order, as he later stated, to "obtain a direct answer to certain perplexing questions."[69]

Moses's essays, collected posthumously in *Yahvism and Other Discourses* (1903),[70] impress the reader as literate and thoughtful, and as permeated by a liberal, almost romantic view of man and God. Adolph Moses was preoccupied with ethical issues and offers sermons on the self, selfishness, and self-realization, sermons that might have been preached successfully, or effectively read in therapy sessions, a hundred years later. Needless to say, Moses regarded the "ceremonial laws" of the Bible and Talmud as dispensable means to an end, but in an essay called "Ceremonialism" (1894), he did defend the dietary laws (as practiced in ancient times) as deriving from a "democratic" impulse in biblical Judaism — namely, that the people were expected to observe the same rules as the priests. In "Yahvism" (1894), a discourse delivered before the graduating class of the Hebrew Union College, Moses defined the "truly genuine American Israelites" as having "completely emancipated themselves from the yoke of the ceremonial laws."

Like all the Reform rabbis of his era, Adolph Moses regarded America as both haven and harbinger of liberal enlightenment, and cited as "America's Contributions to World Civilization" the moral fiber of the country, its economic strides, and its emancipation of women. In the spirit of Isaac Mayer Wise, he regarded the American people as highly receptive to the message of Judaism. Thus, in "The Religion We Offer to the Gentiles" (1896), Moses attempts to win sympathy for Judaism by attacking Trinitarianism for its irrationality and for dividing people and nations into the believers and the damned. He praises liberal Christian denominations that have shed such views.

Indeed, a subtle but perceptible polemic with Christianity runs through his discourses. In a Yom Kippur sermon, "Losing God and Finding God" (1900), reprinted in this book, Moses actually co-opts terminology from Christian texts (including hymns) and theology: "seasons of distress," "ministry of sorrow," "Thy will be done," "abounding grace," "gospel of mercy and holiness," "bleeding heart." He thus claims back for Judaism and for the Jewish People a theology of suffering which he clearly found compatible with the doctrine of classical Reform Judaism that the Jews, the "people of humanity," have the mission to spread "ethical monotheism" to the world, by example and even by martyrdom. "Today," he concluded, "we pray for the peace and moral advancement and happiness of all the peoples, even those that torment and persecute the children of Israel."

In 1897, Adolph Moses presented his own convictions in a discourse entitled "Why I Am a Jew," which affirms pure monotheism over and against the incarnation doctrines of Christianity, as well as Judaism's this-worldly trust in human potential as opposed to the Christian doctrines of original sin and other-worldly salvation. Moses insists that dogmaless Christianity is really Judaism, and that the Unitarian Church is actually a branch of "Yahvism," even though its members "still coquette with the peculiar dogmas of Christianity."

Adolph Moses did not share the nineteenth-century mindset, reflected by most of his colleagues in the American Reform rabbinate, that God's will was revealed in an historical process of evolution which brought people to gradual appreciation of higher truths. In the preface to his little volume *The Religion of Moses,* he stated his basic affirmations about Judaism and firmly attacked contemporary assumptions to the contrary:

> I hold, with the biblical tradition, that Moses was in the deepest and widest sense the founder of the religion of Israel. The prophets who came after him did not originate, but only developed and propagated the religion of ethical monotheism first promulgated by the son of Amram. My contention is that Mosaism never was a tribal religion. From the very day of its appearance it was universal in essence and scope. Time was, when such views needed no defense; but nowadays ... [the] rise of true monotheism and of its lofty doctrines is ascribed to the prophets of the eighth and seventh centuries before Christ. The creative work of Moses is reduced to a minimum. The grandest actor in the drama of humanity's onward spiritual struggle appears a shadowy or mythical figure to the distorted vision of hyper-criticism. The greatest religious and moral revolution known to history is by an influential school of modern writers referred back to the mysterious agency of slow impersonal development. The Shibboleth of evolution is indiscriminately applied to all phenomena, and is believed to explain readily even the most extraordinary manifestations and the greatest works of the human mind. Our age refuses to credit great men with great things. There is a blind faith in the progressive forces and the wonderful achievements of the masses.

What we find here is not a repudiation of the liberal doctrine of "progress in history," but rather of the notion that historical process, and not outstanding leaders, brings about such progress. Indeed, in the sermon "Losing God and Finding God," Adolph Moses said that history "is the record of the manifestations of His wisdom, or His attributes, of His all-wise laws, through the minds of superior men, who have felt after Him and longed for communion with His ways."[71] While this view challenges various tendencies in biblical criticism and in social and scientific theory in Adolph Moses's era and since, it does certainly correspond with late nineteenth-century ideas about literary creation which, according to F. R. Leavis, "laid all the stress on inspiration and individual genius."[72]

As for Adolph Moses's aversion to biblical criticism and its onslaught on Moses, we must understand that this is but a natural result of the nineteenth-century Reform emphasis on Mosaic legislation as the basis of religious authority. The emphasis on the literary and historical inviolability of the word of Moses was so crucial to Classical Reform Judaism that its leaders could not even abide the rabbinic interpretations of various pentateuchal texts, which were in many ways as daring as the theories of Bible critics. The Reform stance was most strongly articulated by Isaac Mayer Wise, who consistently regarded biblical criticism as an onslaught on the essentials of Judaism[73] and who actually refused to engage the leading Talmudic scholar, Louis Ginzberg (1873–1953) for the Hebrew Union College, because he subscribed to Wellhausenean views.[74]

Still, Adolph Moses does not seem to regard biblical scriptures as the only, or even as the central, sources of Divine revelation. In "Losing God and Finding God" he declares "the universe" to be "the volume in which are writ the self-revelations of the Eternal." Ostensibly, "universe" includes "the lead of the men of supreme genius who sought Him and his light all their life, who found Him along the path of knowledge and goodness." These geniuses and visionaries were responding to Him who "has spoken to us, and continually speaks to us, through the soul and with the voice of the path-finders of humanity, who have sought Him, His light and His truth, His laws of righteousness and love, with all their heart." In this way, even the attributes of God "well up from the soul of man as moral ideas." All nature, including humanity, "is the incarnated thought and will of God."

Adolph Moses's published discourses reflect many of the crucial issues that underpinned nineteenth-century Reform pulpit thought. His most dramatic statement of faith was a lecture, "Who Is the Real Atheist?" (1893), in which he observed that the philosophers who have challenged theological "proofs" of the existence of God have often shown the keenest insight into the insufficiency of human discourse about God. The real test of belief in God, he said, is not use of approved religious language, but conduct, for all religious beliefs and practices find their authenticity in reflecting Divine goodness:

The idea of God implies the idea of divine perfection and absolute goodness. God and goodness are synonymous, interchangeable terms. If we believed that God was not goodness, we might fear Him, but we could not adore Him. A good man would appear to us more worshipful than He. Religion and philosophy agree in holding that morality is the highest manifestation of the Infinite in and through the soul of man…. To believe in God does not mean that we simply allow that He exists, it means that we strive to walk in the luminous footsteps of His holiness, to walk in the ways of His justice, truth and mercy. Every virtuous action is a true act of worship…. To smite and over-throw the vaulting instincts of selfishness, in order to serve the common good of all, is the strongest proof that a God of goodness inspires the breast of man. He is an atheist who professes to believe in God but whose deeds put his faith to shame. He who declares that he considers the Ten Commandments a revelation of God and yet violates one and all, he is the real atheist.

The best theological discourse by Adolph Moses is "The Reasons Why I Believe in God" (1895). He begins by observing that man knows of two kinds of existence: the external, material world of objects, and the internal world of consciousness, feelings, thoughts and ideas. Even if everything we see is illusion (an obvious reference to the philosophy of Bishop Berkeley), we know that *we* exist. Without the idea of existence, nothing is thinkable or possible. The universe presents itself to our minds as a unity; there is an "eternal kinship," an "inborn love" between elements.

The suggestion is that a covenantal model, even a paradigm of love, applies to the elements of the universe, though in the "Why I Believe" discourse Adolph Moses never relates this to the biblical covenants that God made with Noah, Abraham and the Israelites at Mount Sinai. Even when he uses the word "covenant," he is purposely ambiguous. In the Yom Kippur sermon "Losing God and Finding God," Moses admonishes that "selfish isolation" and "blind self-love" are the chief obstacles to communion with the Divine. He therefore engages in some family therapy to foster family love and to warn against the selfishness of entire families vis-à-vis other families in the community and in the world at large. He then turns to the concept of covenant:

> All those that have lost God through narrowness and hardness of heart, all those for whom God is far, because they live in egotistical self-isolation, will find Him by renewing in contrition the covenant of brotherhood with their fellow-men, the covenant of active sympathy with humanity's life.

The covenants of Abraham, and, he suggests, of Sinai, are an "intimation" that family union and family love "must be enlarged in our sympathies to a union of the whole people.... Our heart and mind must at last embrace the whole human family within the circle of our highest interests." Adolph Moses implies that Jews must regard their covenant with God as paradigmatic of covenants within community, American society, and the world community, that Jews must foster and even model such covenant, "rising from grade to grade in dignity and universality" in order to bring Godliness to the world through a kind of group selflessness.

In "The Reasons Why I Believe in God," Moses posits that there is no exception to the "universal law of causality." But the atoms did not just meet and *plan* to cooperate. There must, therefore, be one reality behind them. Thus, both our perception of the universe and scientific laws as we understand them point to a supreme being. (The causality argument is, of course, as old as Aristotle's case for the "unmoved mover.")

Given the existence of that supreme being, we are still faced with problems before we can affirm the God of Israel. Is that being a rational self or a blind force? Adolph Moses points out that if the one is not spiritual power, we are *ipso facto* bound to materialism. We would not have a God whom we could adore. But we must reject the notion of a material base to our existence. Consciousness as we know and experience it is not like any form of material being. Feeling, thinking, and willing are not mere motion, are not comparable, let us say, to magnetic force. Our very self is consciousness. If, as Huxley observes, consciousness is not derived from matter or from force, it must, Adolph Moses concludes, be of God.

In a very clever twist of argument, however, Adolph Moses concedes that biology reveals that even the human mind requires nerves, blood, and matter in order to function. Would it seem, therefore, that our alleged bondage to the material world is not an argument to be easily dismissed? And if God is mind, would He not require nerves, braincells, blood, etc.?

Here, Adolph Moses obviously draws upon his training in the medical laboratory. He observes that microbes have feeling and brains, and yet do not have nerves, etc. (Is God, therefore, to be compared to a microbe? Adolph Moses does not even attempt to make a qualification!) Moses adds that although man's brain is the most complex organism, biologically speaking, physiology cannot even begin to explain consciousness. The elements out of which the brain is made cannot explain the mysterious force behind it. While our experience alone cannot tell us what is possible, we know enough to be able to conclude that mind cannot spring from matter. Something can't emerge from nothing. Hence, again, we must affirm the origin of mind in God.

So runs Adolph Moses's ingenious affirmation of God, which begins with an almost Cartesian affirmation of consciousness ("I think; therefore I am") and yet employs medical training to give materialism a straw man's victory in order to debunk it. His discourse on belief testifies to the theological creativity that characterized many American Jewish pulpits in the last century, and that still impresses and delights the reader.

NOTES

1. See Adolf Kobler, "Jewish Preaching and Preachers, A Contribution to the History of the Jewish Sermon in Germany and America," *Historica Judaica*, vol. 8 (Oct. 1945), and Bernard N. Cohn, "Early German Preaching in America," *ibid.*, vol. 14 (Oct. 1953). See also Bertram W. Korn, "German-Jewish Intellectual Influences on American Jewish Life, 1824–1872," in A. Leland Jamison, ed., *Tradition and Change in Jewish Experience* (Syracuse, N.Y.: Syracuse University Press, 1978).

2. New York: Macmillan, 1918.

3. I have limited my investigation to Jewish thinkers who at no time abandoned Judaism. Some individuals, like Solomon Schindler and Charles Fleischer, both rabbis of Temple Israel, Boston, made interesting theological statements but then abandoned the Jewish fold. (Fleischer later returned.) See Arthur Mann, ed., *Growth and Achievement: Temple Israel 1854–1954* (Cambridge, Mass.: The Riverside Press/Trustees of Temple Israel, 1954), pp. 45–83.

4. My major biographical source on Lilienthal is David Philipson, *Max Lilienthal — American Rabbi, Life and Writings* (N.Y.: Bloch, 1915), pp. 1–132. On David Philipson, see his autobiography, *My Life as an American Jew* (Cincinnati: John G. Kidd and Son, 1941), especially the index references under "Lilienthal, Max."

On Lilienthal's advocacy of Reform in his son's congregation, see Fred Rosenbaum, *Visions of Reform: Congregation Emanu-El and the Jews of San Francisco*, (1849–1999) (Berkeley, CA.: The Judah L. Magnes Museum, 2000), p. 71. This well-researched synagogue history reads like a novel, and is a model both of fine writing and of discretion in presenting controversy and scandal.

On Lilienthal, see Karla Goldman, "The Path to Reform Judaism: An Examination of Religious Leadership in Cincinatti 1841–1853," *American Jewish History* (March 2002), vol. 90, no. 1, pp. 47ff.

5. Philipson, *Max Lilienthal*, op. cit.

6. On the background of Ansche Chesed, see Hyman B. Grinstein, *The Rise of the Jewish Community of New York 1654–1860* (Philadelphia: The Jewish Publication Society of America, 1945), pp. 49ff.

7. On Lilienthal, Rodeph Shalom and Shaarey Hashamayim, see the Index references in *ibid.*

8. On the architecture of the Mound Street Temple, see Rachel Wischnitzer, *Synagogue Architecture in the United States* (Philadelphia: The Jewish Publication Society of America, 1955), p. 76.

9. In Philipson, pp. 391–397.

10. My chief biographical source on Gutheim is Bertram W. Korn's article in *Encyclopedia Judaica* (1971), vol. 7, p. 986, col. 2, and the attached bibliography. On Gutheim's association with Isaac Mayer Wise and his ties to New Orleans, see Fred Rosenbaum, *Visions of Reform*, p. 16. See also Karla Goldman, *op. cit.*, pp. 39ff.

11. Rev. James K. Gutheim, *The Temple Pulpit, A Selection of Sermons and Addresses Delivered on Special Occasions* (N.Y.: Jewish Times, 1872), pp. 95–103.

12. See Psalm 34, and Robert Gordis, "The Social Background of Wisdom Literature," in *Poets, Prophets, and Sages: Essays in Biblical Interpretation* (Bloomington: Indiana University Press, 1971).

13. My chief biographical source on Rabbi Kalisch is the memoir by his son, the late Samuel Kalisch, a justice on the Supreme Court of New Jersey, in the work he edited, *Isidor Kalisch, Studies in Ancient and Modern Judaism* (N.Y.: George Dobsevage, 1928). Kalisch earned an honored placed in modern studies of Jewish mysticism when he translated, in 1877, the early Kabbalistic work *Sefer Yetzirah* (third to sixth century) into English.

14. See Lloyd P. Gartner, *The Jews of Cleveland* (Cleveland, Ohio: Western Reserve Historical Society, 1978), pp. 33 ff.

15. See Louis J. Swichkow and Lloyd P. Gartner, *The History of the Jews of Milwaukee* (Philadelphia: The Jewish Publication Society of America, 1963), pp. 43–44.

16. These are anthologized in Kalisch, *op. cit.*

17. Kalisch, pp. 110–134.

18. My chief biographical source on Frederick de Sola Mendes is Moshe Davis, *The Emergence of Conservative Judaism* (Philadelphia: The Jewish Publication Society of America, 1963), pp. 349–351. In the section of the book in which the sketch of Mendes is found, there are several biographical sketches of leading nineteenth-century "historical school" rabbis which are invaluable to students of the period. In fact, the Davis volume marked the groundbreaking of the field of nineteenth-century Jewish intellectual history.

19. Frederick de Sola Mendes, *Tyndallism and Judaism* [Pamphlet] (New York: Congregation Shaaray Tefila, 1874).

20. See James G. Heller, *Isaac M. Wise — His Life, Work and Thought* (New York: Union of American Hebrew Congregations, 1965). See also Andrew F. Key, *The Theology of Isaac Mayer Wise* (Cincinnati: The American Jewish Archives, 1962), and Wise's own autobiographical work, *Reminiscences,* ed. David Philipson (New York: Arno Press, 1973), reprinted from the 1901 edition originally published by L. Wise and Co. See also Karla Goldman, *op. cit.*, pp. 46 ff.

21. See James G. Heller, *op. cit.*, pp. 192 ff.

22. Isaac M. Wise, *The Cosmic God* (Cincinnati: Office of "The American Israelite" and "Deborah," 1876).

23. *Ibid.*, p. 60.

24. *Ibid.*, p. 32.

25. *Ibid.*, p. 34.

26. *Ibid.*

27. *Ibid.*, p. 35.

28. *Ibid.*, p. 36.

29. *Ibid.*, p. 37.

30. *Ibid.*, p. 136.

31. *Ibid.*, p. 139–40. Wise goes on to describe how the "Logos of History" exacts retributions for crimes (144) and is identical with what the ancient Hebrews called *ruakh ha-kodesh* or "the Holy Spirit" (145). The "Logos of History" also manifests itself in genius, which allows history to progress. See pp. 144 ff.

32. *Ibid.*, p. 138.

33. *Ibid.*, p. 148.

34. *Ibid.*, pp. 157–164.

35. *Ibid.*, p. 167. Wise declares that he agrees with Maimonides that creation *ex nihilo* is not indispensable to Judaism, and that matter can have pre-existed with substance. (Actually, Maimonides is ambiguous on the subject, maintaining, as Wise notes, that both creation *ex nihilo* and pre-existing matter are conducive to logical proof. Yet Maimonides seems to lean toward the former belief, in accordance with tradition.)

36. My major biographical source on Felsenthal is Emma Felsenthal, *Bernhard Felsenthal, Teacher in Israel* (N.Y.: Oxford University Press, 1924). Though edited with a memoir by Felsenthal's daughter, this volume is a paradigm for objective and helpful memoirs, collected works, and annotated bibliographies. For more on Felsenthal, see Morris A. Gutstein, *A Priceless Heritage: The Epic Growth of Nineteenth Century Chicago Jewry* (N.Y.: Bloch, 1953), pp. 111–2, 197, 232, 375–76, 395, 405–7.

37. The phrase comes from Isaiah 40:3.

38. On the architecture of Zion and Sinai congregations, see *Faith and Form —Synagogue Architecture in Illinois: An Exhibition Organized by the Spertus Museum* (Chicago: Spertus College of Judaica, 1976), pp. 39–40, 45.

39. See "The Origin of Judaism and Its Three Epochs," in Felsenthal, pp. 156–7, 162–3.

40. Cited in "Selected Writings," *ibid.*, p. 250.

41. *Ibid.*, pp. 218–27.

42. *Ibid.*, pp. 177–87.

43. My biographical sources on Kohut are as follows: Ismar Elbogen, "Alexander Kohut," *American Jewish Year Book* 1942–3 (vol. 44), pp. 73–80; Moshe Davis, *op. cit.*, pp. 344–7; and the memoirs by Barnett A. Elzas, Max Cohen, and Maurice H. Harris in Alexander Kohut, *Ethics of the Fathers*, ed. Barnett Elzas (New York, 1920). On Kohut's scholarship, see Gotthard Deutsch, "Alexander Kohut's Contribution to Jewish Scholarship," in Kohut-Elzas, and George Alexander Kohut, "Memoir of Dr. Alexander Kohut's Literary Activity," in *Tributes to the Memory of Rev. Dr. Alexander Kohut* (N.Y.: Ahavath Chesed Congregation, 1894). For bibliographies of Kohut's writings, see George Alexander Kohut, "Concerning Alexander Kohut: A Tentative Bibliography," in Ludwig Blau, ed., *Festschrift* (in Hungarian and Hebrew) of the Jewish Theological Seminary of Budapest (Budapest, 1927), pp. 200–212, and "Selected Bibliography of Alexander Kohut," in *The Alexander Kohut Memorial Foundation 1915–1968* (N.Y.: American Academy for Jewish Research, 1973).

In addition to becoming the chief defender in America of traditional Judaism, Kohut was able to complete the *Arukh Completum*. On that event and its effect upon the Kohut family, see the memoir by Rebekah Kohut, Kohut's second wife, who raised his eight orphaned children after his untimely death, and became a leading Jewish personality in her own right: Rebekah Kohut, *My Portion, An Autobiography* (N.Y.: Thomas Seltzer, 1925), pp. 162–4.

44. On Kohut's polemic with Kohler, see Philip Cowen, *Memories of an American Jew* (N.Y.: International Press, 1932), pp. 405–7 and Rebekah Kohut, *op. cit.*, pp. 78–86.

45. On Leeser, see Moshe Davis, *op. cit.*, pp. 347–9.

46. On Raphall, see *ibid.*, pp. 356–8, and Israel Goldstein, *A Century of Jewish Life in New York* (N.Y.: Congregation B'nai Jeshurun, 1930), pp. 110–26.

47. Alexander Kohut, *Ethics of the Fathers*, tr. from the German by Max Cohen (N.Y.: The American Hebrew, 1885), pp. 29–42. See also Kohut's original preface to the work. The pages in the Elzas edition are 19–30.

48. Actually, the literal dictum in *Pirke Avot*, attributed to Simon the Just, does not refer to the "world of Judaism," but to the "world."

49. See "The Fence Around the Law," pp. 17–27 in the Cohen ed. (translated as "The Hedge Around the Law") and pp. 10–18 in the Elzas ed.

50. My chief source on Gottheil is the comprehensive biography by his son, Richard James Horatio Gottheil, *The Life of Gustav Gottheil — Memoir of a Priest in Israel* (Williamsport, Pa.: The Bayard Press, 1936).

51. *The Unitarian Review* (January 1887), pp. 1–12. Richard Gottheil cites a letter in response to this article on pp. 131–2, but refers to the article itself only briefly on the bottom of p. 131.

52. Another celebrated polemical work, the culmination of the American Reform Jewish critiques of Christianity, is Abba Hillel Silver, *Where Judaism Differed* (N.Y.: Macmillan, 1956). See also George L. Berlin, *Defending the Faith: Nineteenth-Century American Jewish Writings on Christianity and Jesus* (N.Y.: State University of New York, 1989).

53. My chief biographical source on Joseph Krauskopf is William W. Blood, *Apostle of Reason: A Biography of Joseph Krauskopf* (Philadelphia: Dorrance and Co., 1973). For reminiscences of Krauskopf's preaching and "missionary" activities among East European Jews, see Israel H. Levinthal, *The Message of Israel — Sermons, Addresses, Memoirs* (N.Y.: Lex Printing Co., 1973), pp. 145–6, 186–93. On Krauskopf's battle with Jacob Schiff over the National Farm School, see Philip Cowen, *op. cit.*, p. 325.

54. Reminiscences of Krauskopf's early years at the Hebrew Union College can be found in Max E. Berkowitz, *The Beloved Rabbi: An Account of the Life and Works of Henry Berkowitz, D.D.* (N.Y.: Macmillan, 1932), pp. 6–10; and in David Philipson, *My Life as an American Jew* (Cincinnati: John G. Kidd and Son, Inc., 1941), pp. 22–3, 55–6, 69.

55. Both series were published: *Evolution and Judaism* (Kansas City, Missouri: Berkowitz and Co., 1887); *The Jews and Moors in Spain* (Kansas City: Berkowitz and Co., 1887).

56. These and other highlights of Krauskopf's ministry in Kansas City are carefully reconstructed by Frank J. Adler in *Roots in a Moving Stream: The Centennial History of Congregation B'nai Jehudah of Kansas City, 1870–1970* (Kansas City, Missouri: The Temple, Cong. B'nai Jehudah, 1972), pp. 57–78. This 466-page volume is a fine and yeoman congregational history, and should be regarded as a model for congregational histories and for local Jewish histories.

57. Cowen charges that *The Jews and Moors in Spain* was lifted from John W. Draper's *Intellectual Development of Europe*. See Cowen, *op. cit.*, p. 53.

58. See Joseph L. Blau, "An American-Jewish View of the Evolution Controversy," *Hebrew Union College Annual*, vol. 20 (1947), pp. 617–34. See also Stuart E. Rosenberg, "Some Sermons in the Spirit of the Pittsburgh Platform," *Historia Judaica*, vol. 18, part 1 (April 1956), pp. 61–2.

59. Krauskopf, *Evolution and Judaism*, pp. 315–30.

60. Joseph L. Blau notes in *op. cit.* three major flaws in Krauskopf's *Evolution* lectures: (1) that he was inconsistent in his view of God: "God sometimes appears as depersonalized power, natural law, and sometimes as personal divinity"; (2) that he "evades the Darwinian questions of the struggle for existence and survival of the fittest"; and (3) that he approaches evolution merely as a vehicle for Reform polemics.

61. My chief source on Liebman Adler is the fine biographical sketch of him by Bernhard Felsenthal and Herman Eliassof in *History of Anshe Maarabh* (Chicago, 1897), pp. 40–5. Other background material may be found in Morris A. Gutstein, *A Priceless Heritage*, pp. 101–4 and the index under "Adler, Liebman."

62. Liebman Adler, *Sabbath Hours* (Philadelphia: Jewish Publication Society of America, 1893), editor unidentified. The editor's introduction indicates that Adler intended the anthology for the education of Jewish women.

63. The name *Dankmar* was reportedly a combination of the German, *Dank* ("thanks") and the Hebrew, *mar* ("bitter"), since the mother died in childbirth. Dankmar seems to have inherited his father's upright and amiable disposition. One finds a "Biographical Sketch" of his life in Hugh Morrison, *Louis Sullivan, Prophet of Modern Architecture* (N.Y.: Museum of Modern Art and W. W. Norton, 1935), pp. 283–5. For Sullivan's early impressions of Dankmar Adler, see *ibid.*, pp. 49–50. Robinson cites Frank Lloyd Wright's fond reminiscences on pp. 80–1. On Dankmar's engineering and acoustical genius, see *ibid.*, pp. 90, 102–3, respectively. Liebman Adler is discussed briefly in *ibid.*, pp. 124, 283–4.

64. Cited in Felsenthal and Eliassof, pp. viii–ix, and in Morris Gutstein, *A Priceless Heritage*, pp. 103–4.

65. *Sabbath Hours*, pp. 1–7. The other sermons anthologized here, "The First Verse

of the Bible," "The So-Called Fall of Man," and "Immortality," appeared in the same volume and thus were published in English in the same year.

66. My chief biographical source on Adolph Moses is Hyman G. Enelow's introduction to Adolph Moses, *Yahvism and Other Discourses* (Louisville, Kentucky: Council of Jewish Women, 1903) and the article on him in the *Universal Jewish Encyclopedia* (1942), vol. 8, p. 11, cols. 1–2.

67. Adolph Moses, *The Religion of Moses* (Louisville, Ky.: Flexner Brothers, 1894).

68. Enelow, *op. cit.*

69. See below, "Why I Studied Medicine," and also, "Who Is the Real Atheist?" and "Losing God and Finding God," from *Yahvism and Other Discourses.* Another leading Reform rabbi, Aaron (Albert) Bettelheim (1830–1890), the father of Rebekah Kohut, also studied to be a physician while ministering to his congregation, and combined both professions. See Rebekah Kohut, *op. cit.,* p. 18.

70. All references to Adolph Moses's writings, unless otherwise stated, are to this volume.

71. *Yahvism and Other Discourses,* p. 120.

72. F. R. Leavis, *The Common Pursuit* (N.Y.: Penguin Books, 1952), p. 183.

73. James Heller, *Isaac M. Wise,* pp. 530–3.

74. See Harry H. Mayer, "What Price Conservatism?—Louis Ginzberg and the Hebrew Union College," *American Jewish Archives,* vol. X (Oct. 1958), pp. 145–50.

I

MAX LILIENTHAL

Rabbinical Codices, or the Shulchan Aruch (1856)[*]

I am coming now to the rabbinical codices or the *Shluchan Aruch*. The supreme principle directing your opinion in this province you have clearly defined by the sentence (*Occident*, Nov., 386) *"The plain reading of the rule of the Shulchan Aruch prohibits it, and no sophistry can wipe it out."* By this autocratic and dictatorial assertion you have declared the inviolability of these codices. This, your opinion, is founded on the obsolete medieval notion of an immediate trust in any authority whatever. Without admitting any critical or historical investigation like the kings and nobles of *"Dei gratia,"* you refer to your old books and titles, exclaiming: "Here is the law, sanctioned by the reverence and obedience of bygone centuries; we have to adopt it as we have inherited it; we have no right either to abolish it or even to winnow and sift it. The *Shulchan Aruch* is my guide, and any contradiction of this premise is plain and open heresy."

The spirit of our age, however, unwilling to yield to ukases, replies: Let us examine this your autocratic prohibition. Is the *Shulchan Aruch*, as it is presented to us, a divine revelation, so that no sophistry can wipe it out? No, it is not. Is its entire context a complex of mere direct traditions *(Halachah leMoshe Mi-sinai[†])*? No, it is not. Does the *Shulchan Aruch* contain nothing but the plain *Halachoth* of the Talmud? No, it contains also the continuous additions and accretions made

[* "Letters on Reform Addressed to the Rev. I. Leeser," No. V., December 26, 1856. The Shulhan Arukh ("Set Table") is the classic code of Jewish Law, prepared in the sixteenth century by Sephardic scholar Joseph Karo, and rendered authoritative for Ashkenazic Jews through glosses by Polish scholar, Moses Isserles.]

[† "A law attributed to Moses at Sinai,' that is, a very well-established usage. See Kiddushin 38b.]

by a host of rabbis down to the latter centuries. Was it adopted *in toto* by all the Jews throughout all centuries? No, for the Portuguese Jews follow the opinion of Rabbi Joseph Karo only, while the German and Polish Jews adopted the additions of still later authorities. Hence even from your standpoint it would be permitted to strike out half of the *Shulchan Aruch*, by rescinding all but the plain reading of the rules of Joseph Karo. By this proceeding one full half of our onerous customs and usages would be done away with, they being founded on no other authority than on that of the Polish scholar Remah,* who imported into that codex the manners and customs of the Jews then living in Poland. This importation, having neither biblical nor traditional foundation, but merely the spontaneous consent of his and the following generations, can be declared void of any legal authority as soon as this consent of submitting any longer to these unfounded accretions is withdrawn. Hence without any sophistry whatever, but by virtue of good right and title, at least one-half of our *Shulchan Aruch* can be wiped out as soon as the people are willing to assume this legal authority.

But probing the question still deeper we must ask: What course have we to pursue, when we can prove that legal decisions, as compiled in the *Shulchan Aruch* in course of time have shaped themselves in open contradiction to the plain reading of the rule of the Bible and tradition, and of abolishing developments of later date, that nowadays have become onerous and conflicting with the demands of the time?

You will reply that there are no decisions of that kind. Well, then, I will give you but a very few examples, and matters of fact will substantiate my charge:

1. The scrupulous and minute form of our giving divorce. The plain word of the Bible reads thus: "When a man hath taken a wife, and married her, and it come to pass that she finds no favor in his eyes, because he hath found some unseemly thing in her, then let him write her a bill of divorce and give it in her hand, and send her out of his house." (Deut. xxiv, 1.) The sense and meaning of this biblical command, of providing the dismissed wife with a written bill of divorce, is no other than that she might be furnished with a document entitling her to be married to another man.

[*Moses Isserles [note from original editor, Rabbi David Philipson. In the edition reproduced here, this note was originally signaled with a superscript 1.]

In full accordance with the plain reading of the Bible the Talmud, therefore (*Treatise Gittin*) maintains, that after the charge for giving a divorce has been substantiated, the bill of divorce may be written by anyone whomsoever, in any language and form, provided that it expresses the sense of the divorce, be signed in a legal form by witnesses, etc.

Please compare with this plain legal proceeding the minuteness and the difficulties for writing a divorce detailed in our codex *Eben Haesar.* These go so far that by the most insignificant mistake by the *Sopher* (scribe) the entire bill is declared to be void of any legal validity. Would a reform of this proceeding be antibiblical and antitraditional? Would it be beyond our legal right if we would draw up a formula in plain Hebrew, and translate it into the vernacular of the country, without paying any attention to these obsolete directions?

2. The abolition of the second day of *Yom Tob.* The Bible never and nowhere commands it. The Talmud tells us plainly that these traditional days were introduced merely because the days were not fixed by mathematical calculation, but by the monthly observations of the new moon; and as the messengers sent by the proper authorities for carrying the information as to what days had been appointed holidays could not reach the distant communities in proper time, these second days were instituted to prevent a desecration of the biblical holiday. The Talmud says clearly this is no legal obligation, but a mere custom dating from later times.

The mode of fixing the holidays having entirely changed nowadays, the calculation of the almanac being correct beyond any mistake, the second day of *Yom Tob* being burdensome to a great many of our merchants, tradesmen and mechanics, there being no legal objection raised either by the Bible or tradition, why should we not advocate and sanction a reform when so imperatively demanded, as was done only a few years ago by the Jewish merchants of Italy?

3. The reading of the entire Pentateuch in the synagogue every three years. The Bible ordains (Deut. xxxiii, 10–13) the reading of the law every seven years on the Feast of Tabernacles in the year of release. The Talmud (*Megillah*, fol. 39b) states plainly that in Palestine the Pentateuch was read every three years, for they did not care as we do for the mere reading, but that the portion might be understood by the congregation; and hence they appointed a *Meturgeman* who translated and explained every verse in the vernacular of the country to the attentive listeners.

What meaning has the hasty, unintelligible manner of our reading? Why should we not adopt and advocate a reform, entirely in accordance with the Bible and tradition and in harmony with the demands of our time? What reasonable objection can you raise to such an important and telling improvement of our service? Here, then, sir, you find three examples of decisions, entirely in contradiction with the plain reading of the rule of the Bible and tradition; what reasons or what laws will you adduce for censuring congregations that are willing to adopt such reforms, and to carry out such a radical change of our *Shulchan Aruch?*

You find yourself, then, in the following dilemma: From your standpoint you must assert, either that the legislative power has ceased with Bible and Talmud, or that the same has been bequeathed also to future generations. If it did cease with the first authorities, then certainly we are entitled to abolish the interpretations of later rabbis; and if it did not cease with them, and every successive generation be endowed with the same authority, then we too are entitled to do away with what they have added. Hence, whatever side of the question you advocate, you are logically bound to repeal your autocratic assertion, "the plain reading of the rule of the *Shulchan Aruch* prohibits it, and no sophistry can wipe it out."

I know all the objections you will raise even against this dilemma, and will examine them with the greatest impartiality.

First you will object: "How will you compare the rabbis of our age with those gigantic minds, the eminent Talmudists, the men of unbiased piety of bygone ages; your comparison is lame, and no one will grant you the same authority he willingly concedes to those paragons of learning and religion." Why not, dear sir? Without pointing out the impropriety of imputing to the present rabbis either deficiency of knowledge or want of true piety, I shall refer you to one of your own acknowledged authorities, the Talmud itself, that provided beforehand against such a bar to all progress, against such unlimited reverence of bygone ages. In Treatise *Rosh Hashannah,* page 25b, we read: "It is said (Deuter. xvii, 9) thou shalt go to the priests and Levites and the judge, that will be in these days; now certainly a man can not go to a judge who was not in his days, but has to go to the judge appointed in his own time, so that thou mayest not say (Eccles. vii, 10) that the former days were better than our own." *Rashi* and *Tosephot* corroborate this attitude, and hence this, your objection, is waived by the authority you cite.

But you continue: "Were the rabbis of old at least not as sound and great scholars as those of our time? Why, then, did they arrive at conclusions so widely differing from those of the modern rabbis?" The reply, sir, is a plain and simple one. The cause of this difference is to be found in the difference of the spirit of the respective ages. They acknowledged and submitted blindly to any rabbinical decision whatever, while in our days every authority before being recognized is put to the test of a critical investigation. They started when giving their decisions from the supreme principle *Kol mahmir tavo alav berakhah,* "the more severe the better," while our time starts from the opposite principle *koha d'heiteirah adif,* "the alleviating and disburdening decision has the legal preference." Hence the difference of the times and the results.

But you continue saying: "People are not yet prepared for such a change; you confuse them with your theories; you cause a religious revolution, pregnant with the most fatal results; better leave everything *in status quo;* the doubts engendered by the result of progressive science have taken hold of many a mind, have undermined the faith in the legal foundation, and are urging imperatively the required change. By your masterly inactivity you will foster hypocrisy, the results of which — indifference and atheism — will be a thousand times worse than all reforms." No, sir, if the masses are not yet sufficiently prepared for the changes unavoidably in store for us, it is the holy duty of the Jewish ministry and press to enlighten them on every subject, to build a bridge from the existing order of things over to the newly discovered truth, to assist them in overcoming the travails of the present state of transition, instead of misconstruing an obligation to uphold what time has declared obsolete. As soon as right has been proved to be right, let it be openly declared in spite of the insinuations or the opponents. Such an unanimous and hearty cooperation of all professional men will soon remove the obstacles thought to be insurmountable, establish the right of reform on legal and rational grounds, and restore peace and harmony.

Summing up, then, I deem the reform of the *Shulchan Aruch* to be justified beyond any objection. Therefore, I pause for an answer, which, no doubt, will be given with that impartiality and absence of passion that is befitting a contest, the end and aim of which is the glorification of truth and not of our humble selves.

II

JAMES K. GUTHEIM
The Spirit of God in Man (1872)

Take to thyself Joshua, the Son of Nun, a man in whom there is
spirit.

(Numbers xxvii, 18).

In my last two expositions of this text, I have endeavored to define
the term *ruah* or spirit, the possession of which qualified Joshua, in an
eminent degree, to succeed his great master as leader of the people, to
marshal their hosts for the occupation of the promised land. I have
tried to show, that every man is endowed with this spirit of God, to
whose voice he must listen, in order to overcome the spirit of selfishness, which is lurking in the human heart; I have endeavored, to expose
the fallacy of the wide-spread phenomenon, according to which every
man is apt, to regard himself as the centre, around which the whole
world is revolving; and have drawn the irresistible conclusion, that only
those deeds, which are devoid of selfish motives and ends are emanations of the spirit of God within us, are entitled to be characterized as
good and noble.

It is owing to the prevalence of the spirit of selfishness, that we
meet with so little elevation of sentiment, and that comparatively few
seem to be conscious of their high origin and destiny, their capacities
of excellence, their relation to God, their interest in eternity.

The spirit of God, which is operative in man and by the prompting of which all that is good, great and noble is accomplished, the spirit
of philanthropy and love, is confined to neither age, country or people, but is active, though in a limited degree and in isolated instances,
at all times and in every place. Judaism does not favor pessimism; it
abhors the idea of general depravity or original sin, but emphatically
teaches the God-like character of the human soul. Hence we are justified

in assuming, that the spirit of God is revealed and is manifested through man, just as much in our day, as at any previous period of history. We easily recognize this spirit by its *reverse.* Every manifestation or action, which excludes selfishness, is the product of this spirit; but wherever selfishness predominates, you look in vain for this spirit, for it is wanting.

Let us illustrate this proposition by a few examples.

The spirit of God is called the spirit of wisdom. What is wisdom? It is the choice of laudable ends and of the best means to accomplish them. Its scope is not limited to the individual, but embraces the welfare of the whole; is not bounded by our temporal existence, but includes time and eternity. While estimating material advantages and possessions at their comparative value, it is the chief aim of wisdom, to promote the intellectual and moral growth of mankind, its end the foundation of general good. The spirit of wisdom is essentially the spirit of benevolence.

Now contrast with this spirit of wisdom, the spirit of *worldly prudence,* by which most people are animated and which they apply to practice — a spirit which sternly asserts individual claims and rigidly aims at securing selfish ends— and you will no longer be at a loss, to discern the spirit of God, that should be reflected in our works. The prudent man may be just and moral, and yet be far from being benevolent and religious.

Justice differs from benevolence, not in its nature, but in the circumstances, under which it is exercised. Both justice and benevolence have the same object, the general good; but justice is limited to those cases where public good prescribes a clear, precise and unchanging course of action; while benevolence or its daughter — mercy, is exercised in circumstances, to which no definite rules can be applied, and in which the general good requires, that the individual should be left to his own judgment and discretion. Thus true justice is something more than that petty honesty, which seeks nothing but self, and which is contented with regarding such established principles as cannot be violated without incurring punishment or disgrace. The whole nature of justice is *impartial, diffusive benevolence.*

It may be observed, that, if it be the nature of justice to avoid, whatever is clearly opposed to our neighbor, it is unjust, in our dealings with others, to desire and seek more than the value of our services and commodities. Mutual benefit is the object of all human relations, the very end of trade or commerce. We know, when our neighbor contracts with us, that he expects an equivalent. We know, that he renders his services, or makes a transfer of his property for some adequate valuable consideration, and we have no right to offer as an equivalent, what we certainly know bears no proportion to the services he renders or the property he transfers. A just man, animated by the spirit of God, will never lose sight of the interests of his neighbor. He will not, indeed, feel himself bound, to take the same care of another's property and interests as of his own — for this is impracticable. He will suppose, that every man, who possesses common understanding, knows best his own interests, and on this ground he will deal with him. But when he certainly knows, that his neighbor is injuring himself, that a proposed contract cannot be attended with mutual benefit, he has no right to presume that his neighbor is taking care of himself; he has no right to be determined upon realizing the fruits of his shrewd and sharp transaction. As surely as he regards the rights of others, he will feel, that he has no right to offer as an equivalent, what he knows has no proportionate value.

Yes, it is but too true, that justice unconnected with benevolence is not worth possessing. It is the growth of selfishness, and knaves may boast of it. That man, who makes his own private interest supreme — who monopolises all honors, emoluments and profits that appertain to his province — who cares not how much his neighbor suffers, if only his individual interests be advanced, — who can take pleasure in gains which, he knows, are necessarily connected with the loss and injury of others— who, under pretence of leaving his neighbor to provide for himself, will impose upon him as an equivalent, what he knows to be worth nothing: that man may talk of integrity, and hold high his head in a prudent, mercenary world, but he knows not the meaning of justice. He never felt that *generous* regard to right, that noble appreciation of religion and benevolence, which is of more worth and confers more happiness than all the gains of selfishness.

If such be perfect justice, so incorruptible, what reason have we to fear, that there is little of this principle, when we see the expedients and precautions, which are adopted to prevent men from abusing a trifling or important trust, from sacrificing the interests of their neighbor to a trifling or important gain! We carry our own shame on our own foreheads. Most of our civil institutions grow out of our corruptions and delinquencies. We cannot live without mutual dependence, and yet we are forced, to hedge each other round, to bind and shackle each other, to institute inquiries and to watch with anxious caution, less [lest?] we should abuse each other's necessities, and take advantage of trust, to betray it. At this very moment, here and elsewhere throughout the country, in the General, the State and Municipal government, active investigations are carried on, to ascertain, to what an extent the public functionaries have betrayed the various trusts confided to them. Yes, is it not suggestive, is it not humiliating, that a necessity existed for the appointment of a "Committee on Frauds?" — If men were, what they should be, if all were animated by the true spirit, we should find in every man a guardian, instead of an invader of our rights and interests. We should want no better security than our neighbor's word, and no better witness than our neighbor's conscience. Imagination dwells with delight on this state of peaceful, unsuspicious, undisturbed enjoyment. Is it never to be made a reality? Will the era never dawn on the horizon of man, of which the prophet speaks, "They shall do no hurt nor destroy in all my holy mountain, saith the Lord —?"

It is the glorious design of civil institutions to concentre public strength in support of individual right, to guard the interests of the feeble by the majesty of the State. But no government can fully accomplish the end of its institution. No outward penalties can supply the place of an inward principle of benevolence, of genuine religion. They, who have power, can always find some opportunity of abusing it. Judaism, the exponent of true religion, an emanation from God, emphatically holds, "whoever saith: What is mine, is mine; and what is thine, is thine; pronounces a doctrine of Sodom." True religion forbids us, to abuse any circumstance, which puts our neighbor in our power, or to extort his consent to injurious measures, or to reduce him to the necessity of sacrificing his property, by threatening him with evils, to which we are able to expose him. It recommends the weak and poor to our protection. It renders the defenceless hovel of poverty as sacred as the palace of affluence. It makes the cause of the oppressed our own, and animates us with generous zeal, to rescue the helpless from the grasp of the oppressor. It calls on us, to frown on the base, to separate ourselves from their fellowship, *har-hek mi-sha'khen ra* [lit., "to keep far away from an evil neighbor"], to keep none of their counsels, to follow none of their examples. Men are prone to stoop to successful villainy. They seem to forget the steps, by which wicked men have ascended to eminence. They have only eyes for the outward splendor and seeming prosperity, in which successful villainy is revelling. But the spirit of God within man is inflexible. It can give no countenance to dishonesty and wrong. It looks through the false splendor, with which the selfish are surrounded, and sees and detests their baseness.

A man animated by this spirit takes a firm, elevated ground. He does not cling to every shadow of right. He does not take advantage of ambiguity of expression, to beat down what he knows to be a substantial claim. He does not abuse the ignorance of his neighbor and uphold, by legal subtleties, an unfounded demand. He does not press even his undoubted rights too close, lest he should border upon injustice. He reverences the laws, as they are the guardians of right. He holds nothing merely because the laws do not take it away. He seizes nothing merely because the laws do not prohibit it. His motto is not: I will take all the law allows me. He considers, that laws do not create right, that there are eternal principles of truth and rectitude, to which all civil laws must be reduced as their standard; and to the spirit planted by God in the human heart and revealed in His holy word, he refers all his actions, which relate to his dealings and his intercourse with others.

There is a natural law, that whatever belongs to the earth, presses towards its centre. You may pick up a stone, and fling it high in the air — it is sure to fall back to the ground, from which it was taken. A mysterious force in the dark bosom of the earth irresistibly draws it down, as it attracts every object and every particle, that belongs to the earth. In a similar way does *selfishness* act in man. It is the power of *gravitation* in the human heart, a power, which, if left uncontrolled, would fain attract to its centre all *earthly* objects, means and appliances and hold them fast with iron bands. Selfishness is thus synonymous with darkness of soul, frigidity of heart, spiritual death.

But there is another law of nature, which governs the operations of *light*. Its power is not exerted in drawing all things to its centre, but is, on the contrary, manifested, by shedding its rays, and pouring its warmth on all objects within its reach. This power preeminently, exclusively resides in the spirit of God within man. It is manifested in our diffusing the light of knowledge, in our pouring forth the warming rays of sympathy, of virtue, of benevolence, of true religion. It does not contract, but expands the heart, inuring it to all that is good, and true, and noble, and divine. O, that such a light would burn in every heart. "Would to God, that the whole people were prophets, that the Lord would endow them with His spirit." [Numbers 11:29]

III

ISIDOR KALISCH
Divine Providence (1874)*

The subject of my lecture this evening is the Doctrine of Divine Providence, demonstrated by reason; that there is a government or superintendence of the Universe by a Supreme Being who orders everything in nature for the best interests of his creatures. I believe that earnest meditation on this great and lofty topic will be a matter of the highest moment and attraction to all, irrespective of sex, age, creed, rank, condition or profession.

It will inspire us with sublime and noble sentiments of the grandeur of the divinity, the glory of God's perfection and the immensity of His government; it will bring home to our minds with a deep impression the truth of the biblical assertion: "The work of the Creator is perfect; He is righteous in all his ways." It will awaken in us a sense of our proneness to error and delusion; it will teach us how to conduct ourselves in the different conditions of prosperity and adversity that await us in the fluctuating waves of the sea of life; it will convince us that all is tending to a glorious issue, and that we shall consequently improve each of these conditions to wise ends, important purposes; it will show us how to value the blessings God bestows upon us as well as to appreciate the evils He inflicts, and to bear them better; it will make us feel the momentous import of the seemingly paradoxical principle of that venerable ancient savant, who taught that it is incumbent upon man to bless God for the good as well as for tribulation; it will teach us that we should always endeavor to find the silver lining to every cloud of life and cultivate a rational and habitual serenity and cheerfulness of temper — not extravagantly elated in pros-

*Lecture delivered at Nashville, Tennessee.

perity, nor pusillanimously depressed in adversity in seasons of sorrow, even when keeping the bed of anguish and death; in time, it will thus induce us to be contented with all sublunary affairs how and whatever they may be and thus enjoy life and endure it.

Though men in all ages have entertained various and discordant opinions as to the number and character of the Deity, they agree nevertheless on this point, that the affairs of the world and of men are objects of divine attention and care. It is not only inculcated in us by many passages in the Bible, but was also taught by the ancient philosophers, as for instance by Zoroaster, Socrates, Plato, four to five centuries before the Common Era, and also by a great many others.

Cicero, who lived 106 before the Common Era, in his *De Natura Deorum,* represents Balbus speaking of the existence of gods, "Quo concesso, confidentum est, earum consilio mundum administrari," as "that taken for granted, it must be admitted, that the world is governed by their decree." (Lib. II, 30.) The stoic Epictetus, in his *Enchiridion* (Manual §44) says: "Take notice, that the principal and most important duty in religion, is to possess your mind with just and becoming notions of the gods; to believe that there are such supreme beings, and that they govern and dispose all the affairs of the world with a just and good providence."

Many philosophers maintain, that the doctrine, that the world came into existence and is preserved by the ideal Eternal Good, originated in such a wholly inner life of human intellect that, except showing its source in the human spirit, nothing can be uttered when proving it except irony against every mind, saying anything against it, or putting anything wrong in the place of it. This assertion, philosophically correct as it is, does, nevertheless, not satisfy the popular mind.

We hear generally the repeated question: If there is a kind providential care of the Most High over every creature that he has made from the lowest worm that crawls in the dust unto him that uses and rules many a natural power, how does it come, that there are so many evils in this lower world?

I will try to answer this in a plain and popular manner and I call your attention to it; for the doctrine that there is not only a general but also a particular relation between the All-kind Creator of the Universe and His creatures is of the highest moment, being the foundation and life of all practical morals and religion and consequently the basis of all human welfare.

Yes, it is this maxim alone, that gives meaning to feelings of disinterestedness, noble and heroic deeds, justice and virtue, and makes it reasonable to look to God, when we are in need and sorrow, or struck with fear and tribulation.

The fact, however, that there are so many evils and imperfections, miseries and misfortunes in this world, agitates not only the speculative mind of antiquity and is still embarrassing all those who dwell nowadays on this topic.

They could and cannot refrain from asking: How is it possible that there should exist any evil under the care of a beneficent, everhelping paternal ruler? If He leads and protects man from the cradle to the grave, why does He allow all kinds of man's sufferings? Zoroaster in his reflections on the origin of evil which troubles man in innumerable forms, a meditation from which philosophy arose in the childhood of nations, laid down the principle that there is an original author of the light, Ormuzd or Oromasdes, the Good, and an original author of the Darkness or Evil, Ahriman.

The first, he taught, is the source of all good and the latter of all bad events and occurrences in this lower world, and founded on this doctrine is his whole religious system and statesmanship.

Socrates acknowledged a Providence with the other attributes of the divinity which have reference to good government of the world without, and in particular of man, without giving a full explanation of the questionable points.

Plato composed the first intelligent essay on Theodicy.

He maintains, that the evils in this world cannot be attributed to God, since they are the product of the unformed and variable, and of the acts in conflict with our ideas, by which conflict, life and development are brought to pass in the world; but that God adopted all the measures necessary for overcoming evil.

The followers of Zoroaster, the Manicheans, adherents to a gnostic system which is a mixture of Parseeism and Christianity, established by a Persian, named Manes, in the year 270, maintained that there are two equal and eternal supreme principles, the one Good or God in the realm of light which produces all the happiness, the other evil Hyde or the devil in the darkness of matter which produces all calamity.

The Gnostics who pretended that they were the only men who had a true knowledge of the Christian religion held that the world intelligible and intellectual is derived from an imperfect Eon or substance emanating from God which Demiurg, the governor of the Eons, created and hence from this comes evil.

The Syrian followers of this system held that matter is an eternal and self-existing principle of evil.

Those whom the Psalmist mentions in Psalm lxxiii, Epicurus and others, for instance the Saducees, according to Josephus, deny the existence of a God altogether. Others maintain that everything happens by chance, and finally others thought that all takes place through a blind, inevitable necessity, called fatalism, that can not be resisted by anything or can it be explained.

All these opinions denying a Providence have been occasioned by the idea that the existence of evil upon earth is incompatible with a kind Providence. Since it is, as I have already remarked, still shaking our faith in the doctrine of Divine Providence, I will endeavor to investigate what is that which we usually call evil.

Inquiring of those who are complaining of evil upon earth, they will surely answer, if they do it sincerely, as follows: They see with great horror the triumph of wickedness and defeat of right, "truth forever on the scaffold, wrong forever on the throne." Ah, they will continue, how often is he who performs truly his duty and does much good in secret, shamefully derided, misjudged, slandered, pursued and oppressed, and he who is a selfish, deceitful, crafty man, crowned in all his undertakings with fortune and success.

Why? If there is a living, providential ruler above, how can this happen? Why does he allow, that this or that man perish in the fight for human right, justice and liberty? What misconduct, wrong or iniquity was this honest and brave man guilty of, that his whole property, earned after much toil and trouble, fatigue and anxiety and by a thousand drops of sweat, should become suddenly a sacrifice of war? What sin has this or that infant committed that it is brought up in the greatest poverty, and when its parents are gone, must wander like an outcast from house to house to ask for assistance? And who is able to enumerate all the lamentable sacrifices which death demands? Alas! Love is snatched away from love and heart is torn from heart.

The inconsolable mother sinking down in a fainting fit upon the corpse of her sweet darling whom she bore with pain and reared with motherly tenderness, breathes in vain her burning grief and anguish.

The tears she wept intensely, and the deep sighs she sent praying to heaven for his or her recovery, all in vain.

The child lies before her like a withered flower and with it died away the contentment of her heart, the ornament of her life and her greatest enjoyment on earth. Why did not Providence care for her agony and grief? Why had she been forsaken by the almighty, paternal Governor? How? they continue to ask, are not the elements waging war upon one another? We see very often tempests agitate the sea and plunge by their fury thousands of men into the depths where they find a watery grave. We hear of devastating thunderstorms passing over whole regions and fields and destroying in a few moments all the hopes of many an honest farmer who is working hard for his livelihood.

We read often reports, that inundations caused by the rising of rivers washed away many families with their houses and destroyed them in the flood.

Yes, we read sometimes accounts of earthquakes by which whole cities with all their inhabitants, the good and bad, innocent and wicked, just and unjust, have been buried.

Are not all these facts incontestible proofs that there is no Providence, and all the teaching about it a deceptive means of reason and a self-invented emollient of sorrow and pain? But if we examine all this considerately, we will perceive, that all the doubts thrown over the belief in a Providence proceed from the tendency to form our judgment from present appearances, rather than from consequences and connexions. This may be illustrated by several examples.

Let it be supposed, that the first signal was given for a railroad train to start at the very moment that a passenger was to board the train; he stumbles and breaks a limb. He and the spectators of such an incident might call it an evil; but its consequences show that it was not, since having to stay at home that the broken limb may be cured, his life was saved. The train was wrecked and many passengers were killed and maimed.

Or a vessel is ready for sea. Some prospective passenger or someone near and dear to them, meet with accidents which prevent them from sailing. The vessel founders at sea and all on board are lost. At the time of the happening of these casualties, they appeared as great evils; but the subsequent disaster to the vessel proved they were not.

Many similar events occur to my mind; but as it is impossible for me to mention them all, I refer you to biographies and to ancient and modern history of the nations, where you can find them on nearly every page.

In many instances, however, the particular divine government is doubted on account of one-sided contemplations of the physical evils, which exaggerate them extremely.

It is very easy to make the annals of evil voluminous; because the world is very large.

But would the number of evils appear still so great, if the good were also taken into consideration and compared with it?

If we would place the sum of the pleasant and agreeable feelings opposite the sum of the unpleasant, the number of the latter would surely appear very small. We would then comprehend, that there is considerably more welfare prevailing on earth than suffering. We would also become sensible of the fact that the agreeable sentiments are natural and the disagreeable unnatural, and therefore the latter are easily noticed and the former overlooked.

In moments of distress, when a man is dejected and distracted and discontented with himself and his circumstances, he is forgetful of all the good and agreeable that has fallen to his lot. His holiest convictions become confounded, and he denies the perfection of the sublunary world, because looking through the clouds of unpleasant feelings, as he does, he cannot perceive it. He declares, that the world is full of imperfection, a mere valley of misery; because he is illhumored and annoyed.

And how many evils attend the superstitious follies of mankind. They subject men to imaginary afflictions and additional sorrows, that do not properly come within our lot. Omens and prognostications are handed down like a hereditary disease from generation to generation. Thus for instance a screech-owl at midnight on the top of a house alarms some family more than a band of wild Indians met on the plains.

I remember that in Germany, where there are many pedestrians, if an old woman happens to cross their path or a hare run across their way, it strikes more terror than if they would meet a roaring lion.

Some people, when starting on Friday, are tormented by anxious thoughts, expecting surely bad consequences of a journey on such an unlucky day. Others lose their self-possession at a party, when the salt is spilt and it falls toward them.

I attended once a dinner party that was full of enjoyment and mirth, when suddenly an old woman unluckily observed that there were thirteen of us at table.

The remark struck a panic terror into several who were present, so much so that one or two of the ladies started to leave the room; but an acquaintance of mine arose and remarked: "Friends, be easy and cheerful! Our blessed Union affirms, that thirteen is a lucky number; because not one of the thirteen States that commenced the political and social Union perished, but on the contrary they have grown to the number of thirty-seven; and instead of portending that one of the company shall die, it plainly foretells that our assembly will enlarge its circle all the time."

Had not my friend found this expedient to break the omen, I question not but half the women would have fallen sick that very night.

Besides this, we often occasion ourselves physical vexations and troubles which can be avoided altogether, or at least a great part of them; as for instance, war with its train of cruelties and havocs, the consequences of selfishness, intemperance, ambition, hostile temper, etc.

Sometime we hear or are complaining of an evil which is merely negative. It consists in the disappointment of our wishes concerning beauty, wealth, power, strength, skill, genius, schemes, plans. But these and similar adornments and treasures of life can not be granted to all.

For in the first place, it lies in their nature to cease giving us pleasure, if all become possessed of them, and in the second place, were they fulfilled, they would often tend to make us a prey to calamity and ruin.

We will be convinced of the truism of this remark, when we review with a reflective mind all the strange, joyful and sad events of our life. We will find out by our own experience that sickness was often better for us than health, and the season of disappointed hopes better than the season of success.

Looking back upon them, we will then exclaim with the greatest astonishment: Behold, this was the hand of Providence which always led and restrained, guarded and supported us!

We shall see that all which we once considered adversities and evils were in reality blessings.

We shall become aware, that if this or that of our most ardent desires had been fulfilled, we could not enjoy our present fortune and happy circumstances.

We shall further perceive, that we have sometimes wished for something, worked and prayed for it incessantly, which, if we had received, would have proved a ruin to us and others.

It must therefore be admitted that we are seldom able to judge aright of the present circumstances.

And hence, surely, there is nothing that befalls a man without a beneficent cause and no troubles come upon him that were not the means employed by a divine care to bring him to the possession of exceeding good. Yet there is another point why we find so many evils in this world. It is, that we mistake often the preponderant value of many things and therefore call them evils. It is true, that hurricanes make great ravages; but they purify the atmosphere from unhealthy mephitis.

The thunder often does great damage; but it promotes the growth of vegetation.

We hear an earthquake spoken of as a horrible scourge reducing flourishing cities to a mass of ruins and revolutionizing the whole neighboring countries. But we must not forget, that usually before such catastrophes take place due warning is given for a long time by gales and tornadoes, or by hollow noises and subterranean rolling thunder, so that we may take refuge for safety in a secure place. And are not the earthquakes and volcanic eruptions, as the geologists state and prove beyond doubt, the cradle of new, more developed creations, since the beginning of the earth?

Furthermore it is necessary, that Providence speak sometimes to men in thunder, tempests and earthquakes, in order to remind them of His mighty power and the weakness and frailty of all the human works they are boasting of, and that there is a ruler of the universe who established the natural laws which must obey His will.

This statement is clearly corroborated by the following fact.

It has been proved by modern investigations that the thickness of the earth's crust is not quite twenty kilometers, and consequently this thickness is, in comparison to the whole mass covering it, like that of a sheet of paper that covers an artificial globe, or as the rind of an orange is to the pulp.

This crust is filled with a fluid five times heavier than water, and has a temperature that can reduce everything to vapor.

History tells us what that white glowing matter in the womb of our planet is able to produce.

Hence, were there no Providential hand that restrained and regulated this furious power, our earth could not exist a single moment.

We read graphic accounts of fearful conflagrations which have spread fast, as for instance that of Chicago and Boston, and we ask why did not God, having been the only one who could help, put a stop to it?

But do we also consider, that our question means to say something else: Why did not God let the fire, the nature of which is to consume all that is combustible, become weary of consuming, that is, why did not He change the nature of fire?

Or when we ask, why did not He send heavy showers to extinguish it, or why on the contrary did a wind blow a gale that drove the flames upon such rows of houses as stood close together, and why did the Lord of tempests not command the wind to shift to another direction, we ask here again nothing else but that God shall intermeddle with nature. Natural law rendered it necessary, that there should be no clouds discharging themselves at that time, and nevertheless we ask both.

Nature required that a tempest should blow then, and we want that God should have silenced it and should have performed a miracle.

But this could not and can not be; for the Almighty and All-wise allows the laws of nature, which He has established, to pursue their course without interruption.

And when we all know very well, that the wheels of the great natural machine lock well into each other, that if one wheel of this machine were stopped for a moment, if one spring should yield its elasticity, what a general confusion would take place, and into what an uproar the whole world would be thrown.

Hence there has not been and never will be a pause in the operation of any natural law.

There is a kind Providence, and without precaution and discretion, there is merely danger; without pain, there is no gain and without work no reward.

The Divine Wisdom wanted to force man by the law of necessity to give up laziness and to make use of the spiritual gifts which were showered upon him.

This is the reason that the beasts of the field were furnished with their clothes, their hairy furs, and the birds were covered with feathers to give them shelter against cold and the inclemency of the weather and man was left entirely naked and unprotected. This is the reason that Providence gave to all animals their natural weapons to be able to defend themselves against their enemies.

They received remarkable strength and an extraordinary swiftness. Man, however, was not provided with anything to brave the horn of a bull, the paw of a lion, the sting of a scorpion, but he was blessed with understanding and reason.

He must invent and procure himself clothes and weapons. Thus he is forced to use his intellectual powers in order to become the Lord of the animal kingdom, to cultivate the barren soil, to build villages, towns and cities, and to devise and establish wholesome laws for social life.

It is therefore a blind trust in God, carried to excess, if anyone neglects his work, hoping that God will supply him with all that is good and necessary, without his own labor. It is an idle piety to believe to effect all by saying many and long prayers, or to wait for a lucky chance to gain wealth, honor and respect.

The Creator has not endowed us in vain, with various faculties. We have to use them, and according to a natural law the good will produce the good, and evil must be the concomitant of evil in order to restrain it.

Man must not grumble against God's dispensations but against his own doings, in consequence of which he has very often to suffer, and this is not only demonstrated by past occurrences in all ages, but also by our own experiences in the course of our own lives.

Look at those who are possessed of an inordinate desire for honor; they are dying in a perpetual battle and uneasiness. Look at the miser; he is perishing near the source. Look at the licentious and fast living, the poison with which they have corrupted their blood and destroyed their nerves speaks stridently from their features and dissipated looks.

Behold the drunkards! They are stamped by their vice and having been tormented by different diseases, dull in sense and spirit, they drop early into their graves.

Behold the malicious and treacherous! They are shunned, have no faithful friend, fall, and everybody is glad of their ruin.

Look at the proud spendthrifts. They become impoverished and must go begging to those whom they formerly disdainfully overlooked.

Now, if you would like to know, how it happens that there are some who in their lives are neither quite happy nor quite unhappy, let me endeavor to tell you. It seems to me, that it is the result of an inclination not to be base enough to be entirely bad, or a lack of moral courage to be entirely good.

They waiver betwixt faults and virtues; hence between contentment and troubles of all kinds. The good which they perform rewards them just in the same proportion, as the wrongs which they have committed punish them and expose them to the most disagreeable circumstances.

If one wishes to be entirely happy, he must not be satisfied to be but half good.

Therefore, not the Divine Providence, but the vicious one himself is the creator of his own misery, his diseases, uneasiness and despondency.

The virtuous one, however, is wont to consider only that the end and aim of his life is to elevate and ennoble his spirit, that nothing belongs to him but his immortal soul, and everything else, such as rank, dignity of office, wealth and erudition, beauty and skill, health and sickness, friendship and persecution, material fortune and misfortune, are merely means to gain the one last and highest purpose.

If one familiarizes himself with the idea, that nothing which he is possessed of externally in this world will last; but that everything is loaned to him, and that even the best of friends, parents, brothers, sisters, consorts and children are also only loaned and allowed to walk with him a certain time, he will triumph over his unfortunate circumstances, be they ever so sad and mournful. He will not know nor perceive any evil in this world.

It is objected, that the slaughter of great numbers of animals is inconsistent with the loving kindness of a Providence.

But if we consider this closely, we find that the misfortune of a brute is not so great as we imagine it to be. It is rather a proof of God's kindness, that being necessary to exist for food, it is also permitted to share the boon of life.

It seems to be a great misfortune, that men are born weak and helpless and are weaker than the most irrational beings.

But if a child could shortly after his birth break away from his home and take care of himself, what would become of his education and culture of mind?

Yes, even physical troubles, which are inseparable from human nature, are a source of a thousand pleasures which we could not enjoy without them, such as appeasing hunger and thirst, and the agreeable recollections of having endured many pains and woes.

Therefore people very correctly say pain "is the best spice for seasoning life," because it impresses more deeply on our feelings the value of pleasure and heightens the sentiments of agreeable circumstances.

And apart from this, bodily pain is necessary to indicate the part of the body which is afflicted, thus enabling us to become aware of the diseased place and disorder and to use remedies for curing it.

Many evils, however, exist only in our imagination, representing to us the painful feelings of others, such as the aspect of death and the convulsions of dying persons.

It is indeed a sad aspect, seizing us with horror when we witness violent contractions of muscles; but it is after all the mere production of a blind fancy. For putting ourselves, full of vigor and longing for life, in the situation of the dying, we feel an immense sorrow which they do not know of, and we suffer pains of which they are not sensible at all.

Not dying itself, but merely the thought of it is horrible to men.

Finally, physical evils are themselves an excellent means to promote the moral education of mankind. Like a fire which consumes when touching us but which is nevertheless our greatest benefactor in providing light and heat, they afford us a great sphere of activity wherein we can exercise and develop all our noble faculties to the highest degree.

They give us many occasions for noble and magnanimous deeds in perseverance, sympathy, and so on; enhance our moral merits, form and cultivate our character, and call our attention to spiritual treasures, awakening our mind to, and establishing in us, the ideas of God, eternity and immortality.

Thus we see that the temporal good overweighs generally the evil.

Let us now investigate whether the moral evils prevailing upon earth are compatible with the doctrine of a Divine Providence, or not.

How, asks the skeptic, can a world harboring malice, iniquity and all kinds of transgressions of the holiest rights, be governed by a wise and powerful Providence?

As an answer, we put to him these questions: What do you call the world? Is mankind the world, and the history of human life the whole history of the human race? Should God create no men at all or should He call into existence only such who can not infringe on the right and good? Or should He always oppose every transgression or action produced by a passion originating in a mistaken view? Indeed, were this to take place, God would have to perform miracles incessantly and derange every moment the whole wise and beneficent economy of nature.

And then, again, if God should always check the evil chosen by the created free will of man, the noblest thing upon earth would be wanting, namely—freedom, and such an immediate hindrance would stop only the execution of the evil design, but not the depravity of the will.

Hence, the Creator employed for the suppression of evil such means as could exist together with the nature of man thus revealing His wisdom.

He opposes the outburst of evil by its bad consequences producing external pain, and He enthroned conscience as a judge in man's bosom that it also should suppress it by inward pain.

Evil shall restrain evil.

It is further objected, that the fortune of the vicious and the misfortune of the virtuous are irreconcilable to a wise and just, Providential care.

But are we not deceived as to our judgment concerning the virtue of others? We can only judge of the actions, but not of the motives which are hidden in the recesses of the heart.

Again, our opinion of the fortune and misfortune of others is very liable to error, because the wicked very often knows how to conceal his uneasiness and his agitated state, and the virtuous makes no ostentation of his peace of mind and soul.

Nay, to many the fortune that has fallen to their lot becomes after a time a scourge and severe punishment; while the misfortune that has been visited upon them promotes after a short interval their welfare, and places them in such happy circumstances as they never imagined or dreamed of.

It is also said, that a Divine Providence is irreconcilable with the free will of man.

For admitted that God has prescience of all events and human action, leading them with an Almighty power to reach a certain aim, how is it then possible for men to act at discretion?

To this we reply, that God's decree to govern the universe has no past and the actions of man have in the sight of God no future, that is: in the spiritual world there is no difference of time.

And should some one ask: If Providence does everything for us and delivers us from dangers and bestows upon us all kinds of blessings, what is the use of our own industry? Are not human endeavors and foresight superfluous?

To these queries, I should answer, that God foresaw our activity and took it into account, since experience teaches us that human activity is requisite, as belonging to the natural means through which Providence works.

If we have done all that is in our power, we must then resign ourselves to the Divine Providence, whether it will allow us to reach our aim or not.

And indeed! All good success of our endeavors depends generally upon circumstances which are not in our power, but which are wisely ordained by the Most High.

Having shown, that many things appearing to us as evils have to be called good, if considered with all their consequences from different points of view, I must now remark, that it would be an arrogance of human reason to try to explain the divine admission of evil into this world.

For we know of the Universe nothing more than we do of a particle of dust, and of eternity hardly one second, and consequently it is not quite certain that all which we call misfortune is a calamity for those who have to suffer it.

I will illustrate this by a story of an ancient writer. He tells us of a man who having a house for sale, carried a brick to market to exhibit as a specimen.

You may, perhaps, smile at his folly, in supposing that any purchaser would or could judge of a whole house, which he never saw, by so small a part of it.

But would not we be guilty of much greater folly, should we attempt to form an opinion of God's conduct from that little part of it which we are able to discover?

In order to form a correct opinion of it, we ought to have a correct view of the whole. We must be God ourselves, equal to Him in wisdom, knowledge, power and goodness, to be able to review the Divine works accurately.

It follows, therefore, from all I have said, that the doctrine of a Providence that has control over all human affairs and directs them, if necessary, according to wise laws of the good to the good, is irrefutably correct.

And as a sick man must trust in a skillful physician, though he knows not the nature and properties of the medicine prescribed for him, or as it is reasonable for a blind person to follow his guide, so is it reasonable for us to submit and trust implicitly to an infinitely better Being, though His dispensations appear to us sometimes mysterious and perplexing.

Trust in Divine Providence is the key which is given into our hands to unlock our paradise upon earth, and we need only to use it in order to gain admittance.

I will add only a few words more, namely: that this consoling truth is also corroborated by ancient and modern history.

If we look into its records, we see men and nations coming and passing away like rising and setting stars.

There is a constant changeableness; but there is also plan and law.

As the remotest stars, whose light does not reach the earth, are nevertheless counted and do not belong in vain to the solar system, so is likewise the case with the least in the horizon of humanity. Their most secret deeds exercise an influence on the whole.

Thus is the good generally lasting and the evil transient.

So for instance we perceive, that when the last sun-beam of culture was extinguished in the Byzantine empire, Providence then prepared Spain, France and Germany, in order that a new morning should begin to dawn there, and the whole West of Europe made much progress in the second part of the Fifteenth Century that the days of the Alarics, Attilas, Generics, Hildebrands, Dshingirkare and Tamerlanes could never return again.

Here, on this side of the Atlantic shore, a new world was opened to the nations of the old. Our beloved country, the United States, is more and more developing itself, as its population, commerce and culture increase rapidly.

Power and liberty, arts and science, dwell together within its boundaries, and the welfare of every citizen without distinction is guarded by civil and religious liberty.

It is an asylum for all the oppressed and dejected wanderers from every land; because traditionalism or the Holy Books, which were the center and rule of all teachings in all Christian empires upon earth, were and are here not considered as a source or standard of philosophical knowledge and political law.

The separation of Church and State was declared in our Constitution in unequivocal terms, and the exclusive right of giving the last decision on all subjects was and is entrusted to reason.

The heroic fathers of our country, who framed our Constitution to make us free from all tyranny and to bring about the most happy state of a true, universal brotherhood, founded their great and salutary principles, not on the Bible which can be understood and explained in different ways, not on any teachings of any book or creed, but on intellectual power, natural rights, high talents for arts, and the moral law engrafted in the consciousness of man by the Author of the Universe. Ninety-eight years of prosperity of our Union, unequalled in the history of the whole human race, show as clearly as the meridian beams, that the established principles are aided and protected by Divine Providence, and they are progressing and developing more and more and there is no power in the world, which can ever clip or dwarf them.

Philosophy and science, with which the All-wise and All-loving Father has blessed our age, combined with their powerful ally, the press, will always wage war against all clerical drawbacks, corrupt politicians and simple minded religious dreamers and enthusiasts, who endeavor like polyps with their tentacles to meddle with politics, and nestle, wherever it is possible, their absurd ideas.

Yes, this brilliant constellation in the serene sky of our happy Union will with the sun-beams of truth, throw light upon the works of darkness and legal intolerance in all its relations and bearings and conquer them forever.

Indeed! Philosophy, science and an enlightened press, those modern monitors of reason which are plying on the stormy ocean of life, will render our free institutions secure, and no creed, religious party or sect will be able to stop the human spirits leading us with the rapidity of lightning onward and upward.

The nations of old have successively flourished and faded. Assyria, Babylon, and Persia, Jerusalem and Carthage, Greece, Macedonia and Rome played their parts on the stage of history and withered; but upon this our own great, growing nation, enlightened and humane, rest the hopes of the world to bring about light, culture, liberty and a true brotherhood. It seems to be the only one that has been divined by Providence for this great mission.

And surely we will not be disappointed; for its special, Providential care and guidance were visible to all who witnessed lately the great rebellion of slavery against freedom and the complete victory of the latter.

Let us then acknowledge, that the current of events is under the influence of God's ruling care, prescribing the courses of nations and individuals, so that all shall concur to the fulfillment of his holy will; and happy are we who live in this blessed Union, that is evidently destined by Providence to become a model republic for all nations and to lead in the march of intellect, rendering great services for truth, beauty and justice and achieving gigantic progress in the civilization and culture of mankind.

IV

FREDERICK DE SOLA MENDES

Tyndallism and Judaism (1874)

The Haftarah (portion from the Prophets) of to-day is taken from the first chapter of the book of Malachi, the last of the Prophets both in canonical order and in course of time. Malachi lived, as you are aware, during the time of Nehemiah, about 440 years before the common era, and among the newly-returned exiles in Palestine. Great dissatisfaction and complaint were rife by reason of the desolate, and straitened circumstances of the fresh colonized country; poverty reigned to such a degree, that the usual tithes for the support of the Sanctuary were not delivered. The prophet, in the first chapters, seeks to give his brethren consolation, by comparing desert Edom, punished for its cowardly cruelty towards Judah, with the desolate Palestine, and pointing out how unfounded was the belief that God had forsaken his people utterly. He then passes to a severe castigation of the priests of the Sanctuary, who, in the general disorder of affairs, strove to better their own condition, by substituting worthless cattle for the sacrifices, in place of the people's more valuable offerings. The prophet reminds the tribe of Levi of its original destination and duty: — "*The law of truth was in his mouth, and falsehood not found in his lips, in peace and equity he walked with me, and many did he turn away from iniquity; for the priest's lips are ever to keep knowledge, and the law are they to seek from his mouth; for he is the messenger of the Lord of Hosts.*" (ii, 6; 7)

This failure of the Priesthood to keep within the lawful bounds their duty bade them mark out for all men, the bounds of probity and rectitude, is not singular. From the time of Samuel down to the Exile, many there were who thus proved unfaithful to their priestly charge.

Isaiah, Jeremiah and Ezekiel; Hosea, Amos and Zachariah, besides Malachi, are some of those orators bold enough to declaim against over-weening priestly might. The deeds of blood and violence that stained the Sanctuary during Israel's later monarchy, are known to you, and 1800 years ago, while the cruel Roman lay encamped around the Holy City, the parties of the Priests and Patriots weakened and decimated each other in fierce and fatal slaughter.

With the sins of the Priesthood of other faiths, and since that period, we have nothing to do; they concern us not. But there is a more dangerous species of priestly sedition, not unknown to former ages, which in truth threatens us as well; it is the unfaithfulness of the priests of knowledge, whose dereliction, affecting all faiths which shun not the light of modern progress, touches Judaism as well. The worship of materialism, the adoration of stocks and stones and animal life is not extinct since the days that the son of Torah preached in Mamre's plains; our modern Abraham's occupation is not yet gone.

But we should be careful of falling into extremes; let us temper our zeal with charity, and pause, ere we utterly stigmatize and condemn the opinions of our fellow-man. Not so has the greater part of the religious world acted on a recent occasion; the so-called Christian community has comported itself, in the sense they use the word, most unchristianly; "crying havoc, and letting slip the dogs of war" theological, of war most pitiless and unreasoning, upon the misconstrued and distorted assertions of a man of Science. I allude, of course to Professor Tyndall's recent address before the British Association, and if I venture here to subject this remarkable pamphlet to open criticism I trust that the personal respect and gratitude I owe to the man I am proud to own as Teacher of Science, will not blind my vision to its manifest faults and short-comings.

Deprecating then the hasty zeal which has led many to condemn the essay at once, and irretrievably, let us turn to the authenticated version, and follow the Professor's course; then, and not until then, will we hazard our opinion.

The Professor commences with the beginning, accounting for the propensity of man to turn his thoughts and questionings towards natural appearances, by an impulse inherent even in *primeval* man. From what man knew as true, he formed theories of what he did not yet know; he thought he saw, for instance, the sun cross each day over the sky, and from that experience formed the theory, the truth of which he never could know from actual observation, that the earth was stationary and the sun and planets moved over it or round it. So from their observations of themselves and their fellows, men formed theories of the government of the whole universe; when anger ruled, they saw the features grow dark, the mid light of kindness fade from the eyes; so when the tempest raged, and they saw the skies enclouded, obscuring the light of the golden sun, they said the God of the Sky was angry and was driving away the Sun-God. "The rule and governance of natural phenomena were ascribed to unknown imperceptible beings they knew not, but whom they imagined as a species of human creatures, retaining all human passions and appetites." This formed what is called the anthropomorphic state of religion, the man-shaped, that is, the grade when the Creators and Rulers are supposed endowed with human form and attributes. The Professor gives no illustrations, but we know that this state continued long; the Lacedaemonians always during war, put up their petitions very early in the morning, in order to be beforehand with their enemies, and by being the first solicitors, preengage the gods in their favor. The people of Tyre when besieged by Alexander, (333 B.C.E.) threw chains on the statue of Hercules, to prevent that deity from deserting to the enemy; on the death of the Emperor Germanicus, (19 C.E.) the people were so enraged at the gods, that they stoned them in their temples, and openly renounced all allegiance to them. These examples show conclusively how human, how terribly human, was the idea of a deity in those days. But there were glorious exceptions; far in the depths of history we find men of exceptional power separating themselves from the crowd, rejecting these man-shaped notions, "and seeking to connect natural phenomena with natural principles." They pursued a different method; not believing, for instance, that when it thundered, a Sky God was angry, they inquired, what first natural causes produced the sound we call thunder. The earliest to give the theory of "First Beginnings" or causes as it is called, precision and completeness, was Democritus, and his system is explained and followed by the professor through those of Epicurus, Lucretius and others. According to them "the universe was built up of atoms, individually without sensation, and governed by mechanical laws," not by a superior being or God. The Atoms built up bodies; "not after sage deliberation; but from all eternity they have been drawn together, and after trying arrangements and unions of every kind fell at length into the arrangement we see them holding now." This is certainly the grossest materialism. From belief in an infinite member of gods, one behind every natural event, Science had come to accept inert, insensible Atoms without any God at all.

Into contact with the second state, Judaism's sublime conception, the revealed doctrine of *One God* was brought, rejecting alike the palpable absurdity of Polytheism: absurdity, for no order or regularity can be obtained when everything is governed by independent and capricious deities; as well as the unsatisfactory and unintelligible blank of Materialism, without any God. Judaism taught, "in the beginning God created heaven and earth, the earth was without form and void * * * * * and the *spirit of God* hovered over the deep" chaos and gave it form and order.

Many newer atomic philosophers now made a compromise: while accepting the constitution of atoms, acknowledged God as the great *First Cause* of these atoms, and arranger of the laws that bind them. The Professor meanwhile passes to the doctrine of that school of the present day which numbers among its votaries Darwin, Huxley, Spencer and himself, the doctrine of Evolution; of Development. Tyndall accepts the atomic theory, that the world is built of atoms, and indeed, from recent discoveries in Chemistry and Physics, any person of intelligence will grant it.

So far the most religious, nay the most bigoted, may go with Tyndall. The world and its contents, animate and inanimate, are built up of little atoms, but who or what gave those atoms form, who or what governs them now that they have form? And here it is we must part with Tyndall and his school. Let us examine their logic.

The Professor's keynote is contained in the sentence, "Life without matter, without material atoms, is never found; we know nothing of the *spirit* which Theology assumes as the Animater and Ruler of matter. Since we cannot, from our actual experience, form an idea of this spirit, we refuse it our belief, do not acknowledge its existence." Here the school produces its motto and watchword: "What we cannot conceive, we cannot believe to be." The question remains, if not spirit, *what* causes life and its manifestation in these atoms? Tyndall must answer "There is no spirit, therefore these atoms are ruled by atoms, by themselves, *atoms* cause life." He here approaches the doctrine of a very small school which believes that life needs no creator, but can be brought about by physical means, such as warmth, light, etc. The doctrine is unsupported but by a very few experimentalists who probably delude themselves. Tyndall does not enroll himself among them, and he can only answer "the cause of life is an insolvable mystery, the development of some inherent tendency in the atoms to life." But the question is unanswered yet: "who or what implanted this inherent tendency, who endowed dead matter with it? He will not allow God, a spirit, this would be giving *man's shape* again to the idea, which Democritus combated; we know he says, no spirit and is severe against those theologians who assume a benevolent living Deity, watching as if with benevolent eyes, the course of events. He forgets that Theologians do not intend to clothe the Deity with human attributes; being human they are forced to use human expressions; *Dibera torah bilshon bene Adam,* taught our Jewish Sages, *Religion speaks in human terms.* Men found that all that happened was for the best, that calamities were averted, or changed into blessings, that the whole bias of the world was toward happiness, how could they express this experience otherwise than by saying "Somebody or Something of benign attributes, watches with all-seeing eye over the course of events," yet surely no one believes that the wondrous and incomprehensible Deity possesses human organs of vision, or human sympathies; it is but our mode of expression.

Tyndall and his school come to a dead halt and imagine there is nothing to carry them further; they come to this mysterious influence and cannot comprehend it, and because they cannot conceive it, they will not allow its possibility. Like the pigmy insect crawling over the leaf of a plant that reaches the edge and peers down into space, they can descry the root but cannot reach it from this position, whereas in truth, if the insect would but turn toward the leaf's commencement and origin in the stem, it would find an easy descent. And further, that school is false that teaches the falsehood of the inconceivable, the inconceivable *is* sometimes true. Indeed, we cannot conceive black to be white, nor is it; but could our forefathers conceive the Antipodes, that on the other side of the globe there are men standing with their feet opposed to and towards ours. And yet is it not true? Our fathers could not conceive that a hundred miles could be traversed in a couple of hours, and yet is it not true? Could they imagine an answer to a message can be received over ten thousand miles in half an hour, and yet is this not true? No, our power of conception progresses with our knowledge, and where for the moment it comes to a halt, then God has pitied and provided for our inability by giving us Revelation. Hence religion does not oppose even science's latest teachings, but rather sup-

plements them; when the mind mourns with the Psalmist, such knowledge is too wondrous for me, too lofty. I cannot attain to it — all is
dark; then religion proclaims, "Come, then house of Jacob, let us walk
in Divine Light" — Isa.ii.5. So may we be mindful of this ever, when
we hear of new attacks, forsooth, as they are called, upon religion. We
know the word of the Lord stands forever, the Law of God is perfect;
and warned against joining in the instant cry of excommunication and
anathema, let us remember, "The lips of the wise man scatter knowledge but the heart of fools is unreliable." And abstaining from substituting worthless human theories for precious Divine ones, so shall
personified Religion say of our priestly race: — The law of truth was in
his mouth, and falsehood not found in his lips; in peace and equity he
walked with me, and turned away many from iniquity, for the priest's
lips are ever to keep knowledge and the law they are to seek from his
mouth, for he is the messenger of the Lord of Hosts.

V

ISAAC MAYER WISE

On Metaphysics
(from The Cosmic God) (1876)

I. GOD IN NATURE

LADIES AND GENTLEMEN. — In eighteen lectures previous to this we have been guided through the labyrinth of nature and history by induction solely and exclusively. We have examined facts and attempted to expound them within the bounds of the law of causality. The result of this investigation was unraveled to our cognition, wheels within wheels in the marvelous mechanism of nature and history; facts which stand behind this world of sensual realities as their efficient and final causes. The main fruit of our researches is the existence and substantiality of a force in nature which is life, freedom, will, and intellect, and also government and justice in man's history, universal and super-human. Is the force the first cause of nature, *causa sua?* Imagine it as Kant's intelligible world, Hegel's absolute idea, Schopenhauer's will, Hartmann's unconscious will and intellect, Volkert's panlogism, Venetianer's panpsychism, or Mr. Tyndal's [Tyndall] "unknowable," after all various constructions of the same substance; is it the first cause? Is it the unconditioned *(Das Unbedingte)* and conditioning *(Das Bedingende)*, of which all objects of nature are the conditioned *(Das Bedingte)*? In case this question be answered in the affirmative, the next question is, what do we and can we know of God, nature, man, and their relations? How do we explain the progression of history, the duties of man, and the final cause of both? These, in my estimation, are the main questions of metaphysics, viz., the nature of the cause or causes which exist, figuratively spoken, behind physical nature, behind the mechanism of this cosmos and its parts, which are the effects thereof.

The term metaphysics in philosophy is of accidental origin. The first compiler of the writings of Aristotle found the works of that great master mind divided in logic, aesthetics, and physics, and placed last of all, hence behind physics Aristotle's principal work, and named it, therefore, metaphysics. Therefore, the province and limits of metaphysics have been variously understood by the philosophers. My definition is my own.

In metaphysics, the inductive method will not reach, to ascertain all reason is capable of ascertaining. Inasmuch as metaphysics undertakes to lift up the veil of nature, and to expose to intelligence that which is behind that veil as the cause of causes, the inductive method will do well; but where it begins to expound the nature of that cause, which is no sensual object; there are the limits of the law of causality, hence also of induction; there the province and methods of pure reason begin, and nothing else will solve that problem of problems. There are certainly more methods of cognition than philosophy expound[s] and science applies. Knowledge precedes science, and cognition is prior to philosophy. Mankind knows vastly more than science and philosophy have utilized and systematized. The child sucking its nutriment performs mechanical feats, which only after thousands of years science began to construct. The entire material of philosophy in all its disciplines consists after all of the spontaneous productions of the mind. Philosophy discovered the form, it invented not the substance of its contents.

There is room left for genius to carve out new methods of cognition. Do I not know it *a priori?* I know that there is a God, a Providence, and an immortality, and I know it as sure as I know anything; yet I am not superstitious, ignorant, or credulous; I know all the methods of cognition and evidence in philosophy and science; still I may fail in convincing others of the correctness of my convictions, simply because the methods of cognition and evidence are not exhausted.

The most prominent and most profound metaphysicians in history are the Hebrews, not only those who wrote the Biblical Books, but also those who wrote the apocryphal, profane, and rabbinical works between 300 years before and 300 after the Christian Era, in Palestine and Egypt; and those of the Moorish-Spanish period from the tenth to the fifteenth centuries. They furnished the whole material, which metaphysicians have cast into the philosophical form, from Aristotle down to our days. Take away the Hebrew material from metaphysics, and what is left of it, is its formal portion, into which some indigestible dogmas are artificially pressed.

And now returning to our problem, we must discuss, force once more. The forces co-operate in producing teleological centers. Whatever is a *causalnexus* is also a teleological center. Whatever object of nature we may examine represents a number of forces co-operating, co-ordinate, sub-ordinate or both. Take for instance any piece of common coal, and you have in it cohesion, attraction, gravitation, heat and light differentiated, hence also electricity and magnet. These forces are in the coal, immanent and permanent, insulated from the body of the universe, and bound together to constitute that particular object, that piece of coal.

How do those forces meet and how keep together to constitute that particular object? Only one of the three possibilities will explain the phenomenon: Either the forces bear in themselves, by affinity or attraction, the converging tendency and coherent nature; or all forces are actually but one, differently modified by chemical causes; or there is a superior and governing force, which unites and keeps bound together various inferior forces, to constitute and sustain intact any given object of nature. The convergence of forces is impossible, because they are variously connected in various limited objects, to the exclusion of any further connection with other forces or more force. If convergence was in the nature of all forces, they must unite indefinitely, so that there could be only one kind of objects with the same qualities precisely, and all matter must at last unite to one lump. Besides, death, decay, dissolution, or even the transition of qualities would be impossible on account of the constancy of force: so that the forces once united to an individual object must, by virtue of their convergence, remain forever intact; which we know not to be the case.

If we admit the unity or correlation of forces dematerialized, in their cosmic state, still this unity of forces exists not in their materialized state, in the objects of nature; for we can expel a force from a body, make it cosmic, and the other or others remain therein. You lay a piece of magnetized iron in the fire and expel the magnet, while other forces remain intact in the iron. You stamp a rock to dust and expel its cohesion, while the other forces remain in the material. By heat or electricity you reduce a solid to a liquid and a gas finally, and expel the force of gravitation. So nearly every force may be expelled, dematerialized and made cosmic, from any object of nature, without injury to others.

Besides, if there was a unity of forces in matter, it could present but one kind of quality, which we know not to be the case.

Consequently only one possibility is left, viz., there is a superior and governing force which unites inferior forces in various relations and proportions, to form and to sustain intact the various objects of nature, each of which is a teleological center; and as soon as the influence of that superior force is withdrawn from any natural object, the remaining inferior forces, by their inherent tendency, strive to become again cosmic, which changes the respective bulk of matter in death, decay, dissolution, and would end with the reduction thereof to its elementary or cosmic state, if not arrested by that superior force. So, and not otherwise, life and death, differentiation and indifferentiation, being and dissolution, convergence and divergence in all forms can be understood. Therefore no object of nature can be duplicated by human ingenuity, simply because that superior and governing force is not, and most likely will never be, under man's control.

I beg you, ladies and gentlemen, to take particular notice of this point: The natural objects themselves, granite or tree, diamond or beast, metal or man, pebble or sun, forcibly and irresistibly suggest the necessary existence of a superior and governing force, by which each and all of them become, are, and return to, the cosmos. This superior and governing force is as evident to our mind as our self-consciousness, and as perceptible to our senses as the natural objects themselves are. What Aristotle called *morphe,* the form, that something which makes every particular object to what it actually is, with those peculiar qualities which it manifests, is the superior force which governs all others and modifies matter and inferior forces accordingly. This is no hypothesis, no theory; it is law, universal and undeniable.

I beg leave, ladies and gentlemen, to remind you that in biology we have discovered a similar superior and governing force of organic kingdoms, which was called there vital force. Then we have ascertained that vital force, life, will, and intellect are in fact one substance with these discernable attributes. Then we have ascertained in the teleology of history that the same force is also the Logos of History and Justice, commonly called Providence. Now we have established an analogous force, governing and superior, also in the inorganic kingdoms. Also here is will as the profuse variety of the objects of nature demonstrate; hence, also here is freedom. Also here is intellect, as the presence of will proves; and as every object of nature is in itself a teleological center, being co-ordinate and sub-ordinate to the cosmos, its law, order, and harmony. Also here is a genius of inorganic nature, which combines, proportions, shapes, and overrules inferior forces, to bring forth and to sustain these objects of nature and with them also the cosmos. Hence either these various superior and governing forces are identical, or we have arrived at the existence of several Gods, one of organic and another of inorganic nature, one of nature and another of history. I say "gods," although this word is still postulated only; but I will prove hereafter that the term is used in its proper signification.

Ancient nations understood this quite well, therefore their gods or genii for every class of natural objects, and their superior gods presiding over those inferior spirits, to account for the order and harmony in the cosmos. So the Kabbalistic Jews had their presiding angels, not only over the various elements and forces, but also over the special classes of natural objects, which play a considerable part in the philosophy of the Middle Ages. One of them was the *Sechel hap-poel,* the active or energetic reason, the Genius of Man and History, *Metathronos* who was Paul's pattern in shaping his Jesus.

It had been partly shown before, that the Logos of History manifests the same laws precisely as the Genius of Inorganic Nature; therefore we called history the continuation of the earth's creation. With man's appearance on earth, physical creation closed and mental creation began; the pedestal was finished and the statuary was placed upon it. Geology proves this abundantly.

As far back as science permits us to look, we can only think of matter in its primary elements, isolated, with no force acting upon it. Whether this matter in its zero state was in God, outside of Him, or created by Him, is a question of no particular importance to us; therefore I postulate, it was. Chemistry knows of elements only; atoms or molecules are creatures of science or imagination; elements only are thinkable or imaginable. These elements, however numerous, must have existed as parallels without convergence. No force being in them, there was neither affinity nor attraction. The first act of creation of this or any other solar system, this or any other planet, was the compression or concussion of these elements. This produced heat, and in such immense quantity, that the facit of its calculation sounds fabulous; yet the collision of the elements must have produced an amount of heat corresponding to the mass and the force of concussion. Now all the elements, say of this earth, were one chaotic mass of burning liquid.

With heat there came light, electricity, and motion, the unity of which is doubtful no longer. So first was the *Tohn* [*Tohu*] *Wabohu,* viz., the parallels of elementary matter in space. Then "God said let there be light and there was light," *i.e,.* there was heat, light, electricity, and motion, convertible into one another. Electricity, of course, must have been dynamical, now known as galvanic. Frictional and magnetic electricity could develop only after the mass had cooled off and metallic formations had ensued.

With the compression or concussion of the primary elements, the force of cohesion, chemical affinity, and molecular attraction was also imparted to the chaotic liquid, developing gradually, in which there was action and reaction in the form of contraction and expansion. Contraction may be the reaction of expansion by the mere contact of the fiery liquid with cold space; or expansion may be the reaction of contraction by the rarified and porous state of the heated liquid, and this may translate heat into light, electricity, and motion. At any rate only one force was originally imparted to the elements, by which the creation and formation of this earth was effected, and from which all the other forces were gradually developed. Therefore in our days the correlation of forces in their cosmic state is doubted no longer in science. All physical forces are a unit.

After a brief reflection, however, we discover that the force of compression must have preceded the force of expansion; for the very first act of creation was the compression or concussion of the elementary parallels. In fact, expansion became a force, after compression had united elementary matter and imbued it with force. It is in the nature of force to strive perpetually to become cosmic, to separate itself from the material objects, in which it is kept isolated by the superior and governing force. So it is in the nature of matter to dissolve into its primary elements, unless kept together by force, these two tendencies form[ing] the groundwork of the force of expansion, therefore before force and matter were united, and the parallels of matter were compressed to a body or bodies, there could be no force of expansion in them; hence compression is the original force. Here then we have precisely the same force at the bottom of creation, which we have discovered as the superior and governing force in all objects of nature, viz., compression, forming and preserving intact all objects of nature, of which all other physical forces are derivative, consequently subject to its control. Also planetary attraction and repulsion are reactions of the force of compression, in fact all creations and preservation result from compression, but we can not enlarge here on this topic.

One force in this earth is, all others are reactions thereof; and this one force was originally the impulse imparted to the elementary parallels of matter, by the substance. And so we have arrived again at one substantial force, in the creation and preservation of all natural objects, or if this is identical with God, at the existence of one God. This first creative impulse is represented in the Bible, thus: "And the spirit of God moved upon the face of the waters"; not in the water, but upon its surface, because it was the force of compression; not God Himself moved upon the water, but His spirit, wind, *pneuma,* will, because it was an impulse imparted to the elementary parallels.

This first impulse could not have been the work of chance or casualty; for in all which comes within the cognition of man, in organic or inorganic nature, in history, or even in imagination, there is not one phenomenon without a cause. In fact, the human mind is incapable of thinking of a causeless effect. Causality is not a mere category of the human understanding; like space, it is a reality, inseparable from all which is, was, or will be. Hence the first impulse given to the elementary parallels must have proceeded from a cause, and all phenomena developing from that impulse to this moment must form one consecutive chain of cause and effect, although each object is a *causalnexus.*

An impulse is an action; an action is a function; and a function is in a substance only. Nothing can do nothing. Something only can do something. Hence the primary force which imparted the creative impulse to the elementary parallels is a substance, outside and above the earth and its forces, for which we have no better appellative than super-mundane.

There can be nothing in the effect which is not also in its cause. The cause in this case is super-mundane, consequently psychical; hence the forces themselves must be psychical, which in their action and reaction upon matter became materialized, and dematerialized again in their cosmic state. So we are enabled to form a clear conception of the origin of physical forces and their *quality.*

We have now pressed the question onward to two psychical substances, one above inorganic nature and creation, and another above organic nature and history. We could well enough close here with the reasoning of Maimonides, Descartes, and Spinoza, that there can be only one psychical substance; or, calling the substance force, we could at once refer to the universality and unity of force; and we would have arrived already at the existence of one God. Still I have more evidence on hand, of which Maimonides, Descartes, and Spinoza made no use, and propose to produce it in my next lectures.

II. LECTURE, NATURE'S GOD

LADIES AND GENTLEMEN.—I believe it may be set down as a general principle, wherever we have before us two or more effects, we have no right yet to postulate two substantial causes; for the difference of effect only points to a difference of functions, but by no means also to two substantial causes. Again the unity of the idea in any continuous chain of cause and effects excludes the possibility of two first causes. The material universe and the history of man are known to us as such a unity.

If these propositions are true, and I do not recollect that they have been doubted, then we need not prove the unity of the two postulated gods of our last lecture, viz., the Genius of the inorganic kingdom and creation, and the Logos of the organic kingdom and history. Any division of the first cause could be conceptional only, never real. Every dualism, trinitarianism or polyism in the first cause is necessarily false.

In the special question before us, the analogy of the different phenomena points distinctly to the identity of the cause. The main force in the inorganic kingdom becomes phenomenal in the form of contraction and expansion. The contraction or compression, we have noticed as the continuous activity of the primary force, of the impulse imparted originally to inert matter. Expansion, is the inherent tendency of matter, to dissolve into its primary elements, to fall apart and become cosmic. This is not a force, but a negative thereof, a first, passive, and zero condition which produces no effect. All phenomenal effects are resultants of active forces, which are derivatives of the first impulse, the superior and governing force, known to us in the form of contraction or compression. This is self-evident to the chemist who reduces solid to liquid, liquid to gas and ether, by expelling the forces from matter, which he liberates and reduces to its primary, passive and zero state, as far as he can.

The same main force, however, becomes phenomenal also in organic nature, only that it develops new functions. It is attraction and repulsion, positive and negative electricity, north and south poles in the magnet, centrifugal and centripetal power, or however it becomes phenomenal. We observe the same fundamental action in the cell or even protoplasm, contraction and expansion, and by it accretion and secretion, internal motion and external limitation. This is the fundamental function of all organic life. Then it re-appears in animal instinct, in man's selfishness and social nature, as well as his struggle for personal freedom and patriotism, to be at the same time an independent individual and a dependent citizen of a large, populous, and powerful community, which is the primary cause of all history, with its two similar elements of conservatism and progressionism. It is always the same fundamental principle of contraction and expansion, only that a variety of new functions of the same cause become phenomenal under new circumstances. Hence, we have not the least ground for the supposition of two first causes.

Nor, indeed, is there any reason to think of another first cause somewhere outside of this solar system, as we know the same force and matter to be universal. If there is anything certain in the teachings of astronomy, it is beyond a doubt, that light, motion and attraction appertain to all celestial bodies. Those forces being derivatives of the first impulse, the superior and governing force, hence the same first cause everywhere; although in the materialization of force, other derivatives may be active on other stars, and produce modifications of matter unknown to us.

Again, by the spectrum analysis and by the meteors or aerolites reaching our earth from different regions, we know that matter is matter everywhere, of the same substance and qualities, although elements, in consequence of other derivative forces, may combine to different compositions in different stars. The possibility of combinations of one hundred elements, and there are certainly rather more than less, is almost infinite; but every combination remains the same matter subject to the same force. So all possible varieties and modifications of matter would not point to a second original cause. Therefore, there can be little doubt, that all celestial bodies, however different their atmospheres, rotations, and relations to this or any other sun, are populated with living beings, in correspondence with those various conditions; and there like here, the last link in the chain must be intelligent beings akin to man.

But aside of all these considerations, the unity of the first cause is proved by the teleology of creation, being, and history. Every stage of the earth's formation, every individual object of nature, and every period of man's history, as we have noticed before, is a teleological center, the end, aim, and object of a design and purpose, a logical sequence of prior causes, back to the first cause. In every stage of the earth's formation and every period of history, as in every individual object of nature, as a necessary part of the cosmos, there is again the germ and efficient cause to the next following ones, and so on from the first impulse imparted to the elementary parallels, to the present stage of the earth and period of history, [.] So and not otherwise we can understand the continuous chain of cause and effects phenomenal in every *causalnexus*, necessarily connected with the law of causality.

Therefore we are entitled at every point not only to the question of efficient causes, but also to the queries why and whereto, at every pause. Naturalists will never arrive at a proper understanding of nature, unless they search after the why and whereto at every stage of creation, and history, the objects of nature and their respective parts. The fact is, while one ascertains the efficient causes of one stage or period, he exposes the final causes of the prior stages or periods. Whatever is efficient cause in any higher stage, was final cause in the lower one. This is the unmistakable architecture of nature and history. Science may not succeed in this or the next century to ascertain in all instances all efficient and final causes; but it will certainly solve one problem after the other, and unless they are infinite, they must certainly be solved one day or another. When the laws of nature and history will be scientifically established we will be enabled to see the final causes, without being prophets, and then the final causes must unravel to us the mystery of the final cause. Nothing is unknowable.

When the first impulse was imparted to the elementary parallels to unite and mingle by compression or concussion, this impulse was the efficient cause; the final cause was the unification of the elements and the ensuing heat of about 2,000 degrees F., taking the medium number between the extremes; and this was stage No. 1. The liquid and radiating fire ball which, from the proper distance, must have looked like a sun, was stage No. 2, to which stage No. 1 contained the efficient cause, and of which it was the final cause. But this fire ball was not to remain in *status-quo.* By the forces evolving from the first impulse and materializing in the fiery liquid, it moved around its axis and in some orbit around the sun. Gradually it cooled off, formed a solid nucleus and crust, the radiating heat carrying off the various gases, formed an atmosphere, thick, heavy and pregnant also with the elements which afterwards formed the outer crust of the earth, and the ocean. When the surface of the young earth was cooled down to about 200 degrees F. the gases attracted from the atmosphere covered the earth, all, or nearly so, with water of a peculiar thickness; and yet there was a division, an expansion, a firmament, between the water on the earth and that above it still suspended in the thick and heavy atmosphere, through which the rays of the sun light penetrated sparingly. It was stage No. 3, the earth was in a condition to bring forth organic beings; and this stage No. 3, was the final cause of stages No. 1 and 2, which contained its efficient causes.

Was this stage creation's objective point? Certainly not. If it had been it must have stopped there, which it did not. New functions of the first cause become now phenomenal, organic beings of the lowest forms are brought forth in the thick and hot water, the lowest forms of vegetables and animals, rising gradually in the scale of evolution to huge monsters. Here the final cause of all former stages becomes phenomenal in the existence of living beings. The first impulse imparted to matter by its materialized derivatives has overcome the primary tendency of matter to dissolve and separate in its elements; there is an earth of one piece, covered with a continuous sheet of water — and attempts now to come forth from its unconscious to the conscious condition in animal centers, to which the vegetables are the state of transition in the gradual evolution and differentiation. Here then we have stage No. 4, the start of conscious centers, in which the force captivated in matter attempts its liberation, after it had overcome inert matter to that extent that organic formation had become possible; and here again stage No. 4 is the final cause of stages Nos. 1, 2, and 3 which contain its efficient causes.

Following up the progress of creation, we observe how the formation of the earth's crust, the change of atmosphere, and the development of vegetable and animal life go hand in hand in the regular routine of cause and effect. As the water is distilling, its sediments settle down to the bottom, the fish make their appearance. As the water recedes and swamps ensue, the amphibies follow, always preceded by their food. As the earth attracts the carbon from the atmosphere, producing huge vegetation, the birds, carbon inhaling, come in existence, food and shelter [having] preceded them. And when the carbon enveloping the earth like a thick cloud had been sufficiently attracted by the earth, sun, moon and stars become visible on the earth. Here we have stage No. 5, the earth covered with rich vegetation, land and ocean populated with radiates, mollusks, and articulates of most beauteous forms, together with fishes, amphibies, and birds, now under the direct influence of the sun and the other celestial bodies, and the earth in its proper orbit. The obscure gloom has passed away and the age of light has commenced on earth. The primary force materialized in the earth is reunited with the cosmic light, has liberated itself from the state of gloomy obscurity. Here is stage No. 5, the final cause of stages No. 1, 2, 3, 4, with its efficient causes in all of them.

Now come the creatures of light, the constant types. Now, and not before, the mammals could make their appearance. Elementary matter had first to be brought so far under the control of the active force before it could achieve its liberation from the materials bonds of unconsciousness. But it progresses rapidly through all transitory forms of the vegetable and animal kingdoms, through all phases of conscious beings, always imparting to matter higher morphic qualities, preparing it for higher formations, until the last triumph is achieved, viz., the unconscious has become conscious in the animal kingdom, with the vegetables as its points of transition; now the conscious becomes self-conscious in man, with the animals as points of transition. The primary force becomes self-conscious itself again, in the self-conscious man, who, knowing all in his consciousness, distinguishes himself from all; and this is his self-consciousness. The first cause has become itself again, the self-conscious psychical cause of all forces and all motion in matter. So the ring of creation was completed with stage No. 6, with its efficient causes in stages 1, 2, 3, 4, and 5, of all of which it is the final cause and teleological center.

But here the work is not finished, for man is not fully self-conscious until he knows all which is knowable, to distinguish himself from all which is, and consequently the work of this cause is not completed with the earth's and other planets' creation. Here begins stage No. 7, man's history. It is the Creator's Sabbath. The work of liberation from matter and the triumph over it, begins in man, by him, and for him. He works on to accomplish the subjugation of matter, the resurrection of self-conscious spirit, the triumph of life over death, of light over darkness, of self-conscious intelligence over blind and inexorable powers of darkness; of freedom, love, and happiness over cold and barren necessity. This is the creation of history, the progress of the primary force to self-conscious existence in the human family, and the stages thereof are well marked in the works of intelligent historians. Therefore the Bible states: "And on the seventh day (not on the sixth) God completed His work which He had made; and He ceased to work on the seventh day from all the work He had made (for here man's work begins). And God blessed the seventh day and sanctified it, because then He had ceased from all His work, which God had created to do" (to go on and on to perfection with the progression of man's history). This stage, No. 7, is the final cause of all previous stages which contain its efficient causes.

You see, ladies and gentlemen, it is all one piece, of one cast, one chain of cause and effects, one design, one object, all of which must have been present in stage No. 1 and in each succeeding stage. All of them were in the first, the last in the first, and all in each, which the ancient Hebrews described as: *Sof ma'aseh b'mahashava tehila*, "The end of the work contained in the first thought."

Here then is one will, intellect, and design, one object and one executive power, one spirit, one piece of inevitable logic, from which no iota can be taken away, none added, and none inverted. Here the bare possibility of more than one first cause falls to the ground. As soon as intelligence claims its right to look upon the cosmos through the law of causality, it is led forward and backward through the unbroken chain to the final cause and to the first cause, which reveals its nature in its own last triumphs, in the self-conscious intelligence of man.

He, the substance, who has imparted this first impulse to the parallels of matter, of this and any other planet or solar system, the impulse from which all forces of nature have ensued, and by evolution and differentiation, constructed this great cosmos, triumphs over all matter in the self-conscious intelligence of man, remains in him and over him, preserving and governing all, shaping all destinies, guiding all and constantly from lower to higher conditions; He who is the Genius of nature and the Logos of history, fills all space and is the force of all forces; He is the Cosmic God, for He is the cause of all causes, the first principle of all things, the only substance whose attributes are life, will, and intellect. Matter is the non-substance, for it has no functions; it is the inert, passive, and imperceptible material, which He, by the forces, moves, shapes, subjects, and governs. He is Almighty, for He is the force of all forces, the cause of all causes. He is omniprescent, revealed everywhere by the ever-active force of all forces in nature, and every motion of the human intellect. He is omniprescent [omnipresent?], revealed everywhere by the ever-active force of all forces in natnre [nature], and every motion of the human intellect. He is omnipres- cent, for He fills all space and penetrates all atomic matter. He is all- wise and omniscient, for He is the intellect of all intellect, its cause and substance. He is the Preserver and Governor, for He is the will, free- dom, and justice. He is the Cosmic God, who is not anthropomor- phous. He is not in heaven above nor on earth below, for He is everywhere, in all space, in all objects of nature, in every attribute of matter, and in every thought of the mind. "No man can see me and live." He appeared to none, because He continually and simultaneously appears to all and through all. He spoke to none, because He speaks eternally and simultaneously to all and through all. He resides nowhere especially, because He is everywhere continually. He had no beginning, because He made it; and no end, because He has no beginning. He changes not, because all changes are effects, and He is the cause of all causes and no effect. He is the Cosmic God, — the only God, — whose name is ineffable, who alone is, was, and will be forever and aye, whose existence none can deny, and whose immensity none can comprehend. We know, we feel His immeasurable grandeur, and worship Him with awe.

    Scientists, here is your God and Lord, whom you seek, and whom to find is the highest wisdom. He is the God found by induction and felt by spontaneity. Philosophers, here is your God, whom to expound is the highest glory of human mind — Kant, and other thinkers, have argued against the anthropomorphous God of theology; the cosmic God is philosophy's first and last substance. Simple-minded men, here is your God, whom you need not seek, for He is everywhere, in you and about you, in every quality of matter and every motion of the mind; where you are, He is; where you observe or think, you think Him. Children, here is your God, in the fragrance of your flowers, in the beauteous hues of vernal blossoms, in the thunder and the whis- per, in heaven's azure dome and the earth's verdant garb, in your inno- cent smiles and your mother's sweet tenderness. Sage or fool, great or little, here is your God, you can not escape Him, and He cannot escape you; He is in you, and you are in Him. Men of all future generations, here is God in the harmony of all human conceptions and knowledge, the God of all, and all eternity, the Cosmic God, the Great I Am, and none beside Him.

Thanks to the Almighty, that He has permitted us to look into the mysteries of His creation; that He has led and guided us through the obscure regions of this material world, onward, forward, heavenward, always on the simple path of induction, to His very throne, to simple, sublime, and eternal truth for all coming generations. Humbly and gratefully I render praise and thanksgiving to the Eternal who has permitted me to conceive these thoughts, combinations, and conclusions, which have led me back home to the one and eternal God. My soul triumphs before Him at this immortal victory.

So far, in this particular point, induction leads. Here deduction begins, and here ends our province at present. But we have three more problems to solve, viz., What is nature? What is man? Which is the relation of God, nature, and man? I propose to begin the discussion of these problems in my next lecture.

VI

ISAAC MAYER WISE

The Addenda to Judaism: Its
Doctrines and Duties *(1872)*

ADDENDUM I

Judaism teaches no dogmas or mysteries, on the belief of which salvation exclusively depends. It maintains that everlasting bliss will be the reward of all those who, from pure motives, do that which is right, and shun that which is evil, according to the best of their knowledge. (Deuter. xxix, 28, and xxx, 11 to 14.)

Balaam's faith and wisdom did not save him when he advised wicked actions to his people. The prophet Isaiah called the Pagan prince Cyrus "The Messiah of the Lord," on account of his excellent virtues. King Saul was the Lord's Messiah, and perished by suicide on account of his wickedness, while the Pagan king Hiram of Tyre was counted by the ancient rabbis among those who entered Paradise alive, so righteous was that heathen in their estimation.

ADDENDUM II

None can comprehend this universe with its forces and creatures. The nature of causes is unknown to man. Life, love, and reason are mysteries. How much less can man see, know, or comprehend God Himself, the cause of all causes, the Governor and Preserver of the universe, the eternal fountain of life, love, and reason.

ADDENDUM III

Whatever is composed has a beginning, and is preceded by the cause of its composition. Its existence as such depends on the composition and its continuance, as the water does on the continued connection of hydrogen and oxygen. Therefore, God, the external cause of all causes, can not be composed of elements, parts, persons, or otherwise.

ADDENDUM IV

Whatever changes is finite. The infinite is immutable. All things in nature change except the laws of nature. The laws testify to the immutability of the Lawgiver.

ADDENDUM V

If the will of God should be withdrawn from this universe, the worlds must suddenly turn into nothing. He who made, preserves, and governs all, is almighty, or the might and power of all.

ADDENDUM VI

Every entity is an idea of God, before it becomes a reality. So God knows all things before they come into existence. All that is, was, or will be, is either cause or effect. The Almighty being the cause of all causes, and all possible effects thereof being evident to the all-wise, God must be omniscient.

ADDENDUM VII

Supreme wisdom and supreme justice are inseparable. The former becomes manifest in laws, and the latter in adherence to them. Again, God's justice to man is grace; and mercy is not only the work of grace, but also the highest justice, where correction has been attained without punishment. God punishes the sinner only to correct him; hence the punishment also is the work of grace. "The correction of God, my son, do not despise, and feel no loathing for his admonition; because whomever God loveth he admonisheth, and as a father (doth to) a son (in whom) he delighteth." (Proverbs iii, 11, 12.)

ADDENDUM VIII

(a) The law of attraction, by analogy, illustrates the government of Providence, extending over the vast whole and each minute part thereof, by one and the same force.

(b) As God's physical laws are intended to sustain life and prosperity, so also His special law for the government of mankind must be intended for the prosperity and happiness of man.

(c) Again, obedience to God's physical laws results in its legitimate reward, viz., life, health, and prosperity; while disobedience is the cause of inevitable evil. The same must be the case in God's government of man. Obedience and its reward, disobedience and its punishment, are linked together as cause and effect throughout the universe.

ADDENDUM IX

To do and love the good for goodness' own sake is the highest degree of moral perfection. God only is goodness, real and absolute; to do and love the good from the motive of love to God, is in reality to do and love goodness for its own sake.

ADDENDUM X

(a) The history of mankind is the testimony of God's justice and grace. (Deut. xxvii, 7.)

It is unsafe to judge the nature of a large object by the manifestations of one of its minute parts. The more of its parts we are enabled to examine the better we are prepared to form a correct idea of the whole. It is unsafe to judge of God's wisdom by the knowledge we may have of one leaf or crystal, although in them as in the universe God's wisdom is revealed. It is safest to observe God's wisdom in the grand total of the universe, the simple causes, grand effects, and the harmony of its heterogeneous parts; although we know not whether from the sun to the mote, the earth to a particle, or from the elephant to the infusorium there is one step beyond the center of creatures. In like manner it is unsafe to judge of God's providence and justice by the fate of one man or by one category of instances, although the justice of Providence is visible in every man's life. It is safest to learn the justice of Providence from the history of mankind, although history is but a meager record of the fate, experience, and transactions of the human family.

(b) Nations prospered in just proportion to their national virtues; they declined and have fallen in consequence of their national vices. (Lev. xxxi, 3, etc., and Deut. xxviii.)

(c) Great revolutions in history always resulted in the progress of humanity. (The exode from Egypt and the revelation on Horeb. The end of king Saul and the reign of David. Israel before and after the Babylonian captivity. The Maccabees and their time.)

(d) Whenever mankind needs expected messages God sends His inspired messengers. (Deut. xviii, 18; Jeremiah i, 4, 5, 9, 10.)

(e) Whenever powerful men influenced the fate of mankind from selfish motives or to selfish purposes, Providence always turned the events in favor of the progress of humanity. (Alexander the Great, his wars and their final results. The motives of the Spanish monarchs with Columbus and the results of the discovery of America.) (Genesis i, 19, 20.)

ADDENDUM XI

(a) The words "Ye shall obey His voice," in the Bible, always signify, man should under all circumstances obey God's revelations in human reason and conscience. Whatever one knows to be right, true, or good, he must have the moral courage to utter and to do. Whatever one knows to be wrong, cruel, foolish, or wicked, he must have the moral courage to denounce and to shun.

(b) The words in the Bible, "Ye shall walk after God, your Lord," signify:

1. Man should diligently inquire into the words and works of God to become wise; for the path of wisdom is to seek God in His works and words. The fear of the Lord is the beginning of wis-

dom; to know of Him all man is permitted to know, is the height of all wisdom; for God is the cause of all causes and the reason of all reason. (Psalm xix and civ.; Job xxxviii, and xxxix; Isaiah xl, 25, 26; Psalm cxi, 10; Proverbs i, 7.)

2. In God's works and words we should learn and admire His wisdom, goodness, and justice, and be prompted to imitate these excellencies; for the path of righteousness and piety is to imitate God's sublime perfection. Happiness and perfection can be acquired only in the path of wisdom and righteousness. Therefore, "to walk after God" is to fulfill our destiny. (Deut. x, 12, 13; Jeremiah ix, 22, 23; Micah vi, 8.)

(c) We can not be all-wise, omniscient, and omnipotent, as God is; still we might be very wise, know much of God's creation, encircle the earth, penetrate the depth of the oceans, roam through immense space, and embrace with our intellect the past, present, and future. We can not be all-just, most gracious, benevolent, and merciful as God is; still we might be very kind, just, benevolent, benign, and merciful, such as no other earthly creature can be. Our will may be so free that we do only that for which we have the noblest motives. Our conscience may be so sublime that we perceive directly the will of God. Our love may be so expanded as to embrace God and His creation, and this is moral perfection, holiness, and happiness.

ADDENDUM XII

Although man according to his body is an animal, he is as such superior to all creatures. This is manifest in his erect posture, keen and intelligent eyes, his fine shaped head, and expressive countenance, and above all in his organs of speech and song, capable of variation of sounds, to express and convey the most sublime thoughts and sentiments.

ADDENDUM XIII

(a) These capacities are capable of so immense a development that man may become a prophet who conceives directly the will and purpose of God in His works and words. (Job xxxv, 11; Numbers xii, 6–8.)

(b) By his intellectual capacities, furthermore, man understands the objects of nature, their utility or inutility; knows himself, his merits and demerits, virtues and vices, desires, hopes, and propensities; he discriminates between what is proper or improper, just or unjust, right or wrong, good or bad.

(c) No earthly creature besides man is capable of thinking of the infinite Deity and His will; for none can discriminate cause and effect to the extent to reach the first cause — God. God revealed Himself to man only. No other of the known creatures becomes conscious of the universe, its laws, its harmony and unity; hence among all known creatures, it is to man first and foremost, that the universe exists. Therefore, he stands so much nearer to the Deity than the other creatures, who know neither Him nor His works and words.

(d) None of the known creatures besides man knows that He knows and reasons on His reason.

Addendum XIV

As long as evil propensities govern man to choose that which is wicked, he is not free; he is under the control of animal appetites and irrational necessity.

Addendum XV

Conscience is innate and universal, and every human being acknowledges the principle, that right is right and wrong is wrong before his own tribunal. The definition of right and wrong, being the office of the reason, necessarily differs widely, without effecting the principle, however.

Addendum XVI[*]

As no matter can exist without the force of attraction, there can be no man without love. The child loves his parents, sisters, brothers,

[*Incorrectly numbered "XIV" in the original.]

teachers, playmates, and benefactors. Parents love their children and teachers love their pupils. We all love our friends, our benefactors, our birth place, our country, etc. Every person loves.

ADDENDUM XVII

Man's soul is immortal, because —

(a) It is the image of God. (Genesis i, 27; ix, 6.)

(b) It expects to be immortal. This expectation is impressed upon it by its Creator, and is therefore universal. (Job xi, 18; Jeremiah xxxi, 17; Prov. xxiii, 18; xxiv, 14; Psalms lxii, 6 and lxxi, 5.)

(c) God has given it desires which can not be realized and qualities which can not be exercised on earth. (Deut. iii, 23, etc.; Exodus xxxiii, 17 to 20.)

(d) The mental and moral qualities of good men increase steadily as their physical energies decrease. (The last hours of Jacob, Moses, Elijah, and Elisha.)

(e) Intellect is as indestructible as every other element. (Job xxviii.)

(f) God being all-wise would not destroy the intellect he created; being all-good He would not disappoint the highest hope with which He impressed us; and being all-just He could not have commanded man only to subordinate his carnal inclinations to his spiritual welfare, if the soul was not destined to everlasting life. (Psalm xvi, 8, etc.; xlix, 16; Ecclesiastes xii, 7; Daniel xii, 2, 3; Deut. vi, 24.)

ADDENDUM XVIII

No man can form a complete conception of the nature of future reward and punishment, as we know only the present state of existence. Still a faint idea may be entertained of it.

(a) The satisfaction and peace of the soul which accompany the recollections of righteousness and piety, follow us beyond the grave, and are a natural reward; but the consciousness of guilt and wickedness is the torment of the wicked on earth and his hell in the future state of existence.

(b) The knowledge that we, by our exertions, sacrifices, and faith, notwithstanding the beguiling allurements of life with its charms and passions, and notwithstanding the perpetual combat in ordinary life between righteousness and wickedness—still maintained our faith and confidence in God and virtue, and triumphing over all obstacles went forth from the struggle of life righteous, pious, and confident in God's justice and mercy, is the triumph of our godly nature, and a sublime reward to every good man. Its opposite is moral wretchedness, the punishment of the wicked.

(c) The consciousness of having developed our moral and intellectual capacities according to the will of God, and elevated ourselves to a higher order of spirits, is of itself a gracious reward, when egotism and carnal passions have vanished. And the consciousness of being one of the lower order of spirits, by our own errors and sins, is a mortifying punishment.

(d) The abilities attained, to enjoy the grandeur and beauty of the intellectual world, is a source of happiness; and the consciousness of its loss is misery in itself.

(e) We have certainly no right to expect of an all-just God, in time or eternity, perfections not attained, blessings not deserved, or gifts which we are not prepared to enjoy.

ADDENDUM XIX

Nature produces poisons of which men can make healing medicines. The swamps and morasses exhale pestilence and death, man changes them into fertile gardens. Primitive forests, extensive wilds, or howling deserts breed and shelter the enemies of man, venomous serpents, and ferocious beasts. But man changes forests, wilds, and deserts into fertile fields, meadows, or flower-gardens. Wind, heat, frost, dew, and rain are inimical to man; but he protects himself against them by clothes, houses, or tents, by cooling shades or cheering fires. He transplants vegetables from zone to zone, and almost as he pleases propagates them. He improves and increases also the animals which he domesticates. Fire, water, and air must do his work, shape metals to give him implements, propel his mills, machines, cars, and ships, and increase twenty-fold his own speed and power. Rocks and mountains are no obstacles in man's way, and rivers obstruct not his path. He arrests the thunderbolt, speaks to distant lands by the electro-magnetic force, paints with the light of the day, and rides upon the pinions of the winds. So man is the lord of creation by God's appointment.

Civilization and prosperity progress in the same ratio among the nations as they realize God's covenant with man.[*]

ADDENDUM XX

This covenant[†] has been disregarded by most all writers on Bible religion; and yet it is the very ground-work of the system of ethics and religion taught in the Bible. It refutes Paganism, which deified natural forces and natural objects, and placed man in subjection to them. It elevates man high above all creatures, and places him to the middle between God and the material universe. He is God's agent on earth and continues His work. It replaces iron fate by the dominion of reason, and lays the foundation to the sovereignty of justice, liberty, and peace on earth. It sanctifies labor, and indicates how, by reason's progress, hard labor will decrease the means of subsistence and security multiply, and civilization advance. It exalts God to the Lord of the universe, and accords to the mind the dominion over matter.

ADDENDUM XXI

The moral law as the foundation of personal and national happiness, is the universal idea in the second covenant.[§] Men living isolated, or in small groups, obedient to the conditions of the first covenant (excepting hunting, pillaging, and ravaging tribes), could not feel the want of a better knowledge of the moral law, which regulates the conduct of man to man as social beings. But with the increase and closer contact of men, a better knowledge of the moral law became a necessity. It was the main lesson, under the second covenant, for the Patri-

[*Wise refers here to the Covenant with Noah (Gen. 9:8–9). In the section that follows (76), he quotes from the Prophets and Psalms to augment the Genesis stipulations with the mandates that it is "man's duty" in "covenant" to (1) "acquire much knowledge"; (2) "work and toil in harmony with this knowledge, for the security and prosperity of man"; (3) "be grateful to his Maker for the reason, energies, dominion and control given him"; (4) "advance in the correct knowledge of God and His will, and lead a life of righteousness, to the best of his knowledge."]

[†God's Covenant with Noah; see previous note.]

[§God's Covenant with Abraham (Gen. 17)].

archs to impart to the contemporaries. However imperfect their knowledge of the Deity may have been (Exodus vi, 3), superior knowledge of the moral law is exemplified in their lives.

ADDENDUM XXII

Israel having increased in Egypt to 600,000 men, had become numerous enough to form an independent nation. Having maintained among a hostile people, under oppression and slavery, his peculiar names,[*] language, traditions, doctrines, and a patriarchal form of government, distinct and entirely different from the Egyptian — Israel possessed the main elements of nationality. Most of the people having been the laborers of Egypt, they were skilled in the arts of that country, as many of their wise men were schooled in the sciences of the ancient Egypt; therefore, Israel possessed also the main element of independence. Having thus adhered to the conditions of the two covenants, God redeemed Israel from Egypt, to fulfill in him the promises of the second covenant, and make with him the third.[†]

ADDENDUM XXIII

Had Israel always obeyed the law of God, its land would have become the great school of humanity. Having sinned it was dispersed among the nations, thus to carry the divine right and light to all parts of the globe. As long as authentic history records, Israel stood on the ground of opposition to all mankind — the struggle of truth and error, justice and injustice, is as old as man — and Israel's sufferings among the nations have proceeded from that opposition. But whenever truth and justice will be triumphant, Israel's opposition and suffering will be ended. "Their seed shall be known among the nations, and their offspring among peoples; all who see them will know them that they are the seed blessed of the Lord." (Isaiah lxi, 9; lxv, 23.)

[*The reference is to an ancient midrash that "the Children of Israel were redeemed from Egypt because of four meritorious acts: They did not change their names; they did not change their language; they did not boast that they were to leave Egypt with reparations; and they did not abandon circumcision." (Midrash Tehillim 114:4)]

[†God's Covenant with the Jewish People at Mount Sinai (Exodus 20). See Wise's hymn, "From Heaven's Heights," Hymn #142, Union Hymnal, Songs and Prayers for Jewish Worship (Central Conference of American Rabbis, 1957), p. 150.]

Addendum XXIV

It is not Israel's political restoration, the re-establishment of a throne, the reinstitution of a sacrificial polity, or the coming of a redeeming Messiah, which the Bible promises or predicts. It is the final and universal triumph of truth, righteousness, liberty, and justice, to which the prophets point. Every person contributing to the achievement of this great purpose is a Messiah and a messenger of the Most High. The habitable world must become one holy land, every city a Jerusalem, every house a temple, every table an altar, every person a priest of the Most High, his own prince, priest, and prophet. This is the kingdom of God, the hope of mankind, the mission of Israel.

Addendum XXV

The Decalogue opens with the comma[e]ndatory, "to believe in one God," and the prohibitory, "to have no other God before Him." The fourth commandment again, opening the duties of man to man, begins with the commendatory, "to sanctify the Sabbath," and the prohibitory, "to do no work on the Sabbath day." This points out how all commandments must be understood, viz., each commendatory includes its prohibitory, and each prohibitory contains its commendatory law. For instance, "Honor thy father and thy mother," includes the prohibitory, not to lift up the hand and not to use insulting words against one's own parents. (Exodus xxi, 15, 17.) Again, "Thou shalt not steal," contains the commendatory, to protect our neighbor's property. (Exodus xxiii, 5.)

Addendum XXVI

No man can in every instance appeal to his own reason and conscience, much less to the reason and conscience of mankind, to decide what is right and good, or bad and wrong in particular cases. Besides, the history of mankind teaches that man never was as wicked as he was ignorant; his motives were better than his judgment. When Eve ate of the forbidden fruit she had even a good motive, viz., to become like an *Elohim*, "to know good and evil;" but it was foolish to believe that any fruit has the power to do this. Those who sacrificed their children to Moloch had the good intention to worship an imaginary god; but they were foolish to believe any god could be pleased by such cruelty. Thus man wished to do right, but knew not to distinguish properly between right and wrong, justice and injustice, virtue and vice. Therefore, God revealed His will to the men of His choice, for the benefit of all mankind, to teach them in all cases to distinguish properly and exactly, between right and wrong, justice and injustice, virtue and vice, to know what is acceptable to God and beneficial to man, and what is abominable before God and injurious to man.

Addendum XXVII[*]

(a) To love God with all our heart means, that all our affections and aspirations should be directed toward God, the Supreme goodness and wisdom; and all of our inclinations and propensities should be subjected to His will, the Supreme justice.

We should love man because he is the image of God; we should love virtue and wisdom because God delights in them; we should love and admire the beauties of creation, because they are the testimony of God's goodness, greatness, and love.

(b) To love God with all our soul signifies that the final object of our thoughts, studies, researches, and speculations should be the knowledge of God and His will, in order to be enabled to do it, cling to Him with the power of conviction, and become truly wise by the comprehension of the cause of all causes.

(c) To love God with all our might signifies that our will and energies should always be ready and active to do that which God loves, and shun that which displeases Him.

Addendum XXVIII

In lonely cloisters or solitary wilds, men and women deceive themselves by the erroneous belief that their contemplative lives, devotional exercises, ascetic practices, and renunciation of society, advance them

[*Wise here offers commentary on Deut. 6: 5 ff., the V'ahavta paragraph of the Shema Yisrael verses.]

in piety and human perfection. Whatever is right and good in one, must be so to all. And yet if all men would lead such a life, civilization would come to a speedy end, and all must return to the solitary life of the savage. This is certainly contrary to the will of God. To neglect the society of man is to neglect one's self. To be good, one must do good to man.

ADDENDUM XXIX[*]

Neighbor here signifies every man; therefore, in the way of explanation, Sacred Scriptures add in the same chapter, verse 33: "If a stranger sojourn with thee in your land, ye shall not afflict him; like the native from among you shall be to you the stranger who sojourns with you, *And thou shalt love him as thyself;* for we were strangers in the land of Egypt. I am God your Lord;" *i.e.,* the God and Lord of all men.

Again, in all cases of justice, charity, and benevolence, the divine laws mention the stranger as entitled to equal rights with the Israelite, that national selfishness or sectarian narrowness of mind construe not the laws of the Lord to the injury of any human being, as those nations did, and partly still do, who are guided by imperfect human laws.

ADDENDUM XXX[†]

Exceptions to this duty are: the defense of the State against rebellion or invasion; the combat for the higher interests of humanity; and the legitimate efforts to protect or save the life, health, or limbs of others, especially of those entrusted to one's care or protection. (Leviticus xix, 16; I Samuel xvii; Jeremiah xxviv [?].)

[*Wise here offers commentary on Levit. 19:18, "Love your neighbor as yourself."]

[†On page 50, section 133, just before this Addendum, Wise writes: "The first special duty man owes to himself is SELF-PRESERVATION; i.e., to preserve his life, health, and limbs, as he is commanded, "Thou shalt not kill," either others or thyself, entirely or in part, at once or gradually.]

ADDENDUM XXXI*

Whatever is right and proper for some, must be so for all. If all would try to live without work, mankind must fall back into barbarism. Still, we are not commanded to do manual labor exclusively. Those who work in science, art, or literature, certainly have a sphere of action useful to man and acceptable to God. But they also should do some manual labor, not only for the sake of their health, but also to honor it before their fellow men. "Labor honors the working man."†

ADDENDUM XXXII

Animals and vegetables also have their stated periods of rest, to regain their spent energies. Fruit trees rest for a season, after one or more summers of production. The soil also must have stated periods of rest, to yield properly. (Leviticus xxv, 1–12.)

ADDENDUM XXXIII

It matters not what particular occupation a man has chosen, as long as it is honest and useful he deserves respect and honor, in the same proportion as he is conscientious in his discharge of duty, and desirous to be useful to the human family to the best of his ability. There is no difference, in this point, between the most humble day laborer and the loftiest genius, each in his proper sphere. Society needs all of them, therefore they are.

"Every man to his service and to his burden." (Numbers iv, 19.)

ADDENDUM XXXIV

The law makes no provisions for beggars, and there should be none. Proper care should be taken of the poor, needy, and helpless, that none need beg. Every person has a right to live, hence also to the means

[*Wise here after commentary on Genesis 2:15.]
[†A paraphrase of the Talmudic expression, "Noble is the labor that honors its workmen." (B. Nedarim 49b)]

of support. If one has more than he needs, he owes support to him who needs it. To refuse it is indirect robbery.[*] The state, county, or municipality must provide for its poor. To do more and better for the poor, needy, helpless, widows, orphans, and strangers, than the state or county can, public societies and charities ought to be supported by every good man. To render immediate help where it is necessary, is the duty of every feeling person.

ADDENDUM XXXV

Biblical laws were changed during the period of history recorded in the Bible; so afterward the laws, amendments, and changes could be made, which are recorded in the Mishnah and Talmud. [Compare Deut. xxv. 5 to 10, and Ruth iv.; Levit. xxiii, 42, 43 and Nehemiah xiii. 13 to 18; Exodus vi. 14, 15, 16, and 2 Chronicles xxxv. 18; Exodus xxvi., and I Kings vii., especially Exodus xxv. 18, and I Kings vi. 23; Exodus xx.4, and I Kings vii. 27 to 37, Exodus xxv.31, and I Kings vii. 49; Exodus xxx. 18, and I Kings vii. 38. The rabbinical passages in support of this paragraph are compiled in "The Israelite," volume 2, numbers 40, 41, 42.]

ADDENDUM XXXVI

Palestine is called the holy land, which it was, because:
1. The whole land was given to Israel in which to practice the laws of the Lord, and prepare themselves for the great mission of conveying divine truth to all men. So the whole land was considered one divine temple.
2. The prophets and psalmists of the Lord, by their holy words, sanctified that land to a temple of truth.
It is natural for every good man to be attached to the land where his ancestors rest in the dust, his glorious history was enacted, his prophets and bards touched the cords of the sacred lyre, and poured forth the glowing effusion of inspired words, and his immortal heroes fought the battles of the Lord; therefore Palestine was the holy land. But it is now defiled by barbarism and impiety; it is the holy land no

---

Wise had originally included these bracketed references in the text.
[*On page 60 in the book Wise indicates that he bases this observation on Proverbs 22:23, "Rob not the poor because he is poor."]

more. The habitable earth must become one holy land; this is the object of the Law. [Zechariah ii, 14 to 17; Psalm cxiii.]

Addendum XXXVII

Symbolic actions are required to convey ideas or sentiments to gross or weak minds; barbarous men express their feelings by wild gestures or gross symbols; words and songs are sufficient to instruct and edify the intelligent and express every sentiment or thought. The sons and daughters of the covenant have the solemn duty to be intelligent. Therefore if the temple of Jerusalem should ever be rebuilt no sacrifice would be made there, as we could not thus be instructed or edified, or serve God with all our heart and all our soul. God by destroying the Temple demonstrated His will that no sacrifices should be made.

Holy observances and symbols have often been changed in Israel, to correspond to the change of taste and intelligence in different generations and places; and must always be changed accordingly, by the proper authorities.

Addendum XXXVIII

The same Bible which teaches us that God is immutable and governs the universe by fixed laws, also informs us that the best and wisest men prayed in hours of affliction and God heard and granted their petition, and there is no contradiction in this. To pray sincerely means to express our full confidence in God, that He can and will fulfill our wishes addressed to Him. This unconditional confidence in and submission to God is of itself a lofty virtue, the elevation of the soul to God, which must find its reward as virtue invariably will. The reward of this virtue is:

Consolation and moral fortitude which he feels who prayed sincerely, as a response from heaven.

The fulfillment of his wishes if they are not against his own happiness, inasmuch as he who prays acquires a moral excellency which brings its own reward.

Often we address wishes to God the non-fulfillment of which results to our welfare. Man is short-sighted.

VII

BERNHARD FELSENTHAL

Bible Interpretation:
How and How Not* (1884)

That a Jew is now permitted, and indeed invited, to speak before Christian ministers of the gospel is a hopeful sign that we are approaching the time in which seekers of truth of the various denominations can work together, harmoniously and peacefully, like true brethren. All study and investigation must have but one and the same object in view, namely, to overthrow ignorance, to emancipate the mind from preconceived, but unfounded notions, and to arrive at the truth. And why should Christians and Jews, Trinitarians and Unitarians not work thus together? There is no Jewish Hebrew grammar, no Christian Hebrew grammar; no Presbyterian Greek language and no Episcopalian Greek language — there is but one and the same Hebrew and one and the same Greek for all. I would even go farther. I would say that there is no denominational ecclesiastical history and no sectarian Bible exegesis. In these fields, likewise, the truth is but one. In church history, it is of course natural that a Jew should be more interested in the rabbinical literature of the Middle Ages and the later development of the Jewish church, than a Christian, in most cases, would be. On the other hand, it is also to be expected that a Christian student will take a deeper interest than a Jew in the study of the history of specific Christian doctrines and institutions. A Baptist will naturally be more attracted by the study of the question of baptism than a Unitarian. But the absolute truth, I repeat, is but one. And so I foresee the time when, instead of our or five theological seminaries in Chicago and its suburbs, there will be but one excellently equipped and excellently endowed institution, with a

*A lecture delivered before the Hebrew Summer School, Morgan Park, Ill.

large number of teachers for the various branches, with libraries and other advantages which may well be compared with those in Oxford and Cambridge, in Berlin and Leipzig. This institution for "theological" learning will, as I foresee it, be connected with a great coming university, and will form an integral part of it. And in this university of the future, by the side of professorial chairs for all other possible departments of knowledge, and under the silent yet powerful influence of the other branches of learning, the "theological" studies will be secured against the creeping in of a spirit of mental narrowness on the one hand, and a spirit of undue haughtiness on the other.

But what have I to say concerning the exegesis of the Scriptures? Is this not to be taught differently in separate denominational seminaries? I answer, without hesitation, *no.* From the professor's chair, the Bible must be explained and studied without any preconceived doctrinal or sectarian bias. History, archaeology, philology, must be the handmaids of Biblical science, and not denominational considerations. Whether in our day a man may marry his deceased wife's sister, or not, is, as a practical question, to be settled by the legislative authorities of the Episcopalian church, in England by the English Parliament. But whether such marriages were allowed, or prohibited, by the Bible, is for the unbiased Old Testament student to say. When and in what manner the rite of baptism should be performed, is to be decided by the councils and other competent authorities of the various Christian sects. But whether the Hebrew verb *tâbhăl* means "to immerse," or "to sprinkle," and whether immersion or sprinkling was the practice among the Jews eighteen hundred years ago, are questions for the Hebrew philologist and Bible commentator, for the historian of Judaism and Christianity, and not for the elders of churches and for delegates to church conventions to determine. These questions *must* be answered and *can* be answered fully, independently of denominational disputes and rituals. And such is even the case in still more important questions of dogma and practice. Professors and learners in the field of Bible science must rise above all denominational bias. A biased teacher will too easily and too frequently darken where he should enlighten, and convey errors where he should give nothing but the absolute truth. Such biased teachers we find among the Jews as well as among the Christians, among the Protestants as well as among the Catholics, among the Muhammedans as well as among the teachers of the two older religions of Semitic origin.

Let me give here a few instances of such expositions of the Bible, tinctured by religious prejudices. Muhammedan theologians find in the Old Testament quite a number of predictions of, and typical allusions to, the prophet of Mecca, where an unprejudiced Jewish or Christian Bible reader would not dream of detecting a trace of such an allusion. They see, e.g., Muhammed alluded to in Haggai 2:7, in these words: "The desire of all the nations shall come." *The desire* (hemdah) *of all the nations* is Muhammed — so the theologians of Islam say — and this is sufficiently demonstrated by the fact that the words *hemdah* and Muhammed are derived from the same root, from the verb *hāmădh*. Is it necessary for us, who do not live under the shadow of the mosque, and into whom Muhammedan teachings have not been engrafted, to show the total fallacy of this interpretation? First, the word *hĕmdāh*, in this passage, cannot mean "the desired one"; its meaning is rather "the desirable objects," "the precious things" (plural), as the verb *(ubhā'ŭ)* is in the plural (*"they* shall come," not *"he* shall come"). Secondly, the whole contextual structure shows that the prophet speaks of the coming glory and grandeur of the new temple, the erection of which had just begun in his time; and, referring to the bright future of the rising sanctuary, the inspired prophet says: "Thus says the Lord of hosts, In a little while I will shake the heavens and the earth and the dry land; and I will shake all nations, and the precious things of all nations, they shall come [i.e., into this house], and I will fill this house with glory," etc.

To another instance of Muhammedan Bible-exposition I call your attention. You know that Muhammedan theology admits the divine origins of Judaism and of Christianity; but at the same time it claims that Islam is also divinely revealed, and that, moreover, it occupies a higher place among religions than do its two older sisters. In support of this doctrine, Moses is brought forward and made to bear testimony! Of the words with which his parting blessing (Deut. 33:2) commences, Muhammedan theologians give the following explanation, "The Lord came from Sinai"; that means, the Lord revealed himself to Israel; for *Sînăy* signifies the Hebrew people; "and He rose in light from Seir to them"; that means, to Christendom also God revealed himself; for *Sê'îr*, the country in which Edom dwelt (see Gen. 36:8 and other places), stands for Edom, and "Edom" came, in the course of time, to be regarded as a symbolical name for Rome, for the Roman Empire, and afterwards for the Christian world, whose spiritual center was in the city of Rome; "He shone forth from Mount Paran"; that means, God revealed himself also to the Arabian prophet, to Muhammed; for *Pârân*, where Ishmael, the patriarch of the Arabians, was living (Gen. 21:21), is used here to designate the Ishmaelite Muhammed. Furthermore, it deserves mention that Muhammed himself appealed to the Hebrew Scriptures, which, he said, he did not come to destroy, but to fulfil, and which, as he argued, for those who had eyes to see, pointed to him: "A prophet from the midst of you, from your brethren, like unto me, will the Lord your God raise up unto you; to him you shall hearken." Thus we read in Deut. 18:15; and, in reference to such and similar passages, the doctors of the Koran ask: Was Muhammed not like unto Moses? Did he not come from Israel's brethren, from the children of Ishmael? Is there not, in the Hebrew Scriptures, the prophecy, and here, in the rise of Muhammed, the fulfilment? Are there not, in the old Bible, the types, and here, in the new Koran, the antitypes? Did not the inspired men of Israel foresee the coming prophet of Arabia?

These peculiar methods of interpreting the Bible remind us of the methods which Persian believers in the Koran employ in the interpretation of the odes of their great national poet Hafiz. Shems ed-din Muhammed Hafiz, as is well known, sang of wine, and of love, and of nightingales, and of roses—in fact, of beauty in every form. Can such poetry be accepted by the ecclesiastical authorities in Persia and by the pious ministers of the Muhammedan religion in that country? Yes, the odes of Hafiz, so they say, must only be understood rightly; it must be believed that they are intended as an allegorical and mystical revelation of things divine. And so their commentators tell us that "the wine" signifies the true faith, and that "the beloved lad" stands as a symbol for God, and that "the intoxication" means pious ecstasy brought forth by a deep contemplation of the divine works and words, etc. This has, indeed, been carried so far, that pilgrims from all parts of Persia now resort to the tomb of Hafiz, and almost regard that frivolous poet as a saint. (Who is not reminded, by these commentaries upon Hafiz, of a number of commentaries, Jewish and Christian, upon the Song of Solomon, Psalm 45, and other parts of the Bible?)

The theologians among the Muhammedans assert that their Bible expositions reveal the real and true meaning of the Scriptures. If now some of them would face us today, and would notice how we shake our heads at their strange interpretations, they would probably say: You are too superficial in your explanation of the sacred books; the "inner light" has evidently not dawned upon you; the "deeper sense" of the Scriptures has remained hidden to you. The Christian mystics speak also of a "deeper sense"; the Jewish Kabbalists speak likewise of mysteries, *Sôd-hôth*, etc.

But do Muhammedans alone interpret the Bible under the influence of their religious prejudices? Jews and Christians also have sinned, and do continue to sin, in the same direction. Not that they sin consciously; not that they pervert the sense of the Bible willfully; they err unconsciously. They *believe* that their expositions are the true ones, the only true ones. And they have not, and in certain centuries gone by they could not have, sufficient philological and other necessary knowledge to prevent them from making errors. We, rising above sectarian narrowness, must now be ready to admit that, in many instances, our own teachers in olden times erred, and that, in many instances, their interpretations cannot stand the light of criticism. Here also we may give illustrations. Rashi, an excellent Jewish expounder of the Bible, who wrote eight hundred years ago (he died 1105), explains the first verse of Genesis thus: "Bᵉrē'shîth, *in the beginning;* 'bᵉrē'shîth' is equivalent to 'bĭshᵉbhîl rē'shîth,' *for the sake of* rē'shîth. For the sake of rē'shîth God created the world. Rē'shîth is then, first, a designation of the Torah; for in Prov. 8:22, the Torah is called 'rē'shîth dărkô,' *the beginning of God's ways.* Rē'shîth, secondly, means God's chosen people Israel; for, in Jer. 2:3, Israel is referred to in the words 'rē'shîth tᵉbhū'ăthô,' *the beginning of God's productions."* Rashi desires, by his interpretation, to set forth the idea that God created the world in order that the Torah should become manifest therein, and be a power therein, and for the further purpose that Israel should, so to speak, have a standing-place, a sphere for his being and his fulfilling his mission in the world. Rashi here followed older Jewish authorities who preceded him with this explanation. We now find little to admire in this kind of interpretation; we think that *bᵉrē'shîth* means simply "in the beginning," and that no other sense, no "deeper sense," no "hidden sense" is contained in it. So much is certain to us, that the author — whether it was Moses, or someone living hundreds of years after Moses — did not think of the Torah, or of Israel, when he wrote down the word *bᵉrē"shîth.* And our object, in our endeavor to understand the Bible words correctly, must now be to find an answer to the question, What did the author at first mean by his words? Of former interpretations, be they by Rashi, or by St. Jerome, or by Luther, or by others, we take respectful and grateful notice, but we do so in the same spirit and manner as historians take notice of old documents, of old scientific views and systems. We carefully examine them; we accept what appears to us good and true; we reject what, according to our understanding, is erroneous. But far be it from us to take everything in them as absolutely true....

We have given a few examples of old Jewish explications which, in the light of modern scholarship, we unhesitatingly declare to be incorrect and untenable and to be colored by Jewish bias. But Catholics, and Protestants also, otherwise quite erudite and quite independent in their studies and researches, show, often enough, in their Bible expositions the mighty influence upon them of opinions and doctrines that were inculcated into their minds when they were young. There have been, and probably there are, Catholic scholars who find in the Old Testament quite a number of allusions to the virgin Mary, the queen of heaven, as they call her, and to the almost divine attributes which are ascribed to her by the Roman church. In the so-called Protevangellum (Gen. 3:15), where it is said that the seed of the woman will bruise the head of the serpent, Catholic theologians found the sense that *she,* the holy virgin, will bruise the serpent's head —*ipsa conteret caput tuum,* as the present editions of the Vulgate read, not *ipse,* etc., the feminine gender being used instead of the masculine, despite the Hebrew text having the undisputed masculine pronoun and verb *(hŭ yᵉshŭphᵉkha)* and not the corresponding feminine forms. Thus a text undeniably perverted is preferred to the true original reading, in order to make a Roman Catholic doctrine more plausible and to give to it a Biblical basis.

Is it different with Protestant Bible expounders? Are the exegetical works of many of them not tinctured by religious prejudices and dogmatical presuppositions? Some of them discover Christ in almost any page of the Old Testament, some of them find the doctrine of the Trinity indicated in the very first word of the Bible—for are not the letters *beth, resh, aleph* of the word *Bᵉrē'shîth* the initial letters of *bēn, rŭăh, 'abh* ("son, spirit, father")? According to some of these exegetes it was the Cross that sweetened the waters of Marah, for is not the numerical value of the Hebrew word for "tree" (Exod. 15:25) or "wood" *(etz=70+90)* the same as that of the word (in later Hebrew) for "cross" *(tzelem=90+30+40)*? And may not therefore the words "wood" and "cross" be interchanged? With some of these exegetes, aye, with large numbers of them, Shiloh, Immanuel, etc., are but typical names of Jesus of Nazareth; for has not "the Church" so taught it for many hundred years? And this is called Bible Science!

But place yourselves, for a moment, in the position of one who had never heard from a Christian pulpit, or from the lips of a teacher, or who had never read in a book of Christian devotions, that "Immanuel" is Christ; and then read that chapter in Isaiah where Immanuel is spoken of. In such a condition of your mind the idea will never occur to you that in that plain, clear oration of Isaiah any reference is made to a divine savior who would come more than seven hundred years later. Before the gates of Jerusalem, in the presence of King Ahaz, and of a multitude of the inhabitants of Jerusalem, the prophet is standing. The prophet says: Do not despair! Be hopeful! Be of good cheer! The Syrian armies and the armies of Ephraim, who are coming from the North, and who threaten you, and who, you fear, will conquer your land, lay waste your country, and destroy your sanctuary, will not succeed. In a few years the danger will all have passed away, and you will not be molested any more by the enemy. And this sign I will give you. Behold yonder young woman (ʻalmăh), she has conceived, and she will bear a son, and she will call his name Immanuel; and before that child will be able to distinguish between what is good and evil, the enemy will have gone, the danger will have passed away, and a time of glory and of peace and of happiness will come for the kingdom of Judah, etc., etc.

Is this not a plain prophetical oration which hardly admits any misconstruction? And yet, not only pious women and devout peasants, but learned expounders of the Bible cling tenaciously to the idea that Isaiah meant originally Jesus of Nazareth! And in order to make this idea more acceptable, they force upon the word ʻalmăh—which means *any* young woman — the meaning, immaculate virgin!

And in such a forced manner other so-called "messianic" passages are explained. I am well aware that many of these "messianic" passages were already understood and explained as messianic and as having reference to Christ by the authors of the New Testament. It would probably be improper for me to say before you, gentlemen, composing my present audience, that the New Testament expositions of Old Testament passages were not always exact and correct. To many of you the New Testament is the very highest authority in everything, and you may say, Thus far a Bible student may go, not farther. Where Jesus of Nazareth has expounded the words of the Old Testament, or where Paul of Tarsus has set forth their meaning, the true and only true exposition is given. If a modern expounder undertakes to give another explanation, not in harmony with the New Testament, he is presumptuous, he has left Christian ground.

Far be it from me to combat in this assembly such a position. So much only I may be allowed to state in this connection, that explanations of Old Testament passages similar to those of St. Paul and the other New Testament writers we find also in the Talmud and Midrash and in the mediaeval literature of the Jews. "Shiloh" and Tsemah ("Branch") were also understood by some Jewish teachers of former ages as having reference to a Messiah. There is, however, a great difference between the Midrash of the Jews and the Midrash of St. Paul, or rather between the position of the Jewish student toward the Jewish Midrash and the position of the Christian student toward the Christian Midrash. The former sees in the Jewish Midrash historical documents showing how the Scriptures were understood by the Jews at certain times of the past; and to him, to the Jewish student, a transitory stage of Jewish Bible exegesis is thereby made clear. The Christian student, however, finds in the Christian Midrash, that is, in the New Testament, expositions of the Hebrew Scriptures, which he does not consider as merely transitory, as merely characteristic of their times, but which have become for him petrified, authoritative, unalterable....

I have arrived at the limit of the time allotted to me, and therefore I must close. The logical conclusion of all that I have said seems to me to be this:

The main question which a scholarly Bible student should ask himself is: What was the original meaning which the Biblical author desired to express by his words? And in attempting to find a correct answer to this question, one laying claim to the title of a Bible scholar should free his mind from all misleading preconceptions, from all sectarian bias. Truth, nothing but the truth, should be his aim.

VIII

ALEXANDER KOHUT

The Foundations of Judaism (1885)

From the day of Revelation, the day destined for the salvation and happiness of humanity, is dated the national existence of Israel. Before that day, the children of Abraham were simply members of a large family, a slave herd without self-consciousness or intimation of the higher Power that rules the destinies of mankind. In Egypt, they were a mere body of men without purpose, spending their energies in the treadmill of forced labor, without ambition or yearning for loftier things, moved only by the rod of the tyrant. Only at the foot of Sinai did they become conscious of themselves and make themselves of significant worth to humanity. With the lightning-flash of Sinai, they felt that they were to be no longer mere purposeless tools, but messengers of a great mission of religious and ethical ideas.

The first, spiritually-illuminating *Anokhi*, "I am the Lord, your God," gave them this sense of self-consciousness. Again was uttered the creative word and light was in their minds, which had so long been encompassed by spiritual darkness. Light was in their hearts, which had been so long insensible to the religious feelings which bring happiness in their train.

> "When God created the world," say the Sages, "it was decreed that heaven was God's heaven, and that the earth belonged to the children of men. But when the Torah was given to Israel, it was ordained that thenceforth those who are below should lift themselves on high, and that those above should descend to earth."*

*Yalkut Psalms #873. [All footnotes were added by Barnett A. Elzas for his 1920 edition of The Ethics of the Fathers, by Alexander Kohut. The notes were originally signaled by superscript numbers, 1–6, which for the sake of consistency have been changed to asterisks for this reprinting of the text.]

How penetrating and yet how elevating is this saying of the ancients! Before Revelation, they used to say that only the earth belonged to the children of men; they clung to the clod, moving only in the sphere of their senses and worshipping Nature. They could not rise to the height of the idea of God. At Sinai, heaven opened itself to man, and from out of the heights the All-merciful stretched out his hand to the child of dust and lifted him to a moral atmosphere. No longer was man orphaned, for his soul could now find its way to the knowledge of the Only One. He had discovered that there was a moral force, a higher Power in the universe, which alone could say: *Anokhi*, "I am." Man had found God, and with the discovery, an end was begun of the errors and confusions of weak, vacillating humanity, and stability was assured. Thus were verified the Biblical words (Ps. lxxv, 4): "Whereas aforetime the earth swayed and its inhabitants were unsettled, the *Anokhi* ["I AM"] which resounded through the world and sank as a higher moral force into the hearts of men, cemented the foundations of the earth and assured stability to its pillars."

And what are the pillars upon which, since the day of Revelation, the Jewish world has rested? One of the Sages has given us the answer:

"The ethical world of Judaism rests upon three things: upon the Torah, upon Divine Worship and upon the Practice of Charity."

Let us now examine these three foundations of Judaism in the light of the Ten Words.

"God created the heaven and the earth only conditionally. The condition was the acceptance by Israel of the Torah. Should Israel decline to receive it, earth and heaven must return to their original *tohu va-vohu*["unformed chaos"]."*

It is an inspiring thought that lies hidden in this sentence. The first divine creative thought and the final cause of creation was moral perfection, the impulse towards which is implanted deep in every human being. The recognition and the realisation of our filial relation to God is the patent of nobility inscribed upon the brow of man created in the image of God, an inscription which should never be obliterated by man unless he wishes to sink again into a condition of spiritual *tohu va-vohu* ["unformed chaos"] and be relegated to moral chaos and anarchy.

Tanchuma Bereshith I.

This moral anarchy, characteristic of the pre-Sinaitic period, has been beautifully illustrated by the Sages.*

"Before offering the Torah to Israel, God offered it to other peoples.
"What is written therein"? asked the children of Ishmael?
"Thou shalt not steal. The property of strangers must be sacred to you."
"We cannot accept the Torah, for we, wild sons of the desert, live by depredation."
Then God offered the Torah to the children of Ammon, who led dissolute lives.
"What is written therein"? asked the children of Ammon.
"Thou shalt not commit unchastity. Marriage must be sacred to you."
"We cannot accept the Torah. From unchastity do we spring and we will not be restrained."
And so God offered the Torah to all the nations of the earth in turn and each in turn refused it."

When the Torah was offered to Israel, he did not hesitate for an instant, and as with one voice, he exclaimed: "All that the Lord hath spoken, we will do and understand." (Ex. xxiv, 7.) Ordinarily we listen first and then, after investigation, we accept and obey. Israel, however, promised to obey the Law of God unconditionally and afterwards to study its precepts: Na'aseh—and then V'nishma. Thus did Israel save mankind; and because of his compliance, he was rendered capable of comprehending God's word. And because Israel was the only people that manifested such comprehension, he was addressed with the words: "I am the Lord, thy God."

The first of the Ten Words, Anokhi, "I am the Lord, your God," is supplemented by the second, Lo ta'aseh: "Make no other gods unto yourselves from that which is in the heavens above or on the earth beneath or in the waters under the earth. Have you, O man, ever conceived, with your intellectual vision, the necessary existence of a God? Then must that God be One—an Only One. Read God's wondrous work in the stars and the planet-sown heavens; wander amid the manifold beauties of Nature; penetrate, if you will, to earth's deepest depths, but do not deify the Master's work. Well may you stand in awe of God's creative power and bow down to the dust in worship of that Wisdom which has brought it forth and which maintains it. Deny the all-embracing lovingkindness of God in creation, and creation is doomed to perish, to crumble into its primaeval atoms (Job xxxiv, 14): "If He but intends it, He can call back His spirit and breath." [JPS translation, 1979]

*Pesikta Rabbathi #21, 99b.

But do not deny! Denial is the cancer that is eating ever deeper into the very vitals of modern Judaism. Because man, with his freedom of thought — the free gift of God — has been enabled to guess at the highest truths concerning God, in his immeasurable conceit, he presumes to deny Him. Therefore the second Word commands *Lo ta'aseh*: "Make no other Gods unto yourselves from that which is in the heavens above or on the earth beneath or in the waters under the earth."

And as this, your God, the One and Only One purely spiritual, and therefore incapable of being represented in any physical form, is only disclosed to your profoundest research, so is He, too, the embodiment of all moral perfection. Hence, the third Word, *Lo tisa*: "Take not the name of the Lord, your God, in vain." Truth is the seal of God; do not desecrate it by deceit and hypocrisy. Seek rather to perfect yourselves by the development of your natural talents and your wonderful faculties.

Therefore, *Zakhor et yom ha-Shabbat*, "Remember the Sabbath day." Do not labor exclusively for the things of earth. You are a citizen of two worlds; let the spiritual portion of your nature have its rightful share in Sabbaths and holy days. "He who labors during the six days of the week and can say on the eve of the Sabbath 'I have completed my work and will now take up my labor for my soul,' such a one becomes a co-worker with God."* For God gave man only his physical existence, endowing him, however, with the possibilities of a spiritual life. Man has the power to develop these possibilities and is therefore responsible for the creation of himself into a spiritual, moral and ethical being. If he thus makes himself the creator of his better self, he becomes, in a literal sense, a co-worker with God.

Thus both in outward form and inner content, the first four Words hang close together. They constitute an elevating means to the great end of self-sanctification and moral perfection. They form the substance of our spiritual consciousness and prescribe our relations with, and our duty towards God; — they indicate, that is to say, our service to God, our form of worship — and as such, they are the second foundation on which the moral order rests and without which no support, no firmness is conceivable.

An ancient teacher, R. Akiba, indicates this truth symbolically:

*Sabbath 119b.

"When you see white marble pillars, do not say that they are only idle show and pretence."[*]

When you have reached the stage when you think that you can dispense with God, when you consider religious worship as so much superfluous ballast, be on your guard; you have lost your bearings; you are simply wandering to and fro, confused by moral error. Therefore, let the Divine Service, the second pillar, be our stronghold and our support.

The third pillar, which supports the edifice of the world, is the Practice of Charity, and a strong support it is. Only through it are the two other pillars, the knowledge and the worship of God really made steadfast. It is, in truth, the foundation of the first Word: "I am the Lord, your God"; because "I am He who brought you out of the land of Egypt, out of the house of bondage." This act of God was an act of benevolence towards Israel. And if the Israelite endeavors to free himself from spiritual slavery and to perfect himself in the service of God, he, too, performs an act of benevolence towards himself. He gains strength and courage in his struggle against sin. Such divine service is at one and the same time service of God and service of self.

But man has also duties towards his fellowmen, the fulfillment of which is of equal importance to the fulfillment of his duties towards God. Hence the fifth Word: "Honor thy father and thy mother, that thy days may be long in the land which the Lord, thy God, giveth thee." This Word concludes the series of duties which we owe to God and is at the same time the transition-point to the duties which we owe to Society. Hence God's name is mentioned in connection with the command to honor our parents, as the Being who implants within our hearts such holy emotions.

Respect for the person and property of others is equally of the highest ethical importance, hence follow the further five Words on the second of the two stone tablets of the Covenant, *Lo tirzah, lo tin'af, lo tignov, lo ta'aneh, v'lo tahmod*: "Sacred must be unto you the life, the domestic purity, the property, the good name, and every possession of your neighbor." To Israel be the glory and the honor of having made these last five Words—the substance of the highest ethical truth and the exercise of which means the practice of love in our daily lives, the basis of his moral code for the individual and the community.

The second half of the Decalogue, it is obvious to everyone,

[*]*Hagigah 14b.*

demonstrates that the more abstract first portion is a product of the highest divine truth and wisdom. Intellectual indolence might say of the first half, that God gave the commandments relating to His existence for His own glory. But closely connected with them follow the latter five that have reference to the well-being of mankind, and these lead but to one conclusion: *Adonai Eloheikhem Emet,* "The Lord, your God, is truth." Truth speaks in the wise commands which direct His will towards us. May they guide our relations to Him, our relations to ourselves and to our fellowmen! May they be the means of firmly establishing the three-fold basis on which our moral existence rests: the Torah, Divine Worship and the Practice of Charity. In the fulfillment of these essential truths, we must find the real purpose of the holiness of our lives and pursue it with unremitting love. That is what our Sages meant when they taught that the Torah should be to us as if revealed to us anew each day.*

In this connection, an ancient writer asks: "How has it come to pass that *Simhath Torah* is celebrated at the end of the *Sukkoth* festival, and not on *Shabuoth*, nearly half a year later than we would have expected? Would it not have been more appropriate to celebrate it on *Shabuoth*, the day of the giving of the Law?" He answers his question with a parable.

> "Israel and the Torah are like the union of hearts between a newly-married couple. They have learned to love one another and vow eternal fealty. But how often does it happen that with the lapse of time the bonds that symbolise the union are broken asunder! They have found, on closer study, that they are not suited to each other and they speak the pitiful words: 'If you go to the right, I will go to the left.' But if, by reason of perfect sympathy and heart-harmony, not only the honey-moon, but month after month pass by in ever-increasing joy, day by day revealing to each new virtues and graces in the other, they are filled with greater joy than on their wedding day."

So it is with Israel. On the day of Revelation our ancestors exclaimed *Na'aseh v'nishma*—"we will obey and understand" the word of God. What would have happened if the Law had proven distasteful to them? Would not the oath of fealty have been overhasty? But Israel has gone to the depths of the Torah. Day and night, week by week, month after month, he has found precious pearls in its immeasurable depths. As they worthily celebrated the finding of this treasure, so six months later they rejoiced at the knowledge of its worth.

*Midrash Tanchuma, beginning of Ki Tavo. See also Pesikta d'R. Kahana, ed. Buber, folio 102a.

IX

GUSTAV GOTTHEIL

The Great Refusal (1887)

Being an Open Letter to Rev. S. Calthrop, and His Article Entitled "Israel's Last Word"

> "The Spirit which I put upon thee, and the word which I placed in thy mouth, shall not depart from thee, nor from thy seed after thee."
>
> *Isaiah lix, 21*

My dear Sir, I have not come to quarrel with you. Your recognition of the service rendered by Israel to the cause of true religion is frank, full, and warm. Its enthusiasm would disarm one more disposed to fault-finding than I am. Still, you do make a charge; and it is one not to be lightly passed over. A "great refusal" implies great guilt. You will not think it unnatural that one whose relation to the charge is that of which the poet sang —

"In whatso'er my people sinned, I'll share

Most willingly the burden that they bear" —

should essay a defense. And, even if he does not succeed in his task, he will at least have shown you in what light such a one as he regards the actions of his ancestors. Counting you as one of those who "love the light, and know it when they see it," he may earn thanks if he sheds a ray of light upon a point so intensely interesting to Jew and Christian alike. For "Israel's last word," as you term it, was Christianity's first word. After that, the two parted company. The story of their separation is one of the saddest recorded. It has lasted now for eighteen centuries, some of which are dark as primeval night, or lit only by the fires of the Inquisition. But, though the shadows of enmity may still linger, friendship is taking its place; and friendship may ripen into fellowship, so that each side may do faithfully and loyally that part of the common duty for which it is best fitted.

What stronger proof that this hope is not an idle one can we desire than the fact that, of the many unpardonable sins formerly imputed to Israel, *one* only remains? History is the great revealer of truth, provided you live long enough and are patient enough to await the slow-found verdict of the *Weltgericht,* the world tribunal, as Schiller calls it. Israel is master in the art of waiting and of patience. Who knows but that this one last sin may also be found to exist in the brain of the accuser rather than in the actions of the accused? You will not object to a friendly suit, opened only for the purpose of ascertaining the merits of the case. It may result in a less severe verdict, perhaps in an acquittal. Not that Israel must needs be free from all blame. No man doth good only, and sinneth not. Why should he expect a nation or class to be without sin? Other accusers may bring forward other charges. My business here is with the one you make, and which you clothe in the following words (p. 293): "The one reproach I charge on later Israel is that she has not recognized her grandest inspiration. It was an evil moment that committed her to this 'great refusal.' The Herod dynasty had debauched and led away from Israel's true longings the men in high places, who were thus simply incapacitated from even understanding Jesus. Upon them rests the bitter blame of having been blind leaders of the blind, when keen sight was the one need of the hour. Such men as Hillel loved the light, and knew it when they saw it. But such men, alas! were not at the helm; and the blind pilots steered for the breakers. If all the hosts of Israel had gathered as one man around the new truth, Israel would have been not only the light-bringer, the inspirer of the ages to come, — though the glory of this must be forever hers, — but she would herself have been the leader in the new time."

Now let us analyze count after count of this indictment. Your first charge is "that later Israel did not recognize her grandest inspiration." I will not here question the epithet "grandest," nor inquire whether the inspiration of the second Isaiah, or of Micah, or of the Deuteronomist, or of some of the Psalmists, had not reached as great a height, nor whether the merit of priority amid much darker surroundings might not be held to compensate for any shortcomings, if such had to be admitted, of these early light-bearers. To avoid involving our inquiry with a mere question of degree, I will let you call it the "grandest" inspiration. But what I will ask you to consider is whether failing to recognize an inspiration, grandest or smallest, constitutes a just ground for reproach? Is it not rather a misfortune, a fatality, a call for pity? for you do not charge it to wilful blindness. As well might we blame a man for being of short stature and not tall, slow of foot and not swift, heavy of speech and not fluent. You charge this spiritual color-blindness to "later Israel." Was the earlier Israel any more keen-sighted? Did the generation of Moses or of Isaiah evince a quicker perception of the grandest inspirations of their times? If you say, This only increases the guilt, and is no defence at all, I ask you to show me one single instance of a people recognizing and accepting an inspiration. When did the *vulgus*, when did its leaders, rally around a new truth? As it was in the time of Jesus and in Palestine, so it was always and everywhere; and so it will be for a long time to come. Why, that which you call the grandest inspiration in Jesus is still hidden from all Christian churches except the Unitarian; and the number of Unitarian confessors bears about the same relation to the hundreds of millions of other Christians that the few followers of Jesus bore to the Jewish nation. To all the Churches outside of your own, the greatness of Jesus consists not in his Israelite inspiration, but in those un-Israelite things that you and your Church deny absolutely. His greatness for them rests on his Godhead, on his vicarious suffering, on his resurrection, on his power to judge the quick and the dead, on his conquest of hell, on his opening of the gates of paradise, etc. Despite your glowing love and veneration for the Galilean teacher, you are a heretic in the eyes of all Christendom, you are a Judaizer, — a name from which so great a Christian as Schleiermacher recoiled with horror. How can you demand that that which is still concealed from the eyes of the Christian world, after eighteen centuries of reading, of preaching, of teaching, and of general advancement in culture, should have been recognized by the Jews at first sight? They, at least, had no right to expect any new revelation. Their sacred book was closed, and the voice of prophecy had long since fallen silent. It had become an article of their creed that "nothing is to be added or taken away" from God's sacred word. How would Christians receive a new prophet, should one arrive in their midst who would reveal an inspiration still greater than that which you see in Jesus?

Nay, more. The grander you make that inspiration, the more you lessen the guilt of the people in not recognizing it. If Jesus so transcended all other teachers of religion that the following eighteen centuries have produced none equal unto him, can you expect that his own time and his own generation should take the full measure of his spiritual stature?

On no firmer ground rests "the bitter blame against the leaders of having been blind leaders leading the blind." Blame, bitter blame, for blindness? Lay it at the door of Him who struck the whole people with such a bitter infirmity. "Keen insight," which you call the one need of the hour, — if it was not found in the leaders, how could they have obtained it? By what method known to you, or to any mortal, can that gracious gift of Heaven be called down? The great German people, some thirty years ago, were as much in need of keen insight as ever were the Jews; yet when the man Bismarck, possessing it in greater degree than any one living, arose in their midst, that nation of thinkers rejected him, derided him, opposed him tooth and nail. He was the best hated and most detested of statesmen, and not until he had startled his countrymen by dealing blow after blow upon their enemies did they begin to divine that a Messiah had been raised for them. If the leaders of Israel were blind, it was their misfortune, and not their fault. Whether they were or not, I shall consider further on.

"It was an evil moment that committed her [Israel] to the 'great refusal.'" Refusal of what? Refusal of that which you call the greatest inspiration? Who ever refused that? The New Testament tells us again and again that the people Israel heard him gladly, gathering around and following him, and that they showed him every respect, and treated him better than any other nation ever treated her teachers. Jesus was not brought to the bar of justice for teaching that God is our father, or that all men are brothers, or that virtue is its own reward, or for denying sheol. No paragraph in the Jewish code stamped these doctrines as heretical or made their promulgation an indictable offence. Far different causes must have been at work to bring Jesus into conflict with the ruling powers, and it is on these other causes that his biographers lay the greatest stress. Without saying anything as to the regularity of the proceeding or the justice of the sentence, it is a total perversion of the plainest facts in the Christian records to make "the greatest inspiration" the object of the great refusal. What Israel did refuse to accept was no more than what all good Unitarians refuse to believe to-day, and what many other Christians, though bearing the uniform of Orthodoxy, openly deny or silently drop from their creeds. The real great refusal stands as good to-day as it stood in the time of its first making; and it bids fair to become better appreciated as intelligence increases, as truth triumphs over falsehood, and the chains of dogma drop from the minds of men.

The next count of the indictment seems to me of itself to exonerate the nation from the charge that is made. If the Herod dynasty, which was an alien one, "debauched and led away from Israel's true longings the men in high places, who were thus simply incapacitated from even understanding Jesus," then let the shades of those tyrants answer for their crimes. The people, surely, had striven hard enough to shake off their hated yoke and break their iron sceptres; and their teachers not only raised their voices against them in fearless opposition, but gave their lives in defence of their nation's freedom. All efforts dashed in vain against the Roman power that stood behind that blood-stained throne. The Roman legions were impenetrable. The Roman wolf lay crouching beneath Herod's seat, with his glaring eyes fixed upon his victim. What could the keenest insight into moral and religious truth avail against the power that held the nation in an iron grip, and that shrunk from no means to crush out the national life of Judaea? A regenerated Jewish nation was the one thing Rome could never tolerate. If Jesus truly possessed the power to revive the waning genius of the people, this alone would have sufficed to make his death desirable to the Roman governor. The fundamental mistake under which the anti-Jewish and pro-Christian mode of reading history labors is that they treat the Jews as a religious community only, whose members might have changed their faith, had they only so willed it, in the twinkling of an eye. They regard them as so few in number that a handful of teachers might have effected the change, had they been men of "keen insight." They measure the Jewish nation by the extent of their own congregations, although, of a truth, their experiences within that small compass ought to teach them what a task it is to transform men's opinions. Just now, some of the best men in your own Church in the West think that they see a great light, and claim a "grandest inspiration." What is its effect upon the Unitarian body, undoubtedly one of the most intelligent, most liberal, and most moral in the world? Its effect is a controversy stirring your Church to its very foundations, and a "great refusal" by numbers of men just as good and brave and free as the preacher of the new gospel. If this can happen in a limited circle, what are we to look for in a similar juncture occurring in a whole nation? Brother Calthrop, you are dealing with a nation of some millions of souls, embracing all variety and contrariety of opinions, with intricate relations in every direction, and who at that time had other things than religious reforms to think of. Its fate was trembling in the balance. The least pretext might have precipitated a death struggle. The least claim to Messiahship, which meant revolt against Rome, might have brought down the sword that was suspended over the nation's head. The utmost vigilance and a sleepless care were necessary; and all "keen-sightedness" was wanted to discover the rising danger, and avert it. That was no time for loosening the national bonds; that was no time for changing beliefs that nerved the fathers to their Maccabean victories. That Syrians, Idumeans, and Romans were the loving brethren of the Jews; that there was no sheol for Herod and his executioners, but that they would be welcome to the bosom of Abraham, — all this must have sounded to patriotic ears, not like a "grandest inspiration," but like an insult flung into the face of the unhappy daughter of Zion. The keen insight was undoubtedly there, but it was not directed to theological distinctions. The grandest moral inspiration needed was patriotism, — a virtue in which the first Christians did not excel. What you say about "the blind pilots steering for the breakers" seems to me — excuse the expression — a mere phrase, or else it is a word whose meaning I do not understand. What breakers? Roaring on what shore? The national shore? These the pilots saw only too clearly, and exercised, as I said, the greatest vigilance to steer clear of them. The religious shore? Well, the ship survived them, and has outridden worse dangers, has plowed more tempestuous seas, and is still afloat, sound and safe. Were they moral breakers? Surely, you will not maintain the old calumny that the Pharisees and scribes were a band of hypocrites, who fattened on the corruption of the people? Their moral teachings are now better known to Christians than they were before, and neither for them nor for the lives of the teachers need we blush. I would ask you to read that history over, keeping in view the prime fact that it is the history of a nation that you are studying. You will then no longer think that "the hosts of Israel" should have gathered like one man "round the new truth." Hosts and truth, — God save us from such an alliance! It conjures up the hosts of Constantine, of Mohammed, of Charlemagne when he converted the Saxons, of Philip II of Spain raging in the Netherlands, of the Thirty Years' War. But perhaps you did not take the word literally: perhaps you only meant the people in general by that Old Testament phrase. Now, tell me, what were they to do? Let us leave generalities and come down to facts. Were the people to close the gates of the temple, cease the offering of sacrifices, disrobe the priests and Levites, scatter the rabbinical schools, forbid the observance of the traditional law, declare Moses superseded by a new prophet, and start a Protestant or Unitarian religion? Were they to abrogate their national feasts, their new moons and Sabbaths, embrace the heathen as brothers, eat, drink, and make merry with them? And was Jesus to be the head and leader of this revolution? And was all this to be done under the unsleeping eye of their arch-enemy, the Roman? If not this, — and no sane man would expect such acts of self-destruction, — what else could the gathered hosts accomplish? Were they to rally around moral truths, religious truths? Theodore Parker certainly preached some glorious truths, so new to his countrymen that his nearest religious kinship cast him out and put him under the ban. Nobler and loftier conceptions of Christianity than Emerson prophesied in his lectures to the divinity students at Cambridge no man of this century ever uttered. Where are the hosts that gathered around these sages? The old truths the Jews held were as yet too high for the world, and trembled upon the brink of destruction; and the nation was to gather "like one man" around a new one!

When the Jews call themselves God's peculiar people, they are either ridiculed or scourged for their arrogance. Yet it is expected that everything should be different with them than with other nations. The virtues of the one are a reproach to the other. When America saved her Constitution by shedding the blood both of her faithful and her faithless children, she is honored for her dead; and well she should be to the end of days! But when the Jews defend their constitution, divinely given as all Christendom believes, they are only blind zealots led by blinder zealots!

Now, as to what you style the truth, I have not space to search the title to that claim. I can only declare my dissent from most of your statements, which appear to me to be misstatements of both Old and New Testament teachings. In respect to the latter, you follow the easy method, the popular pulpit method, and leave out of your reckoning everything that bears against your deductions. You may charge contradictory passages to the later chroniclers of the life of Jesus, or to the writers of the Epistles, and so forth; and, by such picking and choosing, you may spirit away the devil and his host of demons, hell-fire, and the gnashing of teeth in the outer darkness. You may say that you do not believe that Jesus ever said that he will deny before his Father those who deny him before men; and you may banish from your fanciful picture the miracles, the resurrection, and ascension, and many other things that do not accord well with the "grandest inspiration." But this is not the way to arrive at a new truth, or, indeed, at any truth at all. Either we submit to authority, and then there is an end to all discussion, or else we question History for her testimony; and, then, we ought in common fairness to insist upon the truth, the whole truth, and nothing but the truth. Now, every candid critic admits that it is exceedingly difficult, if not impossible, to lay hold of the actual, historical Jesus. A veil of legend, and, worse, of the dogmatical contentions and even sectional rancor of his followers, has spread over the fair figure, and has become almost inseparable from it, like the bandages we find wound around Egyptian mummies. The fact is, as it was said that man creates God in his own image, so is Jesus reconstructed in the likeness of his followers. It all depends upon the glass through which he is looked at and the eye that looks through that glass. In the sphere in which you live and have your being, he is fashioned into the likeness of an ideal Unitarian minister, preaching "light and sweetness" to a select country church, not too far from Boston, of course. This is no low ideal, by any means; and I know and love some of your brotherhood, who come very near to it. But it is no more like the Jewish peasant patriot than Boston resembles Jerusalem or than the religious Hotspurs of the Western Conference, in their *"Sturm und Drang"* period, resemble a quietist rabbi worshipping in the halls of the Talmud. A liberal but true-hearted Jew of these days is, after all, the only person competent truthfully to interpret the character of one of the same kind of long ago. He would, however, be sorely puzzled if he did not find in that character that glow of national pride to which no mortal was more entitled than the Jew of that day, nor the profound veneration for the national law and the national traditions out of which sprang the greatest of national inspirations, if he did not hold it in the highest honor

"The dead, but sceptred sovereigns, who still rule

Our spirits from their urns."

No true man, no true Jew, no true teacher, could ever contrast himself with the founder of the Jewish Commonwealth, of whom he reads in the great book "that there never rose a prophet like him in Israel." He might be good to an individual Roman, and enjoin that duty upon his hearers; but the *Romans* he must have hated with a sound hatred, as the sworn enemies of his people. Not to detest them and to desire their destruction was to prove false to his own country.* The forced antithesis between Moses and Jesus alone suffices to stamp the Sermon on the Mount as a later compilation, made with a very decidedly unpatriotic and anti-Jewish "tendency." You know as well as I that it is no Sermon on the Mount at all. In *The Bible for Learners* (iii, 141), we read: —

"The Evangelist had a special motive for 'fixing upon a mountain for this purpose. He intended to represent Jesus laying down the fundamental laws of the Kingdom of Heaven as the counterpart of Moses, who promulgated the constitution of the Old Covenant from Mount Sinai. Luke, on the other hand, not wishing Jesus to be regarded as a second Moses or another lawgiver, just as deliberately makes the Master deliver his discourse on a plain.'"

This "culmination of Israel's spirit of prophecy" was either unknown to all other writers in the New Testament save Luke or they did not consider it in that transcended light. Otherwise, how could they pass it over in silence? Would their accounts not be like the play of "Hamlet" with Hamlet left out?

And, now one word as to the "last word." If I ask reconsideration, it is not because you do not sufficiently honor us. You acknowledge that, although we failed "to become the light-bringers, the inspirers of ages to come," the glory of this last word must be forever ours. Yet there remains the sad reflection that we have now lived eighteen hundred years after that last word was spoken, — have lived, not as other nations, but a life absolutely unique in history, and have suffered more than any other body of men. All this without saying anything further to the world? The Jews, you must admit, were the only ones that did not bend their knees to the Baal to which gross ignorance, superstition, and tyranny had changed the image of the good, simple peasant preacher of Galilee. They have borne loads which, in all human calculation,

---

*The following letter of Benjamin Franklin (James Freeman Clarke, Every-Day Religion, p. 56) may be cited here, as showing this spirit:-

PHILADELPHIA, July 5, 1775

MR. STRAHAM:

Sir,-You are a member of Parliament, and one of that Majority which has doomed my country to Destruction. You have begun to burn our Towns and murder our People. Look upon your Hands. They are stained of your Relatives. You and I were long Friends. You are now my Enemy, and I am yours.

B. FRANKLIN

ought to have crushed them out of existence long ago. But they did not yield, and did not die; and, though branded as the enemies of Jesus, they were better friends to him than the hosts of his worshippers. Are they nothing as an example, as a verification of the power that resides in a great inspiration? Theodore Parker called the fagot of the martyr the cloud of light that leads mankind through deserts to the promised land of truth and right. For whom were they kindled in large numbers than for the Jews? And when thousands of the hosts of Israel perished in the flames, and with their last breath cried, "Hear, O Israel, the Lord our God is One," is it just in a Unitarian to tell the world that their "last word" was heard eighteen centuries ago, and received from them a "great refusal" so that the whole course of their subsequent history went on a wrong track, and was but a monstrous mistake? Such men as Maimonides, Gabirol and Mendelssohn had still some message to deliver to the world, and "were light-bearers" of their day and generation. But enough for the present. *Deo favente,* I may speak to you again; for, whatever else I may in my Jewish blindness refuse, it shall never be the hand of an honest, upright, wide-souled opponent. And so I press yours and remain

Yours fraternally,

Gustav Gottheil

X

JOSEPH KRAUSKOPF
Evolution and Judaism (1887)[*]

This is an evening for rejoicing. This night we complete a momentous task. Our hearts feel light and cheerful to-night. Not so four months ago. With a heavy heart and with a reluctant spirit we entered then upon our research. We felt the urgent need of this rigid inquiry, yet our mind was haunted by alarming fears lest our search might cast us adrift on a cheerless sea of doubt, and land us at last upon the dismal strands of hopeless despair. We saw the age all aflame with the Doctrine of Evolution. We read its praises and we heard its denunciations. We listened to its panegyrics and we saw it branded as the curse of man. We found that leading scientists accepted many of its premises, and deduced from them very important conclusions. We found that it was taught in our higher institutions of learning, that it permeated our best literature, that it formed the subject for research and speculation of many of our knowledge-seekers, yet we also learned, that all theology was leagued in open war against it, that it was charged by the church with harboring evil designs against all that is most sacred to the human heart, and with desiring to replace God by the reign of blind, unreasoning Laws of Nature.

The conflict with Evolution raised among men of science kindled within us a desire to acquire some knowledge of the fundamental facts upon which it bases its theory; the storm of indignation and opposition, which it raised among the theologians, changed that desire to duty. When on all sides the exultant shout arises that Evolution relegates religious doctrines to the nursery, and proves God to be a pure fiction, duty makes it binding upon us to examine deep into the nature

[*This was the summary lecture (Number 16) in a series on this theme.]

132

of that agency, which is held to be powerful enough to dispel, by one single word, that which has been the immovable rock of mankind these thousands of years. When the history of civilization proves, that thus far, human progress has depended largely upon the influence which religion exercised upon the thoughts and actions of man, and a new theory arises with the professed object of banishing all religious beliefs from the heart and mind of the people, it becomes the duty of all, who have the welfare of society at heart, to thoroughly master the new theory, to be enabled either to refute it, or, if logically forced, to accept it, or to weigh both teachings well in the balance, and to remove from the one all that can not satisfy the requirements of truth, and from the other all that the new doctrine proves false, and thus effect a reconciliation.

It was, therefore, that we entered upon our research, and four long and toilsome months we spent upon it. We traversed the ages. We penetrated into the remotest ends of our globe. We ascended into the heavens and wrested many a secret from yon brilliant galaxies of worlds, that spin breathlessly, yet ever unwearied, through the unfathomable abyss of space, and which had hitherto gloried in the thought, that they placed themselves far beyond the inquisitiveness of man. We laid bare the foundations of our earth, and applied the unsparing instruments of science so long, until they yielded up some of their long-kept secrets. With the magic spell which the laboratories impart to the initiated, we reanimated the countless sleepers of past generations, and never permitted them to return to their eternal repose, until they had made known to us some very startling disclosures. With every new success our mind grew bolder, and our inquiring spirit keener. We dared to pass from the physical to the psychical world, and the results attained well repaid our daring.

And we learned to understand the teaching of the much praised, much attacked, and much dreaded doctrine of Evolution. It took us back through inconceivable millions of years, to a time when this wondrous world of ours was but a cloud-like fire mist. We were told that this nebula cooled, concentrated and formed the sun, which at first almost filled all space. Constant cooling, concentrating, revolving and rotating reduced it to a sphere in the centre of the world. It sent off fire-rings, which formed themselves into planets, and these in their turn, cast off rings also, which became attendant stars to them. In the course of epochs of centuries, our earth cooled, changed from a globe of glowing gas to a ball of liquid fire, and finally, as its heat constantly irradiated into space, a gradually thickening crust began to envelop our globe. At this juncture organic life appeared, manifesting itself in its first stages as microscopic dots of jelly throbbing with life. With the gradual changes which the cooling earth was constantly undergoing, came a gradual unfolding of organic life, struggle for existence, and a tendency, inherent in all animal life towards continuous perfection, aided this unfolding, and thus arose, in gradual rising succession, and increasing complexity of structure, all the various species and genera of vegetable and animal life, from the sea weed to the lily, from the mollusca to man, from the protoplasm, swimming unconsciously in the primeval sea, to the social, moral, religious, rational being in whom Evolution has, in our day, reached its culmination point.

And it taught us still more. It proved that every evidence for Evolution is every evidence for the existence of an *"evolver."* It confessed its inability to explain *"origin."* Having *"matter"* with its inherent properties, and *"force"* with its eternal and immutable laws as starting points, it can slowly unfold the crude to the more perfect, the simple to the more complex, but it is forced to take this matter and force, with their eternally inherent properties and immutable laws, from a *Living and Intelligent First Cause.*[*] It is forced to postulate the existence of some *Supreme Power* behind matter and force, behind life, behind natural laws, behind consciousness, behind reason and volition, and this power, theistic evolutionists name *God.*

And still more it taught. It revealed something of the true nature of this God. It pointed to the reign of supreme harmony, supreme design, supreme intelligence in the universe. It revealed along every step in the march of its progression this God as ever present, ever active, constantly creating, directly all matter — organic and inorganic — and all force — physical and vital — and gradually developing all life from the simplest to the highest, from the crudest to the more and more perfect, from the not-living to life mortal, and from life mortal, through the gateway of death, to life eternal.

And yet more. It taught our heart and mind to worship God. As with the aid of microscope and telescope, scalpel and magic lantern, battery and reagents it laid the breast of nature bare, and revealed God working everywhere for the final good of man, the all-surpassing

[*The text erroneously reads "Causes" in the plural.]

grandeur of the Creator's handiwork, and awe-inspiring proofs of His Supreme Wisdom and Love, the infinite and inscrutable which constantly confront us, and our finiteness, which in this vast embrace of supreme power and intelligence stands out in humiliating contrast, all these humble our reason, they unconsciously but irresistibly teach our head to bow, and our knees to bend, and our heart to lift itself in prayer and our lips to stammer forth words of adoration and gratitude.

And its crowning teaching of all, is its clear and unmistakable declaration that it comes to strengthen religion and not to weaken it. It comes to harmonize religion with reason. It comes to show whither it is tending, what its goal, and how largely it is depending upon rational religion for the speediest realization of its object. It makes it religion's mission henceforth, to so labor with and upon the heart and mind of man, that man may be constantly conscious of the existence of God, and may consistently comprehend Him as the Universal Life, the Cause of All and the Cause in All, Nature's Lord, and the Almighty, the Intelligence and Love Supreme. It makes it religion's mission to constantly stimulate man to frequent spiritual intercommunion with God, by means of worship, for self-purification, and acquaint man with the purpose for which he exists, and to aid him to live in the fullest harmony with that purpose, which is, to constantly unfold and develop the highest and best that in us is, until the God-like is reached.

Therefore is this an evening for rejoicing, therefore, is our heart light and cheerful to night. Rich in the reward of our labor. Harassing doubts have been changed to comforting convictions. Instead of an abstract unthinkable God, we have a God who in everything that exists [,] in everything that is highest and best within us, in everything that tends towards our happiness, our ennoblement, our intellectual and moral unfolding reveals Himself as our loving Father. Evolution the dreadful enemy of all things sacred, proves itself to be religion's staunchest friend, and instead of harboring evil designs against the stay and support of civilized society, it openly declares itself its most faithful ally. It has faithfully kept its promise which it gave to Judaism in the opening lecture of this series. As Goethe dug the beauteous flower, which he chanced upon in the gloomy forest, with all its roots and with exceeding care, and transplanted it into his garden fair, where it still grows and blooms, thus gently and lovingly and thoughtfully dealt Evolution with Judaism. It did not pluck it that it should fade. Carefully it dug it up, root and all, and carried it forth out of the dismal shadow of the primeval forest and transplanted it into a garden fair, where it shall grow forever and bloom to eternity.

It doeth [doth?] seem strange, passing strange, that such a religious standpoint as ours should be attacked as irreligious, and so bitterly, and so abusively attacked as ours has been. It doeth seem strange, and passing strange, that we should have been heralded abroad as enemies of Judaism and as pronounced atheists. In his "Introduction" to *"God and the Bible,"* Matthew Arnold relates the martyrdom of *Polycarp,* bishop of Smyrna. For this trying to introduce Christianity among the heathens, he was accused as an atheist, and condemned to the stake. As he stood in the amphitheater, preparing for death, the Roman pro-consul, pitying his great age, begged him to pronounce the formulas which expressed adherence to the popular religion and abhorrence of Christianity. "Cry," said he, "away with the atheists!" Whereupon Poly-carp, looking around with a severe countenance upon the heathen clamorers, who filled the amphitheater, pointed to these with his hand, and with a groan, and casting up his eyes to heaven, cried: *"Away with the atheists!"* and died the death of a martyr. And drawing his lesson from this narrative, Matthew Arnold makes this truthful observation: "Confident in its traditions and imaginations, this religion now cries out against those who pronounce them vain: 'Away with the atheists!' So deeply unsound is the mass of traditions and imaginations of which popular religion consists, so gross a distortion and caricature of the true religion does it present, that future times will hardly comprehend its audacity in calling those who ajure it 'atheists,' while its being stigma-tized itself with this hard name will astonish no one."

It is true the doctrine of Evolution has necessitated us to renounce a mass of ancient mythology, of Oriental traditions and imaginations, of heathen survivals and bad philosophy, of neo-platonic mysticism and of dark age superstition. It proved the fallacy of the belief that the Bible was either written by the hand of God or by the hand of men under the dictation by the mouth of God. It proved the absurdity of Biblical mir-acle stories. It refuted the Biblical theory of special creation. It is opposed to the belief that multitudinous species of organism that now exist, and that have existed from time to time, were specially created. It is opposed to the belief that God took clay and shaped it into a man of flesh and bone, with new fibers and ganglionic cells, with lungs, intestines, blood vessels and secreting glands, and all, strange to say, resembling in nearly every detail those of the highest species of the ape family. It is opposed to the belief that woman was formed out of the rib taken unawares from Adam. It is opposed to the anthromorphistic God, a human-like, personal God, who acts, looks, speaks, feels, tempts, resents, rewards, takes vengeance, repents just as a man does, with the only difference that his power, for good or for evil, is infinately superior to that of man. It is to those who impose so degrading a caricature of God upon religion that evolution says: *"Away with the atheists!"* and not to us.

It is to those who brand us as infidels, because we insist upon discriminating in religious beliefs and practices between the essential and non-essential, upon severing the eternal from the transitory, the universal from the local, the original from the borrowed, the rational from the untenable, that Evolution says: *"Away with the atheists!"* and not to us.

It is to those who brand evolution as blasphemous, as poisoning the minds of youth, as forming the recruiting grounds for anarchy, because it teaches that there are deficiencies and inaccuracies in the Bible, that it contains much that no longer satisfies the requirements of truth, much that belongs to a dead past, that the dead must be replaced by the living, that the Bible did not come down to us for our instruction in scientific knowledge, or to rear cosmic philosophers, but to fix upon our heart and mind the eternal moral truths that it contains, and which alone give it its importance, it is to those who brand these teachings as infamous that Evolution says: *"Away with the atheists!"* and not to us.

Yet, after mature reflection, we find that the attack with which Evolution meets everywhere is not at all surprising. Its teaching is new, and as such it must share the common fate that awaits all new doctrines. Never, within the knowledge of man, have the masses cheerfully welcomed a new thought. The innovations that have yielded unto mankind its greatest benefits have, with the rarest exceptions, had the hardest struggles for securing a foothold. Up to the very threshold of our time, no man ever taught a new idea without being compelled to suffer for his daring. Harvey lost his practice and was accounted crazy when he published his work on the circulation of the blood. The proposition to light the streets of London gave rise to the greatest alarm. When the application of steam to locomotion was proposed, the *Quarterly Review* ridiculed the idea "that people would be insane enough to trust their lives to a machine rushing on at the rate of twenty miles an hour."

When Kant published his thoughts to the world, he was proclaimed "an ignorant charlatan," and Bacon was branded "an atheist in hypocritical disguise, his philosophy a spiritless materialism, uncertain and unsteady in its expression, frivolous in tone, and full of fallacies in every assertion." After Galileo had invented his telescope and had learned through it, that the planets were globes like our earth, his teaching was received with scorn and incredulity. The leading professor of philosophy at Padua absolutely declined to look through the telescope to examine the planets for himself, though repeatedly urged to do so, and he proved "by the strictest academical deductive reasoning" that the planets could not possibly exist. The professor's syllogisms were conclusive to the masses and the evidence of the senses sustained an ignominious defeat. Maimonides, Spinoza and Mendelssohn, the most brilliant triumvirate of modern Israel, were, by their own people defamed as heretics and excommunicated because of their new teachings. When Joseph II., emperor of Austria, (1741–90) yielding to the spirit of his age, removed the degrading disabilities from the Jews, and permitted them to learn trades, and pursue agriculture, and opened the public schools and universities to them, and extended to them all the privileges of free citizenship, his humane spirit raised the greatest apprehension and a storm of indignation and opposition among pious Jews. Public school education and free citizenship, they claimed, would estrange their youth from Judaism, and modern teachings would force Rabbinical studies to the background. To-day no rational being doubts the theory of the circulation of the blood, nor would civilized society relinquish its lighted streets. We trust our lives to railway accommodation, rushing at even greater speed than twenty miles an hour without thought of being insane, and Bacon and Galileo and Kant and Maimonides and Spinoza and Mendelssohn have the honored places in the temple of fame, and the Jews enjoy every human right, without thereby becoming estranged from Judaism, and so, too, will the Doctrines of Evolution, though execrated to-day, be the universally accepted doctrine of all denominations not many decades hence.

Passion and ignorance will never stay the rush of progress. In the fulness of time truth must conquer and reason must triumph. Trickery and hypocrisy cannot prevail forever. A time inevitably comes in the history of every religion, when the false must flee from the altar to the nursery, and the untenable must leave the pages of the Bible and seek a place within the children's rhymes. The anachronistic Church of our day may declaim against the pretensions of science and rail against Evolution to its heart's content, Evolution will vindicate itself and return its revilers into worshipers.* 'The Doctrine of Evolution, even in its widest application, can never affect theology so profoundly as did the heliocentric theory of Copernicus, when it dethroned the earth from its supposed central position of the universe.' Ecclesiastics denounced his theory as impious and absurd, and they did not always confine their opposition to words of abuse; to-day the truth of his theory is admitted, even by the Church, and religion is not the worse for that admission. So will, in its due time, Evolution be the universally accepted doctrine, and no one will regret the loss of the false science, and of the obsolete notions which it replaced. Somewhere in his "Outlines of Cosmic Philosophy," Fisk remarks "that the truth is not yet wholly trite, that the most valuable men of every age are its heretics, that the heresy of one age is the orthodoxy of the next, and that complacent orthodoxy is wont to claim as its allies, to-day, the very men whom it burnt or crucified in days gone by."†

The outlook is bright. When such men as Professors Dana, LeConte, Asa Gray, McCosh, men like Mivart and Wallace and the Duke of Argyle, men like Henry Ward Beecher and Minot J. Savage, all prominently connected with religion, and some of them even with very orthodox denominations, hold substantially to the doctrine of evolution, we are encouraged in our belief, that the blessed day, when the Doctrine of Evolution will form a fundamental article in every creed, is not very distant. We believe with the poet Wordsworth: "What one is why may not millions be?" Though it is at present the possession of only a few disciplined minds, it must eventually become the property of all. The rising sun illumines the mountain peaks first, but, bye and bye, the valleys beneath are as radiant with light as the proudest mountain top. Each age reflects in its belief the predominating tendency of that age. The age in which the doctrine of the "Immaculate Concep-

---

*All real progress is more or less surrounded by trouble. It is the interest of men that truth should live; and after men's cares are over, and the truth has had some time given it to bloom and bring forth its fruit in new and higher forms, men find that it is not wasting, but it has really led on to something better and higher. They get over their panic; and the next generation hearing the truth from the cradle, and seeing none of the objections that their fathers did, they accept it, and the world goes on and goes up.—Beecher's "Evolution and Religion," Lect. XVII.

† It is a familiar thought that the unbelief of to-day is the faith of to-morrow: and yet to-day always condemns the premature to-morrow. The skepticism of honest men unfolds the truth, and becomes the conviction of the aftertime.—Beecher's "Evolution and Religion"—Preface.

tion" was raised to the dignity of a dogma reflects as faithfully the intellectual status of that age, as the age, in which the world's exhibition building of Paris could not hold all the specimens of electrical apparatus, reflects the religious tendency of that age. Evolution is the watchword of our age. Ascend unto the heavens and descend again into the depths of the sea, penetrate into the very center of our earth, and compass, if you can, the vast extent of the universe, it is the same word you spell everywhere; it is *"Evolution,"* and it will profit little to raise a barrier around religion's consecrated ground and say: "Thus far, but no farther."

Gradually men are awakening to a consciousness, that religion exists to influence morality and to unfold the highest of which our natures are capable, and the evolution, in revealing to us the eternally immutable laws of nature, forms the safest groundwork for morality, and in revealing to us an ever-present and constantly-creating God, proves itself a most powerful agent for the maintenance of every one of the fundamental truths which give to religion its permanent value. Gradually men are awakening to a consciousness that a proper knowledge of God, as the Intelligence and Love and Power Supreme, as He reveals himself through natural laws, and a mode of life in the fullest obedience to the will of God, as it appeals to our heart and intellect by means of His natural laws, is the creed and only creed.

The minister with empty head and empty heart, who is content to rehearse empty forms before empty benches an hour or two a week, is not the minister of the coming era. A parrot-like repetition of forms, creeds, prayers, more than half of which neither minister nor congregation believe, is not the service of the future. Gorgeous temples, kept up at enormous expense, for form's sake, are not the temples of the future. That minister, who will kindle within the heart of his people an incessant longing for seeking God and for living in the fullest harmony with His Will, is *the minister of the future.* That service, which while appealing to the heart will appeal to the intellect, which will send forth after every devotion better and wiser men into the walks of daily life, is *the service of the future.* That religion that will carry the flag of science in the van of a progressive people, that will vanquish forever every antagonism between it and science, that will boast of good deeds accomplished more than of the excellency of its creed, is *the religion of the future.*

My task is done. I have not endeavored to formulate new creeds in these lectures, nor to establish a new faith. I have but sought to reconcile Judaism with science. I have added nothing to Judaism, pure and simple, and I have taken nothing from it. I have tried to remove the imposed untenable and foreign and false. Whether wrong or right, increase of years and of learning alone can decide. Till then, Pope's Prayer is mine:

> "If I am right, Thy grace impart
> Still in the right to stay,
> If I am wrong, O teach my heart
> To find that better way."

XI

LIEBMAN ADLER
The Story of the Creation (1893)
Gen. 1:1

In the Jerusalem Targum, "in the beginning" is rendered by "in wisdom." Truly, in the very first word of Holy Writ there is wisdom, since it begins with "the beginning," and leaves untouched all that goes before.

Among the ruins of Nineveh, a library of inscribed stone-flags was discovered. When deciphered, they were found, among other things, to contain a tale of the creation and the story of a flood, which, in many particulars, coincide with the Biblical tales. These ancient accounts from Nineveh may be older than those of the Bible, but the latter excel the former, even as the laconic speech of an experienced sage eclipses the confused bombast of a thoughtless chatterer.

Whereas the Bible is content to begin with the "beginning," the Nineveh document supplies the unknown preceding the beginning with fables and tales of the gods, wildly fantastic and unaesthetic.

The ancients have propounded the question: "Why does it say, 'in the beginning God created,' why not, 'God created in the beginning?' God, the subject, ought to take precedence." The query was considered worthy of various replies, and, with the same idea in mind, the Greek translators have taken the liberty of changing the text. But even when thus transposed, there is wisdom in the words.

The Bible wishes to give man a story of the creation of the earth which he inhabits; it wishes to speak of the "beginning" and not, as does the Nineveh document, tell a tale of the God-head, a theogony. For this reason, "in the beginning" should be more accentuated than "God."

The ancients furthermore ask why the Bible commences with *bet* in *bereshit* ["in the beginning"] instead of with *aleph*, as do the ten commandments. The question is scarcely a brilliant one, but the reply is very clever. The letter *bet* is closed on all sides but one. This signifies that we must not too deeply investigate, we must not permit our thoughts to betray us to the heights of heaven or into the depths of hell; they should not lose themselves in speculation, either about prehistoric ages, or about a future world. Therefore, the Torah begins with neither philosophy nor hypothesis concerning the nature of the Godhead, but with heaven and earth.

Portions of the Bible do not meet with universal approval. But we are apt to forget that its wisdom does not consist merely in what it says, but equally, if not more, in what it leaves untouched. Strictly speaking, it contains no theology, no metaphysics, no mysticism, no heaven, no hell, no angels, no devils, nothing of another world. The Bible, according to its contents, may be divided into natural history, history, laws and ethics.

"In the beginning God created the heaven and the earth." This verse brings the Bible into harmony with the most advanced science. When was the beginning? That is not explained; perhaps millions, perhaps an utterly inconceivable number of years ago. Whence was the earth evolved? From fire? From water? Or from both? The Bible itself is silent on that point. It leaves to science full sway to investigate and decide the question.

The ancients inquire: "Why does Scripture say *et ha-shamayim* ["the heavens"] and *v'et ha-aretz* ["and the earth"]. These words *et* are apparently superfluous; it would be just as correct to say: "*Bereshit bara Elohim shamayim va-aretz.*" And they think that these words signify that heaven and all that is included in the idea of heaven, and the earth with all its potentialities were created on the first day, *i.e.,* indefinite ages ago, but that on earth these forces proved their existence gradually, each one acting in its own time.

We may consider the story of the creation of the universe told completely in the first verse. The further narrative deals exclusively with the earth which we inhabit; not with its creation, but with its development, its evolution. It is no cosmogony, but purely geogony. On the first day, or in the first stage of development, light found its way through the dense vapor shrouding the earth. And there was light! But there was not yet discernible a body whence light emanated.

In the second stage of development, the fluid element was divided into actual water and the vapor that fills the atmosphere.

In the third stage, the last, mighty upheavals of the earth took place. The crust of the earth was sprung open, mountains arose from the depths, while other parts fell into abysses, were filled with water, and formed the seas. And upon the newly-made dry land appeared the earliest vegetation.

In the fourth stage, the atmosphere had become so clear that the sun, the moon and the stars were visible. Finally, in the fifth and sixth stages appeared life, rising from its lowest forms to its highest development in man.

Today, as on each Sabbath, we have solemnly taken the Torah from its case, and have thanked God aloud for blessing us with it; the congregation, Bible in hand, devoutly follows the reading of the portion, and at its close, once more gives thanks to God for bestowing upon us the treasure of the Torah.

And what is this that we have read? It is what in science is known as geogony, the doctrine of the formation of the earth, a branch of natural science. Science — this is the distinction — deals with the creation only, regardless of the Creator; whereas the Torah mentions the Creator: "God said, God created, God made," etc.

What could be more potent in urging the Israelite to investigate and acquaint himself with Nature, than the fact that the Torah, his Holy of holies, opens with a chapter of natural science? It does not begin like our catechisms with, "What is religion?" but it tells God's people how the earth developed under God's omnipotence. Man's earthly weal, his fairest, chastest joys, and his pure, sincere piety are the results of this study. The psalmist, in the 104th Psalm, loses himself in contemplation of Nature, and then his surcharged heart breaks forth into the words: "O Lord, how manifold are thy works! In wisdom has thou made them all: the earth is full of thy riches."

If, thousands upon thousands of years ago, in the infancy of mankind, long before there was any idea of natural science; before the telescope had brought within mortal vision spheres millions of miles away; before the microscope had disclosed a new microscopic world; before the magnet had pointed the path over the seas; before air and water had been analyzed in the crucible; and thousands of other means had brought light and order in the dark bowels of Nature, and revealed a world full of marvels— if, at that early period, Nature was held in such esteem that the holy book, the Bible, was opened with a contemplation upon it; if, at that time, sages and poets, gazing about them and up at the starry firmament, drew thence the inspiration which impelled them to immortal verses and songs of wisdom; how far advanced we must be, we children of the nineteenth century, in which science, with its innumerable discoveries and inventions, has opened so many windows, admitting light into the awful depths of Nature! Alas, we are indeed *children* of the nineteenth century! The ordinary individual — I mean one of the masses of today — is a child in matters of natural science. Yes, we have retrograded. We have, it is true, cast off an immense number of superstitions, of absurd explanations and prejudices held by the ancients concerning the phenomena of Nature. But this is not due to intelligence; there is a different reason for it. The ancients inquired into the causes of things, and if a rational answer was not at hand, the query was silenced with a fable. We do not *inquire;* we are, therefore, safe from all misunderstanding, but neither do we arrive at an understanding of these causes. We imagine that we have advanced; we *have* advanced, but it is not progress; we are prodded by comparatively few thinkers. Ask the masses about any ordinary phenomena of Nature and their causes— about thunderstorms, earthquakes, cyclones, shooting stars, volcanoes, eclipses of the sun or moon. For every one of these, the ancients had an explanatory reply; but were you to repeat that reply to one of the masses of today, his education would lead him to deride the credulity of the ancients; yet no better answer is forthcoming; none is needed, since none is asked for. In social intercourse there is nothing more unbearable than an inquisitive person; but in the intercourse with Nature, the Nature in and about man, everyone ought to be inquisitive, particularly the Israelite; and sound and reliable answers can be drawn from the wells that have been dug and made accessible to all —from a rich, popular literature.

Ah, how woefully has religious thought gone astray! Religion and natural science, which, in the first chapter of the most ancient record of religion, went hand-in-hand, and appeared to possess *one* heart and *one* soul, now regard each other inimically, and, like Jacob and Esau, quarrel about the rights of the first-born. Jacob must bow down seven times before Esau embraces him; and when Esau says, "Now let us go forth together like brothers," Jacob trembles at the thought of such close companionship, and answers, "We may not go together, for my flocks might suffer; go thou first, and I will follow." And when Esau says, "Then shall some of my people remain with thee to guide and protect thee," Jacob replies, "Wherefore? I need it not."

Judaism ought not to countenance this unbrotherly relation 'twixt religion and science. The Bible is science — natural science, history, law and ethics. The Talmud, despite the objections and warnings interposed by some of the rabbis, discusses all the branches of science known in these times, as do the best rabbinical writings of the brilliant Spanish school. Only the German and Slavonic rabbinical schools, during times of unutterable oppression, became alienated from science, as also African and Asiatic Judaism has become estranged.

I am addressing an educated, enlightened congregation, one certainly not accustomed to unctuous sermons from its present preacher. Yet, were I to bring a flower into the pulpit instead of a Bible-text, and attempt to prove the omnipotence of God by showing the structure of the stem, the leaves, the calyx, the corolla, the stamens and pistils, the cells and veins; were I to show that the goodness and wisdom of the Creator are manifest in the drop of honey at the bottom of the cup, attracting the insect, which in its intrusion is covered in pollen, carries the pollen to other flowers, and so fecundates them, etc., you would not be greatly edified. You would say, "Such matters are out of place in the temple of God!"

This is the true reform at which we must aim: we must consecrate both history and natural science, by regarding them as integral parts of religion; —*Bereshit* considered as natural science, must be held equally sacred with Noah,* considered as history.

---

*"*In the beginning,*" the name of the first of the fifty-four weekly portions into which the Pentateuch is divided. Noah is the name of the second portion.-[Tr.]*

XII

LIEBMAN ADLER

The First Verse of the Bible (1893)

"In the beginning God created the heaven and the earth."

Gen. I:1.

Heathens can accept not even the first words of Holy Writ, for, according to their ideas, "in the beginning" the gods were created. The Torahs of the heathens do not begin with cosmogony, the history of the creation of the world, but with theogony, the account of the creation of the gods, and of how one god begat another. After that, how many generations may have come and gone, ere the spirit of research awoke in man, leading him to investigate the origin of each individual creation, and then of the sum of things, the universe, that is to say, ere he reached the idea contained in the words "he created!"

For these words also are beyond the conception of the heathen; he would say "they created." We have revised our prayer-book, substituting "salvation" for "Savior." But a far greater, a far more important and more influential change at the time was that from "they created" to "he created." Nor, indeed, could the heathen say "they created." "Created" signifies the formation of something from nothing, and the power to do this the heathen does not accord to his gods, who may only give form to pre-existing matter. These first words of our Torah, "In the beginning God created," which express a complete revolution in the world of thought, have been given to humanity by Judaism, nor have they yet taken root anywhere but in the soil of Judaism and her daughter-religions. How long, then, may it have been before the human intellect was sufficiently strong and disciplined to sum up manifold creation in two concepts, and to give expression to these in two words: heaven and earth!

Then, for thousands of years, this first verse of the Torah express-
ing, as it does, a spiritual conquest, was conned by mankind. But in
the course of those years, its imperfections have been remedied, and
its misconceptions righted. Divine truth can never be clearly enough
understood, and much less clothed in words, because, for the divine,
we have but a human method of expression. This is shown in the very
first verse of Holy Writ, in our text. "Elohim," which is the concentra-
tion of the blind, heartless forces of Nature, supposed to have been
divided among all the gods, was later transformed into "Adonai," a single Creator, Preserver of the world and Controller of human destinies,
an eternal, omnipotent, just and merciful God, a God that is Providence, an all-providing Father, a holy, superior, intelligent Being, free
from all faults and passions, asking no service for himself, demanding
only that we seek the light of truth, and abide in virtue. Thus, in the
course of time, the incomplete designation of a supreme power, "Elohim," gave way to the more comprehensive "Adonai." So, too, have
misunderstandings been dispelled. Isaiah's prophecy has been fulfilled
with regard to the word "heavens:" "The heavens are vanished like
smoke." Heaven, as the ancients understood it, no longer exists for us,
not *one,* much less *seven* heavens. At the time, it was an enormous triumph of the mind to bring all creation under two heads; as time went
on, the mind included all creation in a *single* conception, and expressed
it in a *single* word: universe, or the even more forcible cosmos.

When we raise our eyes to the glorious azure, which the ancients
called heaven, we, with our modern conception thereof, are none the
less disposed to reverential wonderment, our souls are none the less
attuned to joyous adoration, when we think of the Creator of these glories, of this ether, which at night is illumined by innumerable lustrous
worlds, and in which our earth floats like a feather. Yea, this azure
awakens in us, as did the heaven of the ancients in them, worship and
adoration of the Ruler of the universe, even though the azure no longer
represents to us a solid edifice, the better half of creation, the habita-
tion of superior beings.

The word of God is everlasting, but its interpretation varies. The
word "Shomayim"["heaven" or "heavens"] signifies to us what is
beyond human conception, the supernatural, which the mind sees as
in a vision, the inexpressible which the heart dimly feels. The animal
part of man belongs to the earth. But his higher thoughts and aspirations, his world of ideas, and all that is beyond animal pleasures:

thought, hope, the consolation of immortality, the belief in one God, the constant striving better to understand his being and his will, to live and act accordingly — these constitute our heaven. To earn what we require is earthly; but to earn it honestly and fairly under the most trying circumstances, so to limit our wants that we may not jeopardize honesty and rectitude, *that* is heavenly. To live in wedlock is earthly; but for man and woman to live together in love and faith, in peace and harmony, even though it necessitate daily and hourly sacrifices, *that* is heavenly. To be father and mother is earthly; but to use every endeavor, shunning no sacrifice, not merely to rear children, but to bring them up in the fear of God and on the path of virtue, not only to regard them as the sunshine of the home, a natural delight to the eyes of the parents, but to be ever conscious of the sacred duty to make good, useful men and women of them, *that* is heavenly. To live for one's self and one's family is earthly; but to deny one's self pleasures in order that others may enjoy, to exert one's self that other exhausted ones may rest, to care for others and save them care, and even to risk one's life for that of others, *that* is heavenly. To drift with the tide is earthly, but to stand against the current in the defence of truth and conviction, to stand alone for the right, firm as a rock, even though the tide of public opinion toss and swell around one, and principles totter and sway, *that* is heavenly. Earnest attention to temporal needs is earthly; but to think of the eternal, and to sacrifice momentary good for the sake of eternity, *that* is heavenly.

This heavenly spirit was created as was the earthly. It was the creation of the first day. And in the account of the five days following the first one of creation, we are told of the development of this creation in matters of the earth as well as of heaven.

Thy heaven, oh man, thou carriest within thy mind and within thy heart! Some have only a bit of it, others, all the seven heavens of the ancients: with some, it is clouded o'er, somber and threatening; with others, radiant in its brilliancy. Rabbi Akiba died a martyr, after indescribable torture, yet seven heavens were in his heart. Hadrian's life closed with the blackest skies within his heart, though as Akiba's emperor, he was apparently enjoying the greatest earthly prosperity.

God created the heaven and the earth; but just as the earth became known to man by degrees, a large portion of it being discovered after thousands of years, and much still remaining to be discovered, so it is with heaven, the heaven in the mind, in the heart, and in social life. It must be sought and found. Progress means ever to discover new heavens within us, heavens of knowledge and of culture of heart and mind, patience and fraternity, peaceful and harmonious existence in social life, as well as in the intercourse of countries and nations. This is the sevenfold light, these are the new heavens which the prophet of Messianic times has promised us; and to approach nearer and ever nearer to them is the task of our mundane existence.

XIII

LIEBMAN ADLER

The So-Called Fall of Man (1893)

Gen. III

The Bible suffers from two opposing parties—on the one hand, from the simple piety of those that pay it unquestioning homage; on the other, from its enemies. Both accept the words of Holy Writ, in their literal sense, even in those portions that are narrative and not legislative.

The one class takes it very ill, if we say, "The word has a meaning, but word and meaning are as different as body and soul;" that they consider the most pronounced heresy. The others say, "What absurdity! and that is supposed to be Holy Writ!"

We believe that when the Bible commands and forbids, there is no room for subtle interpretation; there the words embody the full meaning to be conveyed, and whoever attempts to wrest the sense to suit himself, acts dishonestly by the book. But when the Bible clothes its teachings in tales and parables, we agree with Rashi that the words themselves cry out, "Explain me!" With regard to the verse, "This is the book of the generations of Adam," our sages say: "So far as the story of the creation and all that is connected with it is concerned, the honor of Holy Writ demands that we take a hidden meaning for granted; but further on, where questions of practical life are involved, the honor of the Scriptures demands an exact and literal interpretation of its contents."

Thus do we approach the task that we have set ourselves for today's discourse, the explanation of those portions of the Bible that treat of the "fall." (Gen. II:15–17; III:1–7.)

Let us say at once what meaning they convey to us. The first human beings lived their appointed time in happy innocence. Then they began to think, and their innocence was destroyed. Doubt, discord between head and heart, took the place of a calm spirit and serene content.

There is a way of thinking that but reflects the thoughts of others. A child thinks as its parents think; a pupil thinks as the teacher has taught him to think; an individual thinks as those about him think.

There is a kind of thought that subordinates itself to the wishes of the heart, "the wish is father to the thought!"

There is a kind of thought that will make no concessions to the feelings, but would rule as an autocrat; it says to the heart: Repress thy desires, they do not please me. Speculation makes unquestioning enjoyment of life an impossibility.

Speculative thought banishes innocence. The child is innocent so long as it follows the instincts of its heart, and thinks the thoughts of others. But no sooner does it begin to think independently, than its actions become good or evil, it can no longer be called innocent. So what is told of Adam is the natural course of man's life. Every human being, for a time, lives in innocence, in pleasant unconsciousness of right and wrong; if left at liberty, he acts according to the dictates of his heart, and enjoys his existence.

As the young child need not trouble itself about its sustenance, since it is given to it, so with its thoughts: it thinks whatever is given it to think. A child of a quarrelsome disposition may manifest it at an early age, it is true, and live at variance with those about it; may be easily fretted and angered and excited, but within its heart every child is at peace with itself. No sooner has independent thought asserted itself than heart and reason, inclination and duty, gratification and remorse battle for supremacy. Before thought awakens, we live at peace with ourselves; but awakening thought drives us out of the paradise of childhood, to which we may never return.

This Bible story does not betray a disturbance in the plan of creation, as if God had had some other intentions concerning man, and these had been frustrated by the sinfulness of Adam. It raises the veil, and discovers to us the underlying idea of the plan of the Almighty.

It is true, it is a great deal pleasanter to abide in ignorance, at peace with ourselves. We live much more calmly, more content with ourselves and the world, when we do not think, or if we think, think as others do. It is much more conducive to peace to know little. Learning and knowledge, inquiry and introspection bring much disquiet into one's own heart and into the world. The Preacher says, "He that increaseth knowledge increaseth pain," and the German prince of poets:

> "Who thinks not of the morrow,
> To him life brings its gifts,
> And yet he's free from sorrow."

The innocence of *not thinking,* of artlessness is, upon closer consideration, not quite so charming as it would appear. The child is guileless, sweet and good, because it is too weak to do any harm, and because its parents and guardians watch over it that it may not abuse what strength it has. But when the natural innocence of not thinking has grown great and strong, and can no longer be watched, then woe to such simplicity and to its surroundings! Innocence, sentiment, but not reasoning, is the attribute of a savage. The savage is a grown child. The savage, like the child, follows his instincts; he is not troubled and unsettled by thought. And like the child, the savage is self-satisfied, he may wade in blood, but he feels none the less innocent. Not only those that we call such are savages. Whoever allows himself to be guided only by his feelings and instincts, and has not partaken of the tree of knowledge, is a species of savage. Were all men but children, mature only in years, we would have no villages, no towns, — only wigwams.

No; innocence is becoming only as long as man lacks the power to do harm. As the years go by, bringing strength to man in their flight, thought, the serpent, the symbol of the ancients for eternity and wisdom, rears its head, and man enjoys the fruits of the tree of knowledge. He is no longer a child, existing in innocence, not knowing what is good and what evil; he is a divine being, rising above nature; he knows good from evil, and can regulate his life accordingly.

At what period does this change take place? In our religion, thirteen is the age assumed for the male sex, and twelve for the more rapidly maturing female sex, as the boundary between irresponsible innocence, which eschews thought, and the responsibility imposed by the consciousness that independent thought may be exercised. Of course, this is only an approximate boundary line, for many a one may grow hoary, nor cast off the innocence of ignorance.

Our story draws a picture of the human race at the very dawn of the history of mankind — not its fall, which the Church teaches as fundamental truth, but on the contrary, its elevation. On the one hand, it discloses the paradise of innocence: life without moral restraints, truth without investigation, thoughts without thinking, gratification without remorse; no warning, no prohibitory laws, not even a sense of shame to restrain enjoyment. "Of every tree of the garden thou mayest freely eat." But then there is the picture of the tree that man is warned not to touch. This is the tree of thought. If thou partakest of its fruits, thou wilt be like unto a divine being; thou wilt think independently of parents, of teachers and of the times; thou wilt know good from evil. But I warn thee, dearly must thou pay for it. Thought gnaws like a worm at all thy pleasures; the innocent child within thee will die, and thou wilt become as a different being!

But of all trees, this very one attracts man with irresistible power. He partakes of the fruit, and pays the penalty. The careless, thoughtless, joyous Adam is dead; in his place, we see a serious man, upon whose brow earnest thought is mirrored.

It was not intended that man's fate should be characterized by the unbroken regularity of the development of the flower of the field, or of the course of the stars in the heavens. Thought and feeling were to battle within him, and thought with thought. The keen edge of reason was to clip the wings of feeling, and the warm heart was to give of its warmth to cold, cruel, uncompromising Reason, and coax it gently into harmony with life. That which we have lost, the harmony of childhood in the years of innocence, we are to find again in the reconciliation of thought and feeling. This recovered harmony, which is our own merit, even though it be imperfect, is worth far more than the perfect one which was given to us, and which we lost with childhood.

We cannot deny that the tenor of the tale in question is suggestive rather of loss than of gain to humanity; and here, as elsewhere, the wisdom of the people is proved in their proverb: "Not all is gold that glitters." Thought is a double-edged sword, which ofttimes wounds the thinker, and brings misery and unhappiness not only to him, but to the world at large. It can transform rich, luxuriant fields, the scene of joyous existence, into a bleak, barren desert. However, the means to prevent such misfortune is also mentioned. Man is told, "In the sweat of thy brow shalt thou eat bread." When the years of innocence have flown, and thought begins to hold sway, give the boy work, and work also thou as long as thou hast strength, even to old age. Labor is a panacea for all ills; it keeps sound hearts healthy, and heals suffering ones; it keeps thought within bounds, preventing it from straying off into unprofitable regions. Every thinker ought also to be an artisan of some kind, and every laborer a thinker.

Woman, too weak physically, too sensitive in nature and disposition, to battle for daily bread in the cruel world, takes upon herself the responsibilities of motherhood, and the greater part of the cares, troubles and burdens of the home and the bringing up of the children, which latter, alas! often entails anxiety and sorrow. She devotes herself to her children, and sacrifices herself for them all her life; and this complete devotion of heart and soul and thought to her maternal duties protects her equally from temptations of the heart and from undisciplined thoughts. Intelligent mothers are the greatest blessing of the human race.

As our first mother induced the first man to eat of the fruit of the tree of knowledge; as once choruses of women animated David to immortal deeds, and drove a king, whom they did not praise, to despair; as the homage of woman was the one bright spot and the moral support of the knights in the darkness of the Middle Ages, so even to-day much of what men do that is worth doing can be traced to the importance which they attach to the approval of noble women. Whenever we meet a man who is distinguished in mind and deeds above his fellow-men, we may safely conclude that the spirit of an intelligent mother lives in him, a mother that guided her son to the tree of knowledge.

Now, that thought may not completely control man, to the exclusion of heart and feeling, the narrative goes on to say: "And I will put enmity between thee and the serpent, and between thy seed and its seed; thou shalt bruise its head and it shall bruise thy heel." And what is the world's history but a continuous warfare between wisdom and stupidity, passion and self-control, sound judgment and prejudice, civilization and savage instincts? How often is the head of wisdom trodden upon, and how often do critical thought and finical deliberation drag upon the heel of noble impulses!

No, it is not a fall of which we read. A being as perfect as is our God would not create an order of things so frail and destructible that the first man could disorganize the entire system.

The story is rather a mirror of the noble impulses of man; of his striving after knowledge and enlightenment; of his efforts to comprehend the causes of things; of his attempts to demolish every barrier opposing his progress towards knowledge; of his desire for possessions that floods cannot wash away and flames cannot consume, and for this we must not blame Adam and Eve, our first parents, but rather praise our God.

XIV

LIEBMAN ADLER
Immortality (1893)
Gen. XLIX

"There are more things in heaven and earth than are dreamt of in
our philosophy."

Shakespeare's profound observation that there are "things in
heaven and earth," of which man has no knowledge, does not refer to
those natural forces which reason has as yet failed to comprehend,
though undoubtedly true also of them, but to a spiritual world, whose
nature can be grasped neither by physical perception nor by the finest
powers of the human intellect, a world whose borderland we may tread
but in dreams and vague presentiment.

In our discussion of this proposition in regard to "things in heaven
and earth," we shall try not to soar into high and unaccustomed spheres,
but shall remain as near earth as possible, dealing with those problems
that obstruct the path of every thinking being.

Let our text be the assertion of our sages: "The patriarch Jacob did
not die."

Jacob went down into Egypt with seventy followers. During his
seventeen years' sojourn in that land, this number must have increased
considerably. Nevertheless they continued to form one family. The
dying patriarch was as ever its head, holding all its members together.
To his three oldest sons, themselves advanced in years, he addresses
stern words of reproach. He takes from the oldest son the highly-prized
birthright, and no one ventures to remonstrate, much less to gainsay
his decision.

Families are not held together by the force of reason. If such were
the power of reason, if intelligence could bind together the various

157

members of a family, our hold on family life would be as strong to-day as it was in Jacob's time. We have lost nothing of intellectual power since his time; neither has the faculty of reasoning been taken from us. Nevertheless, it would be impossible for twelve large households, with children and grandchildren, to hold together as one family. It is difficult nowadays for the adults of a single household to look upon themselves as one body. The more extended the power of the intellect, the more limited the range of that subtle "in heaven and earth" which we do not understand. Among these things must be reckoned the recognition of the ties of kindred even in the limited degree in which it exists to-day.

No one can have failed to observe that the most intelligent are not the most obedient nor the most affectionate as children; not the most faithful in conjugal relations; not the most self-sacrificing as fathers and mothers—in short, not the ones most cognizant of the claims of kinship. Goethe's correspondence with his mother was carried on through a valet. Moses expected the sons of Levi, whom he had placed in the exalted position of teachers and guides of the people, to have sufficient strength of soul to disregard their feelings for parents, for children and kinsmen, if necessity demanded the sacrifice. If we wish to see true beauty of family life, tenderness in parents, obedience in children, warmth of affection for kindred, we must not ascend too high in the strata of intelligence.

The old world can boast of an entire class of men of supreme culture, with whom, in the United States, only individuals, not a class, may bear comparison. Nevertheless, as a whole, the people of this country may be considered the most intelligent among the nations of the earth, or rather, we may say, this country has the smallest number of uneducated and narrow-minded citizens in proportion to its population. But, on the other hand, it must be said, a chilling indifference, penetrating the very heart of the people, characterizes its family life. The American can not be denied credit for unexampled nobility and public spirit in generous gifts to charitable and educational institutions, but the lack of warmth in family relations may perhaps be one of the causes of this extraordinary liberality. The fortunes of his heirs after his death trouble an American but little.

It is not agreeable to contemplate the consequence of the stronger family feeling existing among the Jews—less readiness in making great sacrifices for the common good; Judah Touro has as yet had no successor.

Intellect is, therefore, an obstructing rather than a fostering element in the recognition of the claims of kindred. Union may exist among the members of a family, even though there be no sympathy among them, no harmony in inclinations of mind and heart. There must, therefore, be some common *soul* element in the family, handed down from dead and gone ancestors, sometimes tracing its origin far into the past, which makes the descendants of a common stock feel a bond of kinship uniting them.

Such is the subtle bond thrown about us Israelites. In spite of our patriotism for the land in which we dwell; in spite of our intimate associations with the professors of other faiths; in spite of the differences among us, in culture, in religious opinions and practices, we Israelites, scattered over the whole earth, as we are, possess a common "something" inexplicable by reason, a prevailing family feature, something that reason neither grasps nor courts. "Jacob is not dead." Jacob's soul continues with his family in immortal life. The soul of Jacob is not exceptional. The souls of all of us continue to live in our descendants. Our fathers and mothers live on in us, and our spiritual characteristics are transmitted to our grandchildren and great-grandchildren. This truth is a ray of immortality itself.

The proof of the existence of a life far removed from the earthly life of reason; of a life unfathomed by the understanding, lies in the very stronghold of the intellect, namely, in science. Can mere *reason* explain how it is that man gives up his whole life to the cause of science? Does *common-sense* ever make such a demand upon man?

How many men of noble character and high attainments, while seeking to extend the domain of knowledge, have met their death in the icy regions of the Pole, in the swamps and sands of Africa! But no matter how many may thus perish, the number remains great of those that, undeterred by the fate of the pioneers, follow in their footsteps. How many Crœsuses of learning have languished in attics, and have, finally, perished in the act of enriching science with the result of their labors! Such phenomena may be included among the "things in heaven and earth," beyond the comprehension of reason.

In our own days, have we not had a sad instance of such devotion to science in the fate of the two men* that sought to do that in attempting which hundreds before them had perished — to tame the strong

---

Donaldson, who, with a companion, made an ascent in a balloon, and never returned.

winds of the air for the use of man? Would cold reason urge man to risk his life in such a cause, were there not, at the same time, a vague presentiment in him of the "things in heaven and earth," of which the intellect can tell us nothing; did not an inward voice whisper to him, "If the worst happen, your body may perish in the venture, but no harm can come to your soul?"

What would science be or what would become of it, if left to the control of reason, which it worships as its god; were it nor for belief in immortality, which it refuses to accept?

In spite of the initial expense of a musical instrument and the cost of instruction in its use, it is not uncommon to find one in our homes, while in scarcely one of a hundred dwellings is there an apparatus for physical experiment; in one of ten thousand, perchance, a laboratory. Hundreds of private tutors in music, in arithmetic, in penmanship and orthography are employed, against one engaged to teach history and natural science.

The education of children is frequently directed solely with a view to their worldly success. The study of history and natural science does not contribute to this end. The poor instruction in these branches offered in the public schools— if, indeed, they be included in the curriculum — is deemed sufficient.

There are, however, some human beings to whom these subjects are of the greatest interest, by whom days and nights are given to the advancement of learning that can bring them no practical gain in a world of reason. Such devotion proves to us that the soul soars in another world even during its life on earth — a world, in which there is no death, though everything above us, in the world of reason and the senses, be hushed, and our friends lament and bury us as dead.

When Jacob called Joseph to his side, and gave him instruction as to the manner of his burial, suddenly the thread of his discourse was broken off, and as though in delirium, he began to speak of Rachel, who had died many years before. In distant Egypt, with the shadow of death already upon him, his spirit hovered over the lonely grave on the road to Bethlehem.

What explanation can be offered for this contact of the soul of the living with the dead, unless we admit the existence of that "something," soaring far above our atmosphere of cold reason, on the heights of fancy and presentiment?

What was the earnest wish that Jacob expressed upon his death-bed? He entreated Joseph to convey his body to the home of his youth, and there bury it beside his forefathers. The task imposed was no light one. Its execution demanded the assistance of quite a little army, for the way was long and difficult. In our days, the bodies of those wrecked off the far English coast were taken up from the bottom of the sea to be laid away to rest in the earth of home, in the western part of this country.

Is this the prompting of reason? Common-sense says: "Let grass grow over the graves. Let oblivion spring up in the hearts of those left on earth. As for the remains still visible to us, let them be removed from sight as soon as possible." Science offers its aid, and builds an oven for the speedy destruction of the body. And it would seem as though the spot in which dust is returned to dust ought to be a matter of indifference.

Is reason not right in its opinion? The world, however, from Jacob's time to the destruction of the *Schiller* in our own day, has refused to become reasonable on this point. It cannot be gainsaid, there is an immortal something "in heaven and earth," which was before our time, exists during our lives, and will continue to be after we have passed away. The deaf man has no conception of sounds, the blind man knows nothing of colors, so it may be that we live in the midst of glories for whose perception we have not the proper senses, and to understand which we lack intellectual strength so long as our *physical* existence continues, so long as the soul, hidden within the body, is limited to the perception of the things in this world.

What we call the future life is not a kingdom of heaven, a preternatural world entirely separate from this one. It forms one world with our own. As long as the soul wears its earthly garb, we can perceive only so much of it as our senses reveal to us, and intellect and reason teach us, and as a "something" tells us— something beyond the reach of intellect or reason. Like a disembodied spirit from another world, it flits across our consciousness; like lightning's flash, it illumines our souls; like a ghostly echo, like faint sounds dying away in the distance, it rouses vague thoughts within us.

A man may presume to doubt the existence of God; he may scoff at those that believe in the immortality of the soul and find comfort in this belief. He cannot argue out of existence that spiritual "something," spoken of by Shakespeare, soaring above the senses and beyond reason. Let him call it an incomprehensible something. To us, it is God and immortality.

XV

ADOLPH MOSES
The Reasons Why I Believe in God (1895)

I.

Let us begin our search after the rational grounds of our belief in God. Let us seek for proofs, if haply they may be found, that there exists an all-pervading, eternal Unity Divine which embraces both the universe and the soul. Let us try to bring into clear view cogent reasons for believing in a supreme Being, in an ultimate Reality and creative Energy of which matter and mind, force and will, the external world of nature and the inner world of consciousness, are perennial manifestations and purposeful self-revelations. Let us for the moment discard all preconceived beliefs and unbeliefs and in all seriousness and solemnity face the problem of problems, as if we were commissioned by mankind to find a solution to it; as if our age depended on us to give a satisfactory answer to the question, compared with which all other questions dwindle into utter insignificance.

We know two kinds of existence, the external material world of things, of objects, and the internal world of consciousness, of feelings, thoughts, ideas. The most awful mystery of all is this very mystery of existence itself. How comes there to be anything at all, matter and motion, atoms, forces, life inanimate and animate? How comes there to be feeling, sensation, thought, or consciousness? Space and infinitude, the home of all being, time and eternity, the stream in which all that exists and happens moves, rises to the surface and disappears; what are they, why are they, why can not we imagine them as non-existent? To be, the eternal, indestructible fact of being in general, of existence universal, beginningless, endless, continuous, that is the question.

We can by no effort of ours bring ourselves to deny that something exists somehow, somewhere. Even if we think that all things outside ourselves are unreal appearances, that this fair world, the heavens and the earth are merely a dream of our mind, yet we doubters and dreamers still exist. You can not think of a time when there was absolutely nothing in existence, nor are you able to think of a time when existence itself shall be annihilated. Take the wings of imagination and fly from star-system to star-system to the uttermost bounds of all known galaxies, beyond the region of the faintest and remotest cosmic cloud, even in the heart of eternal night and silence and cold you are still floating on the waves of being, and are unable to break away from your soul's inseparable companion, from the idea of omnipresent existence. Should you fancy space beyond all stellar regions to be absolutely empty, still space is left, space exists. You can put no bound to space in thought. Beyond the uttermost reach of imagination infinitude stretches, one, indivisible, eternal, pregnant with the seeds of star-births, heaving with the throbs of universal force. You can not conceive a limit set to force. You can not say, only to a certain point in space does it go and can not dart beyond a certain fixed boundary line. Where force is, there dwells being, there are beating the pulses of all-pervading energy. Being, then, has no limits in space or time. Existence is infinite and external. Well may the idea of infinite and eternal existence thrill us with religious awe, and cause us to observe towards it an attitude of speechless wonder. It is the simplest and surest and most universal fact. It is the tap-root of all truths. It underlies all thoughts.

Without the idea of existence nothing is imaginable, thinkable, nothing is possible. Yet it is the mystery of mysteries. We are so near it, it surrounds us, we live, move, and have our being in it. Still it is inscrutable. We are overwhelmed by the thought that whatever is has always been and forever will be. We prostrate ourselves before the unfathomable mystery that matter and force, the very atoms and energies with which we are everywhere in closest touch, of which we ourselves form a living part, have existed through boundless space from eternity to eternity. Before the race of man was born, before the sun, the moon, and the stars were formed, there was the same essence, the same indwelling power was moving through space, combining, dissolving, blossoming, bearing fruit, decaying and awakening to new life and activity through seeming death.

The same substance, the same force, the same laws existed on and on, indestructible, of the self-same identity, ere the universe blossomed into its present living harmony as at this very hour.

Some of the profoundest religious minds of former days have stood like us in worshiping awe before the unfathomable mystery of beginningless, endless, and universal being. They, too, wrestled with the attempt to comprehend the incomprehensible, to express the inexpressible. They adored the infinite and eternal being as the highest Being, as the only Reality. They worshiped it as the supreme Power behind all power, as the permanent essence behind all fleeting appearances. The Bible calls the supreme Being Yahve, "He who is, was, and forever will be." The Most High reveals himself to Moses as "I Am that I Am," "I Am, that is my name." In the theosophical speculations of the later Vedic poets the all-pervading, self-existent essence is worshiped under the name of Brahma. Some of the greatest Greek philosophers called God the Being, *to on,* or the true Being, *to ontos on.*

II.

We have so far considered the mystery of existence in itself, in a purely abstract way. We have been dealing only with the bare, though awe-inspiring, fact that something infinite and eternal does exist, that something, be it matter, force, mind, has always been, still is, and forever will be. But the question of questions is: Is all existence of one essence, are all forms of being one being, all forces one force, all manifestations of energy the outpourings of one eternal Energy? Are all minds lights reflected from the effulgence of one infinite Self? Does the chain of natural causes and effects begin and terminate in a highest cause, in an almighty cause of causes? Is there unity and identity of essence in all diversity of being and multiplicity of forms?

May it not be that every atom has from all eternity been an isolated self-existent being, an individual independent center of force? Thus there would be an infinity of eternal, uncaused existences. We would then have no principles of all-pervading, all-embracing unity which we are seeking and which is to be accounted the first cardinal attribute of the one only Being, of the ultimate Reality.

Nature, as known even to the most superficial observers, shows the assumption of an infinite number of unrelated atoms without any communication with one another to be the wildest of errors, the most senseless of all imaginable blunders. The universe does not present itself to the human mind as a host of countless self-imprisoned, unresponsive atoms and forces which have no relation to one another, which exert no influence upon one another, and do not mutually determine one another. If every atom were absolutely shut up within itself, if all were not bound up by an indwelling principle of unity, they would not be able to combine with and interpenetrate one another. There would be no change whatever. For all change is caused by the chemical marriage of atoms with atoms, of molecules with molecules, and by the thousand other influences which all elements exercise upon all others, be they near or far. There would be no room for the universal play of cause and effect, if there were no eternal kinship, no inborn love between all elements and forces. How could all the parts of the universe, the remotest and the nearest, be connected together as an harmonious whole by the interminable chain of cause and effect, if there subsisted no eternal relationship between them?

The law of causality is of universal validity and admits of no exception. The underlying principle of all science, the supreme truth, upon which all the systems of knowledge rest, is the indestructible belief, that nothing happens within the whole compass of existence, that nothing can take place in the life of nature and man, without an efficient cause. Every fact is the offspring of other facts which have gone before it and stand to it in the relation of parent cause, and every new fact must give birth to others which in their turn are bound to be the seeds of events to come. Nothing great or small that exists or occurs in the universe stands apart by itself, has the roots of its origin and activity in itself alone. Whatever is or happens is joined together by a chain of cause and effect with every part and force in nature and with the remotest past of the world's life. The whole present with all its countless phenomena, with all its multitudinous forms, is the child of the past by an endless succession of evolutions, which are bound up together and determined by the indestructible ties of universal causation. All the star myriads and the fulness thereof form a living harmony, a symphony of forces and movements, of action and interaction, of cosmic growth and fruit-bearing. They ebb and flow together with the all-penetrating currents of omnipresent causation. They are interlaced and intertwined by the unbreakable chains of universal order.

Now the question arises: Why must all kinds of existence obey the law of cause and effect? Why are all atoms, all things, all phenomena, all manifestations of force of every kind, held in the eternal embrace of causality? There must be an all-sufficient reason why all things must act and react upon one another. There must be an efficient reason why all particles of matter or atoms influence one another in a certain unalterable manner, why they combine with one another according to fixed laws which they can not transgress. Why is the behavior of all things toward all others subject to an unchangeable rule and order? On what ultimate ground does the law of causality rest?

It is clear that the law of their mutual behavior, the necessity of acting in a certain way in harmonious cooperation with one another, must lie in the original constitution of all the elements of nature.

Now, if the atoms were from all eternity self-centered individual beings, if they were absolutely the last elements and forms of existence behind which there is no higher reality and controlling power, how should they come to form among themselves those everlasting bonds of friendship, to establish the unchangeable laws of their conduct toward one another? Did all the atoms in the starless foretime once meet in counsel, and did they say to one another: "It will not do for us to remain forever in our state of single existence and unprofitable isolation. We must form an everlasting and perfect union. Let us establish among ourselves a covenant which shall not pass away. Let us unite our forces for ever higher ends. Let us lay down for ourselves inviolable laws to which we shall all yield unquestioning obedience. Let us regulate for all eternity our mutual relations. Let us give up our barren independence and through universal interdependence become fruitful, creative. Let the act of one always affect the others in a certain foreordained way. Let us combine and grow into suns, star-systems, earths, plants, animals, and at last flower into man, who shall translate our elemental compact into thought and call our unchangeable social contract the universal law of causality"?

Surely, the indissoluble unity which binds all atoms together into a living harmony, the immutable laws which hold absolute sway over them all, and determine with unfailing precision all their courses, combinations, dissolutions, evolutions, give proof that the atoms can not be separate and self-determined entities, that they can not be the last elements of existence. There can be but one conclusion: Behind all atoms there is one universal Reality, behind all special forms of existence there is one all-enfolding absolute Existence; behind all finite beings there is one infinite Being. All forces are the manifestations of one almighty Force. This supreme Reality, this infinite Essence and omnipotent Power, we call God. All the world-systems are borne in the same parental arms of this one creative Force. They all rest as children, grown or growing, against the bosom of the same infinite parent Power. All their vital energies and unfolding lives are but incarnations and transformations of the one self-identical Energy, inscrutable, all-sustaining, all-quickening, all-pervading. All atoms and aggregations of atoms must obey the eternal and immutable laws of the universal Self, because they are indwelling parts of it; because they live, move, and have their being in it. All nature proceeds from the same divine Essence; the whole Cosmos has blossomed forth from the same omnipotent Energy. Hence no atom, no finite part, no creature, no star can separate itself from the identity of the Almighty, can break away from the immanent modes and ways of infinite Life. The universal reign of law is nothing but the universal self-revelation of the One infinite and unchangeable Power which is forever at one with itself. The universal law of causality flows from the identity of the one omnipresent and omnipotent Being. The unity of nature springs from, and reflects, the unity of God.

III.

Our argument has so far led us only to the necessary belief in a universal, self-existent Essence, to the idea of an infinite, all-enfolding divine Unity, to the conception of an almighty Power which is the ultimate cause of all that is and happens. The truth which we have brought into light forms the first broad foundation on which all religion rests. And now there arises the most far-reaching of all questions and presses for an answer. Is the infinite and eternal Essence, the supreme Being, the omnipotent Power, an intelligent Essence, a rational Self, or is it merely an irrational entity, a blind force? It is clear that we could not adore a senseless Power, that we could not love a Being that lacks the attribute of reason. We might stand in awe and dread of the Universal power. We might at times crouch in abject fear before the manifestation of its deadly terrors. We might use all possible means to avoid coming into conflict with the inexorable ways of the almighty and omnipresent Being, lest we be crushed by a blow dealt us by its outstretched arm. We might view with speechless wonder the multitudinous forms of inanimate and animate life which the infinite Being assumes. We might with eager curiosity try to discover the immutable laws which govern the universe from center to circumference. But we could not worship and venerate that Power. We could not bow our head in humility before the Infinite as being higher and better than man. For the highest and noblest kind of existence, is reason, the divinest reality is the knowing mind, the most worshipful power is the purposeful will realizing the ends of goodness.

If the Infinite is not a spiritual Power, we are shut up to materialism. The wings of faith are cut. We can not escape from the prison of self and commune in sorrow and joy with the general Soul.

Now what proof have we that intelligence is a quality of the universal Essence, that the all-generating, all-sustaining Power is a conscious Self? My answer is: The existence of thinking and willing beings on our planet, the existence of consciousness in man, gives proof that the ground of all existence must be an intelligent Entity, that the almighty power, of which our minds are manifestations, can not but be a rational Energy.

Let us full earnestly consider that kind of existence which we call Consciousness. What is consciousness? What a question, you will reply. Consciousness is consciousness. This is the only term by which it can be expressed. It is the only definition we can give it. Sensation, feeling, perception, thought, are names denoting various manifestations, simple or complex, of the same unique phenomenon of consciousness. It is absolutely unlike any form of material being, it has no quality in common with any kind of external existence. For this reason consciousness can be stated only to be what it is—consciousness; to be identical with itself only and to have no affinity with anything else.

But is it indeed impossible to compare mind with some physical reality, be it matter or force? Let us just try. All things material have three dimensions, length, breadth, and height. Suppose you ask, How long, how broad, how high is consciousness? Why, you will say, Not even a madman can conceive such a question. Right enough: Is consciousness thick or thin, hard or soft? Is it in a solid, liquid, or gaseous state? Leave us alone, you will cry, with your crazy questions! The attributes of extension and density do not apply to mind. Well, we take note of this self-evident fact and will soon make use of it in our argument. What is the color of consciousness? Is it white, black, red, green, or yellow? Is consciousness warm or cold, sweet or bitter? You exclaim,

Stop putting to us such questions, which sound like the gibberish of madness. But your amazement, your vehement protests, simply make it as clear as noonday that none of the qualities of matter can be in thought ascribed to mind. Now, we know a thing, a being, exclusively by its qualities. Since mind and matter have so far been shown to have no quality in common, therefore they can not be compared with each other, they can not be placed in the same class. Consequently they can not be of the same essence and nature.

Again, consciousness can not be tasted nor smelled nor touched nor seen nor heard. The five senses have no access to it, they can not penetrate to it, receive impressions, combine them into qualities, and by such operations inform us what mind is. On the other hand, all we know of matter, of the world external to us, comes to us as a message of the senses. Without the senses matter of every kind and form would be absolutely unknown to us, the external world would simply have no existence for us. We would be wholly shut up within our self-consciousness. Again, we can not imagine consciousness to be identical with force, such as is manifested in the physical universe. We know force first of all and chiefly as motion appearing in moving bodies. Can you conceive consciousness as a sort of motion? I appeal to your own inward experience. Has feeling, willing, thinking, any feature in common with what we call motion, moving from place to place? Force under certain given conditions is changed from motion to heat. Can you realize in thought that consciousness is nothing but a form of heat? Well, force reveals itself also as electricity and magnetism. Is consciousness perhaps a species of electricity or magnetism? Try to think it out this very moment. Can you say to yourself: As I am observing my consciousness, I feel it to be like the electric currents in a battery or like the magnetic force? Why, your mind at once tells you, that identification is an unthinkable absurdity.

You have the direct and incontestable testimony of your mind that consciousness is absolutely unlike both matter and force. Yet consciousness undoubtingly exists. Your own self is consciousness. Your truest and inmost being is spirit or soul. Whence comes our consciousness? From what ground did consciousness spring? Our minds form part of the universal existence. It did not rise into being by itself and through itself. Our spirit must have its origin and existence in the universal existence. It can not be the offspring of matter and motion or force, because it is in every respect different from them. Only like begets like.

You can by no effort of imagination or thought bring yourself to realize that your mind is nothing but a species of matter or, what amounts to the same thing, a product of matter. You are absolutely unable to think of feeling and will as a peculiar form of heat, electricity, or motion. On this head Professor Huxley writes in his inimitable style: "It seems to me pretty plain, that there is a third thing in the universe, to wit, consciousness, which in the hardness of my heart and head I can not see to be matter, or force, or any conceivable modification of either, however intimately the manifestations of the phenomena of consciousness may be connected with the phenomena known as force."

Since consciousness can be derived from neither matter nor force, we are driven to the conclusion, that it must have its ground and origin in something which is like it, namely, in a superhuman consciousness or a universal mind. Human consciousness can not have sprung into existence out of nothing. For nothing will in all eternity bring forth nothing. We dare not say that mind has from eternity to eternity existed only as human consciousness, as spirit in man. For there was surely a time when the human race had as yet no existence. There was, beyond a doubt, a time, when the earth had not yet been formed and become a fit dwelling-place for rational beings. Mind must, therefore, have existed in the universe before the birth of animals and men on our globe. The conclusion is thus forced upon us that intelligence is an eternal reality. We can not say that it exists only as an isolated phenomenon in some part of the universe and nowhere else. For the universal and infinite existence is one being and power, forever and everywhere identical with its own self; it would, therefore be the height of absurdity to ascribe consciousness to only a part of the Infinite, seeing that the Infinite consists of no separate parts but is an absolute, self-identical Unity, all whose manifestations are revelations of its hidden essence, and self-hood. The infinite and eternal Existence and Power, whom we call God, is thus shown to be a conscious Being or a universal Intelligence, the fountainhead of all consciousness in finite existence. The conclusion of the matter, then: The Eternal is a spiritual Being.

IV.

The argument has, however, not yet fully satisfied you. Your doubts have not yet been completely dispelled. The greatest of all difficulties is still obstructing your path towards a rational belief in an intelligent supreme Power. How can we possibly believe in a universal mindlike Being? How can mind exist without a nervous system, without a brain? All mind-life, which we know of, appears in connection with nerves, and the most highly-developed intelligence is indissolubly bound up with the central organ of the nervous system, the brain. If you destroy a man's brain, his mind manifests its existence in no manner whatever. Let a man's brain be seriously injured, and he becomes a maniac or will sink into a state of death-like sleep. When the heart ceases to beat and no longer sends the current of vitalizing blood to the brain, the body dies and with it the mind seems to vanish into nothing. How, then, are we to believe that the supreme Being is a conscious entity? For the blasphemous idea must of course be ruled out, that there is somewhere in the world a gigantic divine brain communicating with every part of the universe by means of an all-pervading nervous system.

To minds not trained in philosophical thinking, to minds not accustomed to rise above the analogies of sense-experience, these objections appear fatal to the belief in a conscious, absolute, and infinite Being. They are the main considerations, why so many men who implicitly trust their own rough and ready judgments regarding what is possible or impossible, have to their own hearts' grief come to imagine that they do not believe in God.

It is a mistake that the manifestations of feeling and will are absolutely dependent on that peculiar organization of matter called nerves. There are innumerable forms of exceedingly small animate beings, termed microbes, which do not show the faintest trace of nerves. They possess no organs internal and external of any kind. Yet these tiny structureless and nerveless creatures plainly exhibit the phenomena of feeling and willing. They pursue their prey, seize and devour it. They become aware of danger and try to escape from it. By such and similar actions they give unmistakable evidence of discerning and volitional impulses. These facts clearly prove that feeling and willing which are the web and woof of all mind-life can exist without any nervous apparatus. If nerves and brain were the absolute condition and ultimate cause of all mental phenomena, the existence of sentient creatures devoid of nerves and brain would be an utter impossibility. But you will object and say: "Those creatures lowest in the scale of animate life display but the dimmest and most shadowy beginnings of feeling and willing. All developed intelligence, all consciousness deserving that name, is invariably found in closest connection with a brain. The more highly developed a creature's brain, the greater is its mentality. The intelligence of man is immeasurably superior to that of all other living beings, just because his brain is more perfect, more finely organized than theirs. If the world-ground is intelligent, it must be mind of the highest kind, infinitely superior to the human mind. But how can we reconcile the belief in a universal intelligence with the facts of experience which tell us, that there is no consciousness without a brain?"

To this I reply: If the brain could ever be shown to explain the existence of consciousness, your reasoning would have some force. If science could ever demonstrate, how matter organized as brain brings forth mind out of what is not itself mind, there would be some show of reason for asserting that the brain is the parent cause of consciousness and hence that mental life is impossible where the assumed creative force is absent. But will the most minute and thorough knowledge of the structure and composition of the brain ever enable us to say: "We clearly see and observe, how the brain manufactures thought. There is no longer any mystery about the origin and nature of mind"? Suppose we should even succeed in fixing upon the exact spot and the special cells of the brain in which each particular thought takes its rise. Suppose science should one day be able to make visible to the eye every wave and tremor in the brain substance accompanying every thought. Suppose physiology should one day bring into clear view the peculiar set of molecular and chemical changes which occur in the substances of the brain, while a certain set of ideas is passing through the mind. Still such knowledge would in no way explain the existence of consciousness. It would in no possible manner show, how the molecules of matter making up the brain can produce mind which is absolutely unlike matter. For the brain is after all no more nor less than highly organized matter. Over eighty per cent. of the brain substance is made up of the elements of hydrogen and oxygen, which, chemically combined, form water. Nitrogen, sulphur, carbon, iron and other elements are the materials out of which an inscrutable Power has builded the glorious dwelling of the mind, the brain. Now, we have shown that consciousness can not be identified with matter and motion, that it is impossible to conceive of mind as a modification or product of either. Matter in the form of brain still remains matter. It can not transcend its essence and quality and be changed from what matter is throughout the universe, and by virtue of organization give birth to mind. Since, then, the brain does not explain the existence of consciousness and can not be regarded as the generating source of mind, we have no right to hold that under no possible conditions can consciousness exist without a brain, and that consequently the infinite ground of being can not be believed to be intelligent. All that we may say is that under the given terrestrial conditions, as far as we know, intelligence of the higher kind invariably appears in closest connection and interaction with a brain, that the finite human mind, while incarnate in a body, manifests itself through the agency of a complete nervous system centered in a brain. But our sense-bound experience does not justify us in laying it down as a universal and absolute law, that it is impossible for mind to exist outside of a brain.

Our experience alone does not suffice to decide with apodictic certainty what is possible and what is impossible. How shall we determine that something is absolutely impossible? Innumerable things for ages have been universally believed to be impossible which a larger experience has proved to be possible. To talk and be heard at a distance of thousands of miles, but a few years ago seemed to be an impossibility. Yet the telephone has made it possible. To catch the dread force of electricity, to make it carry man's message from one end of the earth to the other with incredible swiftness, to harness lightning like a horse to our wagon, to heat up our dwellings and cook our meals, till recent times was deemed utterly impossible. In Columbus' time no human being considered it possible to cross the Atlantic in iron ships, in less than six days, without the use of sails. In biblical times it was held impossible to measure the earth and weigh it in balances. In our days the length, height, and depth, the weight and density of the sun, moon, and every planet are perfectly well known. Spectroscopy has in our days made possible what two centuries ago was regarded as a self-evident impossibility. The human mind can nowadays ascertain with scientific exactness the number and nature of the atomic elements present not only in our sun but in the remotest stars, whose light travels six thousand years before reaching our globe. The idea of changing air into a liquid and even turning it into a solid till recent times was denied by the strongest evidence of experience. Yet the testimony of experience, so long accepted with unquestioning faith by all men, in these days of ours has proved to be fallacious. According to the data of our given experience it is impossible to transform coal, stones, and other materials into food for man and animals. Yet the science of chemistry, which is still in its infancy, will probably one day be able to change inorganic matter into organic means of subsistence. Countless other things which are now universally believed to be beyond the range of possibility, one day will come to be well-known realities exciting as little surprise as the telegraph and telephone.

What, then, is eternally and absolutely impossible? That which is absolutely unthinkable, which is an irreconcilable contradiction to the indestructible categories of our mind. That is *a priori* impossible which is at war with the inborn ideas of the soul. The most fundamental of these innate ideas is: It is impossible for anything to spring from nothing. The law of universal causality, the necessary belief that nothing can exist or happen without a sufficient cause, is but another expression of the same innate idea. Hence, it is an absolute impossibility that matter in any imaginable form, matter in the guise of nerve and brain, should be the parent cause of mind. Matter having no quality whatever in common with thought, the rise of consciousness out of it would be a new creation out of nothing, which is unthinkable.

Still both matter and mind exist. Neither can be identified with the other, nor can they be derived from each other. The two worlds, the inner world of consciousness and the external world of objects, seem to fall apart. In spite of their intimate relations and interactions these two eternal forms of existence seem separated by a yawning chasm with no bridge leading from one to the other. They face each other as irreconcilable contrasts. Materialism can by no tricks of sophistical reasoning drive mind from its position as a self-existing entity. Idealism can not deny matter and prove it to be a mere illusion. But the human mind can not rest in such dualism. The soul finds no peace in a world divided in itself. The very root of all knowledge is the indestructible and immediate belief that the universe forms a unity, that the soul is co-related to the world in all its parts, that all being is of one source, of one essence, of one energy. The very ground of all knowledge is the innate belief that behind the inner world of consciousness, and behind the phenomena of the world of objects, there is Divine Unity in which they are both embraced and in which their differences are reconciled and disappear. This belief in an all-pervading and all-enfolding Unity which binds together matter and mind in a supreme harmony, underlies all thought. This one Being reveals Himself as nature, and manifests Himself and is present in us as mind. In Him we live, move, and have our being. Yet He transcends both the human mind and nature. He is infinite and absolute. He is not circumscribed by the conditions within which matter exists. He is not circumscribed by the limitations which bound our intelligence.

XVI

ADOLPH MOSES

"Who Is the Real Atheist?" (1893)

Time was—and that time does not by any means belong to a remote past—when atheism was regarded as the most heinous crime of which a human being could render himself guilty. To be accused of atheism meant to be dragged before the tribunal of the state, as was done in the days of antiquity, or before the bar of an ecclesiastical court, as was the practice during the Middle Ages and for nearly two centuries after the Reformation, there to be arraigned as the worst of criminals, compared with whom even a murderer seemed to be an angel of innocence. If convicted, and an atheist was rarely acquitted, he was condemned to die a felon's death. The curses of the community followed him to the place of execution. No tombstone was allowed to mark his resting place. One suspected of atheism was shunned like a leper, and hated as if he were a fiend incarnate. Yet how many glorious champions of truth, how many path-finders of humanity, how many saints of the earth, whose noble lives were the best indications of the belief in a God of holiness, have been persecuted with merciless fanaticism as atheists, as the worst enemies of the human race!

The Greek philosopher Anaxagoras, who taught the profoundest of all religious doctrines, that the universe was shaped into purposeful harmony by an All-wise and Almighty Mind, being accused of atheism was thrown into prison, from which he secretly escaped and then fled from Athens in hot haste. Even his powerful friend Pericles could not protect him against the suspicion and the hatred of the masses. Socrates, the wisest and most pious of all Greeks, whose philosophy marks an epoch in the history of the human mind, and whose life came to be to the Hellenic world what that of Jesus is to Christendom, was condemned by an Athenian jury as an atheist, and in his seventieth year compelled to drink the cup of deadly hemlock. Giordano Bruno, on the 17th of February, 1600, was burned in Rome as an enemy of God. And yet that reputed atheist taught that God is the unity of the universe, the universal substance, the one and only principle, the efficient and final cause of all, the beginning, middle, and end, eternal and infinite. Spinoza, whom Schleiermacher called "a God-intoxicated man," he who ascribed real existence to God alone, declaring all finite beings to be mere manifestations of the Infinite and Absolute, was not only excommunicated by his own co-religionists, but was until recent times universally regarded with horror and hatred as the worst and most dangerous of atheists. The Jews were loathed by the pagans as a people that believed in no God. So utterly fallible and so baneful in its effects has the world's judgment in all times and among all nations proved to be, as regards atheists and atheism. As a rule the so-called atheists of one age become the venerated religious teachers and spiritual guides of after ages. Those that perished amid the execrations of their generation came to live transfigured in the mind and heart of later generations as types of an ideal humanity.

The fact of the matter is, no original thinker, no genuine seeker after truth, has ever been a real atheist. The alleged atheists simply differed more or less profoundly from the theology of those who passed judgment upon them. The Greek philosophers who were indicted on a charge of atheism, did not believe in the Olympian gods, holding as they did monotheistic views. The Jews were hated by the heathen world as atheists, for the reason that they denied the existence of the gods of the Gentiles. Similarly, the men that were hunted down and brought to an untimely end as atheists in Christian lands, only rejected certain dogmas, held by the established churches to be essential principles of faith, without which it was believed religion would be destroyed.

Again, most scientists are reproached by over-zealous theologians with being atheists and teaching atheism. "You teach an atheistic science," they cry. "You leave God out of your astronomy, your geology, chemistry, botany, zoology, and physiology. No mention is ever made in any of your writings of the Maker of heaven and earth." Only blundering stupidity, going hand in hand with blind intolerance, can speak thus. It is not within the province of science to teach religion or metaphysics, to prove the facts of experience by referring them to the highest and last cause, to trace all phenomena back to the ultimate ground of existence. There is certainly no religious mathematics, there is no room for God in a treatise on geometry. The engineer who elaborated his plan for the Brooklyn bridge, was not expected to start with the premise, that all the physical laws on which he based his calculations, measurements, and adjustments, were perennial manifestations of an infinite, eternal, and immutable power, that we worship as God.

It is the sole office of the investigator of nature to ascertain by conscientious observation and careful experiments all the knowable facts within the range of his experience, to arrange them in the order of their closer or remoter relationship, to find the bond of union which binds them all together into a systematic whole, to discover the laws, according to which they live, move, and have their being. It is the function of science to drive the notion of accident and caprice from her entire territory, to show every physical event as flowing of necessity from a preceding physical event as its cause, to demonstrate that no phenomenon in nature stands apart for itself, but forms a necessary part of the whole order of the universe, to connect by a chain of cause and effect whatever is or happens in the present with the remotest possible past of the heavens above and the earth beneath or the waters under the earth. Science is neither theistic nor atheistic. It is as little religious or irreligious as cooking, building, sewing, or plowing. It deals only with what is within the ken of the senses, and its boldest conclusions and theories in the last resort go back to what the senses bear testimony to. Science proper has nothing to do with what is supersensual or beyond the reach of the senses. It does not meddle with questions relating to the origin of things, nor does it extend its inquiry to the ultimate ground of all being. It is exactly where science ends that philosophy begins. The subject matter of philosophy is the infinite and absolute, the eternal ground of all existence, the inscrutable power behind all phenomena, the cause of all causes, the beginning, the middle, and the end of all existence, that which alone is, was, and forever will be. The existence of the Infinite and Absolute is to all systems of philosophy the highest and most certain of all truths.

The idea of the Eternal is incomparably more incontrovertible than the several finite things which we may touch, taste, or smell. The Infinite is to philosophy the only true reality, while the finite is regarded by it as enigmatic, doubtful. And shall we decry these supreme philosophical ideas as rank atheism, because the philosophers prefer to call the eternal source and cause of all existence the Infinite and Absolute, instead of calling it by the name of God? The Hebrew name Yahve, He that is, was, and will be, He that causes all being, corresponds exactly to the philosophic term of Infinite and Absolute. The philosophy of Spinoza, the best hated and calumniated of all reputed atheists, ought to be called, according to Hegel, Acosmism, the doctrine of the nothingness of the world, while reality is ascribed to God or the Infinite alone. What is true of Spinoza holds good of all philosophers, from Thales down to Herbert Spencer. None of them was an atheist, popular prejudice and priestly fanaticism notwithstanding.

"But have not your philosophers," some of you might ask, "asserted over and over again, that we can not prove the existence of God? Has not your master Kant used the gigantic powers of his mind, to demolish, one after another, all the time-honored proofs of the existence of God?" It is not in wisdom that you ask thus. It is because Kant and other thinkers of equal originality stood like Moses face to face with the Eternal and Infinite, that they wished to show that all theistic arguments are either untenable or insufficient. How can we prove that which itself the proof of everything else, upon which all other truths hang, without which all knowledge would be vanity and a striving after wind? To prove means to trace back what is uncertain and doubtful to what is certain and beyond a doubt, to explain the unknown by referring it back to what is known, by showing it to be akin to what is recognized and understood. But this process of proving must at last reach a limit. We must finally arrive at something, a proposition or cognition, which we can not demonstrate, because there is nothing beyond it, in which it might be included or to which it might be linked. It is the supreme truth, the most certain and immediate of all cognitions, it is the foundation upon which all other verities rest, and without the recognition of which all truth vanishes. It can neither be proved nor does it require proof. "The idea of God or the Infinite is this most general truth, which can not be reduced to a more general one. It is the deepest truth to which we can get. It can not be explained, it is inexplicable, unaccountable."

But what of materialism, is it not atheism? Are there not philosophers who derive all life from the lowest to the highest from matter and motion, and deny the existence of mind or anything akin to mind in the universe? My answer is, no serious thinker in our days holds such views. Materialism has been refuted and exploded as a theory of the universe. It does not account for the existence of mind in man and animals. How can mind, which is absolutely different from matter and motion, be the offspring of matter or the child of motion? We can by no effort of thought conceive how matter and motion could be changed from what they are and be transformed into consciousness. It is simply unthinkable. And if all matter is believed to have an inner side to it, to be endowed with the qualities of feeling and the dim germs of thought, then it is no longer matter, but something else, something higher. From whichever point of view we look at it, philosophical atheism turns out to be a mere fiction, a mere delusion of theological zealots.

But who are the real atheists? They whose *conduct* belies their belief in the existence of God, whose *life* forms a glaring contrast to the idea of God. The belief in a God is not simply the highest and most certain of all truths, it is also the greatest and most potent moral idea. The idea of God implies the idea of divine perfection and absolute goodness. God and goodness are synonymous, interchangeable terms. If we believed that God was not goodness, we might fear Him, but we could not adore Him. A good man would appear to us more worshipful than He. Religion and philosophy agree in holding that morality is the highest manifestation of the Infinite in and through the soul of man. Whatever we may think of its origin and development, as it is, it doubtless is the most glorious incarnation of the inscrutable Power, of the Universal Self. To believe in God does not mean that we simply allow that He exists, it means that we strive to walk in the luminous footsteps of His holiness, to walk in the ways of His justice, truth, and mercy. Every virtuous action is a true act of worship. To curb our passions in obedience to the laws divine engraved upon the tablet of our hearts is the grandest homage paid to the idea of God. To smite and overthrow the vaulting instincts of selfishness, in order to serve the common good of all, is the strongest proof that a God of goodness inspires the breast of man. He is an atheist who professes to believe in God but whose deeds put his faith to shame. He who declares that he considers the Ten Commandments a revelation of God and yet violates one and all, he is the real atheist. He who acknowledges that we should recognize no other God beside the Eternal, and yet worships his own poor self as the highest being and places his own interests and pleasures above the highest interests and aims of humanity, he is a real atheist. He who perjures himself, who swears a false oath or utters lies to obtain profit or gain favor, he does practically deny God, he demonstrates that he does not believe in Him "that will not let him go unpunished that taketh His name in vain." Whoever fails to honor his father and mother as the representatives of God on earth, whoever in heartless selfishness neglects his aged parents and refuses to surround their declining years with blessings and comforts, he is an atheist, though he daily bend his knee in adoration to God and sound His praises in the midst of the assembly. He that makes of himself a slave of Mammon, who, in his greed to amass wealth, lets the higher powers of his mind and heart run to waste, verily he is an atheist, he does by his conduct prove that he does not believe man to be a child and image of the Most High, destined to pattern his life upon that of Divine perfection. He that defrauds his neighbors in any matter great or small, who uses false weights and false measures, is an atheist: he does not believe in a God that hates deception and injustice. He is an atheist that deprives the hireling of his wages, and takes away from the needy the fruit of his labor. That man is indeed an atheist, who robs the substance of his fellow-men by violating the laws of the land, or by bribing legislatures to enact wicked laws to favor his iniquitous schemes. Jay Gould[*] was an atheist, although he belonged to a church and was buried by three ordained ministers. Whoever sacrifices duty and conscience to his passions, is a rank atheist. That priest at the altar is an atheist, that teacher of righteousness and faith, whose heart burns with the unholy fire of lust. Though he make many genuflections and lift his eyes in prayer to Heaven, he does deny God in his sinful soul.

All those were real atheists who persecuted their fellow-men on account of their faith, who tortured and murdered the children of God in the name of God. Torquemada and Arbues were atheists, in spite of the fact that they scourged their bodies and sang many litanies in honor of their God. That ruler is an atheist and an enemy of God who grinds the faces of the poor and needy, who oppresses men on account of race and religion, who deprives human beings of the right to earn a livelihood, who withholds from them the means of acquiring knowledge and leading the lives of human beings. The Czar of Russia is an atheist, although he is at the head of the National Church; his wicked counselors deny God, because they rebel against the laws of Divine justice.

[*Jay Gould (1836–1892), American financier and railroad owner, had the reputation of being a "financial preditor" and a conspirator in causing the "Black Panic" of September 1869 on Wall Street.]

He is an atheist who calls darkness light and evil good, who praises the despot, who drives mothers with their babies out of their homes in midwinter, and causes many infants to die of cold and starvation. The irreverend Dr. Talmage[*] is an atheist, though Sunday after Sunday he cuts capers in his pulpit, and calls himself the servant of God. The God of truth and justice is not in his heart, else he could not call a tyrant a benefactor of his people, who causes infinite woe and misery through-out the length and breadth of his land. All those teachers of religion are atheists, the Stoeckers and the Rohlings,[†] who on Sundays preach from their pulpits, "Love thy enemy as thyself," but soon as they step out of their church, do preach and practice hatred and malice, spread calumnies and baneful falsehoods, and excite in the breasts of the masses vile and bloodthirsty passions.

Whoever holds that a man can be religious without trying to be absolutely just, truthful, and merciful toward all men, denies and blas-phemes God. Whoever treats his fellow-men with contempt, and deems them unworthy of associating with him on account of race or religion, is an atheist, because he practically denies that all men are children of one Heavenly Father, who loves them all and whose majesty resides in them all. It is on account of such practical atheism that the cries of the depressed and down-trodden are heard. Such atheism is the parent of infinite woe and misery. Such practical atheism has drenched the earth with the tears and the blood of the innocent. Alas, how many are entirely free from practical atheism? Ministers and laymen, men and women, Gentiles and Israelites, one way or another deny God in their conduct. Oh, let us not glory in the religious doctrines we hold, let us not boast of the principles of faith which we profess. By our fruits alone let us prove that we believe in an all-just, all-wise, and all-merciful God. Let us gird our loins in strength and strive to establish the king-dom of God, the kingdom of righteousness and love on earth. Let us endeavor to make our lives symbols of the perfection of God.

[*Rev. Thomas DeWitt Talmage (1832–1902) was a leading Evangelist in Brooklyn and in Washing-ton, D.C., who visited and praised Czar Nicholas and his family, calling them exemplary Christians at the time they were mercilessly persecuting Jews, and maintained that Jews should clamor for "rights" in Russia rather than emigrate to America.]

[†Nineteenth-century figures Adolf Stoecker and August Rohling were, respectively, a German pas-tor and a Prussian priest-professor who advocated proto-Nazi racism and preached virulent anti-Semitism and anti-Judaism.]

XVII

ADOLPH MOSES
Why I Studied Medicine (1893)

The fact that I have for the last five or six years given whatever time I could spare from the arduous and absorbing duties of the ministry to the study of medicine; the fact, moreover, that the University of Louisville has lately honored me with the diploma of a physician, gives the public the right to inquire, and makes it incumbent upon me to explain, why I have so long devoted time, labor, and thought to a field of knowledge that seems to lie out of all relation to that of religion, which it is my calling assiduously to cultivate. It may surprise you to be told that it was from religious motives, from an intense craving of my soul to obtain a direct answer to certain perplexing questions, that I pursued a course of study that must have appeared to you absolutely useless to a preacher of righteousness, to a teacher of faith in a living God of wisdom and mercy.

Religion and science, the priests of atheism assure us with an air of infallibility, are antagonistic powers. The more diligently you investigate nature according to the strict methods of scientific inquiry, they say, the more readily will faith lose its hold on your mind. They cry: "As long as nature is to you a book sealed with seven seals you will be able to hold fast to the traditional belief in a universal supreme intelligence, incarnate in all existence as the creative and purposeful cause of causes. But as soon as you have learned to open the volume of nature and to read the eternal facts writ therein by the hand of necessity, your faith in the kinship of nature with mind will vanish as an illusion and a dream." Listening to such assertions, I said to myself: "Let me examine for myself, whether a deeper and wider knowledge of nature does indeed teach the rank atheism which is alleged to be the last outcome of science. Let me learn to know as thoroughly and minutely as possible what modern science has ascertained regarding the physical framework of man, which is doubtless the highest manifestation of the universal energy, the last and most perfect fruit that has grown in the world-garden on the topmost branch of the tree of life. Should the study of the anatomical structure and the physiological life of the human body force upon me the conviction, that the world of nature is absolutely different from the world of mind, that there is in the former no trace of the presence and activity of intelligence, I will with an aching heart, yet in obedience to my honest conviction, give up the calling of a minister, which presupposes the belief in an absolute and infinite wisdom of which both nature and the human soul are perennial revelations."

Today, after years of converse with the highest forms of nature, I make the solemn declaration that such converse has made me more genuinely religious than ever, that I have come forth from communion with nature firmly convinced that a supreme intelligence, passing man's understanding, is manifest in the masterpiece of creation, in the human body! Oh, happy hours that I spent in thy temple, O Science, hours of blessedness and prayerfulness, when my spirit felt itself near the creative spirit of the universe, when my soul sang joyfully, "I am wonderfully and fearfully made, O Lord. Verily the body of man is the sanctuary which Thy infinite wisdom has formed. When I consider Thy wondrous work, this mortal frame of mind, which Thy will has fashioned, my spirit is overwhelmed within me, and my whole being bends in adoration to Thee." Life's mystery of mysteries has embodied itself in us, and is become flesh of our flesh, bone of our bone. The infinite Self has woven on the loom of time the living garment of our soul. His creative thoughts have entered as warp and woof into the texture of our corporeal being.

The bony framework, which sustains and bears all, which shelters all vital parts and defends them against contact with surrounding evil, is itself the marvel of marvels, an inconceivably perfect piece of mechanism. What wise adaptation of means to ends there is observable in the whole and in every part! All the laws of mechanics and statics have been called into requisition to build up what is the most elegant and at the same time the most durable, the strongest and yet the most pliant of structures. What seem insurmountable difficulties offered by the law of gravitation are overcome by contrivances incredibly cunning and yet simple withal. Natural obstacles to locomotion are turned into aids facilitating locomotion. Every possible emergency is provided for, every contingency and danger are [is] foreseen and guarded against. There is the nicest adjustment of every part to the whole, the most harmonious cooperation of all the parts to bring about the desired result. Every smallest spot, every elevation and depression, every ridge and groove is put to excellent use, and, in most cases, is made to serve more than one purpose. Every arrangement known to the most advanced science of applied mechanics finds its prototype in the framework of man. And this framework is covered over with a garment of living tissue that can not but fill the contemplative mind with worshipful wonder.

Will I ever forget those hours of rapture and prayerful wonder, when under the guidance of a masterful teacher in the morning, and with the dissecting knife in the evening, I learned to know and understand the marvelous system of muscular bands and ties and clasps which bind and knit together the whole body, and enable it to perform innumerable kinds of co-ordinated motions and purposeful motions, which give it the power to walk and run, to stand up and to sit down, to breathe and articulate sound, to vail or unvail the eye, to grasp and loosen the hand? Who but a designing mind can have directed muscles, at what point they shall take rise, along what lines they shall spread, and at what particular spot they shall fasten their ends, in order to perform their office with the least effort and with the best result? I can not shake off the conviction that it was a creative purpose which gave birth to these remarkable groups of twin muscles, those pairs of correlated and mutually counteracting muscles, of which one invariably bends when the other unbends, one stiffens while the other contracts. Marvelous are the works of the Eternal, and this my soul knows full well!

The muscular system is infinitely more wonderful than the solar system. It bewilders the mind to consider the countless adjustments of means to ends; to contemplate the living unity of purpose which binds all the parts together and causes all their several movements to blend and make the graceful rhythm of vital harmony. I am overawed by, and stand in speechless humility before, the mysterious power inherent in the muscles to contract and retract, to lengthen out and harden at the bidding of the will or in obedience to commands issued by unconscious centers of authority. Who can help believing in an incarnated universal intelligence, as the hidden wonders of the muscular structure unfold themselves under the microscope before his gaze? What no eye has seen and no mind had dreamed of is disclosed therein as the divine architecture, which out of countless myriads of tiniest cells builds up wonderful structures, able to bear the greatest strains, and to perform during three score years and ten and upward an incredible amount of vital work. Invisible to the naked eye, every individual fibre is revealed by the magnifying lense as a most complex organism lying sheltered in a sheath of its own and separated by it from the rest. Millions of fibres are associated together wrapped in a special covering, which welds them together into a unity, and isolates them from the surrounding bundles. And all the thousands of bundles are compacted together into a still higher organic unity of the muscle, enfolded in a living garment which divides off, and keeps its vital functions apart from, the adjacent tissues.

And between the minutest parts there run innumerable tiny rills of blood, bringing nourishment to every cell, overlooking none, forcing their way to the most hidden and remote. The sacred rivers of God, the life-bearing streams of blood, that issue from the lake of the heart, and in rhythmic cadences flow along the foreordained paths to the place whence they flow, whither they are ever returning to flow again! The spirit of Creation is moving over their red waves! By day and by night they hasten with sleepless activity from place to place, bearing in midstream the red purveyors of the vital breath and the white carriers of life-renewing food. To every cell they come like loving mothers to their nurslings, to refresh the faint and to feed the hungry. To each they offer that kind of nourishing substance which it craves and needs for its maintenance and sustenance. To the muscle they give what will make muscle, to the eye what will form eye, to the brain what will transform itself into nerve and brain matter. It is inconceivable to me that accident, blindly groping, blindly striving, could have mixed and combined the elements making up the blood current, and determined their due proportions.

Were there no other witness in nature, the heart alone would testify to searching faith that an Eternal Will organizes itself as an intelligent and intelligible purpose in the living forms of creation. Whatever the fanatical priests of materialism may assert to the contrary, our reason refuses to believe that an organ as marvelously perfect as the heart can be the product of blind mechanical causes. The heart dwells central in the microcosm of the body as the perennial fountain of life. It is nestled between the lungs that are its life-long associates and co-workers in the holy office of keeping the vital stream wholesome and rich. The inscrutable power inherent in nature, which makes for progress and vital perfection, has brought together what in lower orders of animal life form two distinct and separate hearts, and welded them together into an organic unity, making one perfect organ out of twain. Each half, the right and left heart, still discharges as in the early days of tentative creation its own special function in the household of the body, but being incorporate into each other they beat with one pulsation and throb with the same rhythmic alteration of activity and rest. From every part of the body, from the remotest nooks and corners, the blood, which has done its service in feeding and oxygenating the tissues, returns dark in color, short of vital breath, panting after life-renewing air. The rills of venous blood gather themselves into brooks, the brooks swell to many streams, the streams unite into two mighty rivers, which, one from above and the other from below, fall into the upper chamber of the right heart. At the same time the beautiful air-laden, red blood flows from the lungs through four channels into the upper chamber of the left heart. A shock, a quiver, and the dark mass descends into the lower chamber of the right heart, and the red fluid goes down into the lower chamber of the left heart.

Why does not the blood on either side return backward, thereby to cause disease and bring on premature death? Because the universal creative mind has prepared gates and bars which shut of themselves and prevent the blood from surging back and working havoc. Another shock and quiver more powerful than the first, and lo and behold, both halves contract and stiffen, driving the dark blood to the right into the lungs to be purified and renewed by receiving the precious burden of the vital air, and to the left, sending the red stream of life-bringing blood through the broad aortic channel, thence to rush onward, dividing and sub-dividing as it passes on. But why do not both of these streams, after ascending, fall back into the cavity from which they rose? Because the all-wise creative Self put on either side wondrous curtains, which, immediately, after the uprushing of the blood, join themselves together and allow not one drop to return. Within the brief space of twenty seconds all the blood has flown in a circle through the whole body, issuing from the heart through one of its gates, and returning through another. And this tremendous activity the heart carries on by day and by night, in summer and winter, in spring and in autumn, during seventy, eighty or ninety or even a hundred years, and in some few persons even a hundred and twenty years and longer. The heart never takes a rest like the other organs of the body. Were it to sleep but a few minutes, there would be no awakening to the whole body. Yet it sleeps by snatches. After each pulsation there is a moment of silence and sleep. During this brief interval of rest the blood comes to it to feed it and give it strength to take up its all-important work again. Marvelous as is the heart in itself as a master-piece of creative art, no less wonderful are the intimate functional relations which it bears to every part and organ of the body, and most especially to the lungs. The whole body appears as a systematic unity with the heart as its vital center, from which life radiates in every direction to the outermost boundary of the periphery, and toward which all activities far and near are converging.

The very existence and the structure of the lungs are comprehensible only in reference to the service which they render to the heart and through it to the circulation of the blood. They are manifestly means fashioned by an all-wise Will to serve a purposed end; they are made to convey the life-sustaining air from the atmosphere without to the hidden recesses of the heart, and at the same time to carry away the poison from within produced by the self-combustion of the blood. Had not the thousand dissecting hands of science laid bare, and her thousand magnifying eyes made visible, all the minutest arrangements and hidden marvels of the pulmonary structure, the human mind would not believe it, that an organ so ingeniously constructed, so perfectly adapted to a special end, could exist in nature. In the cave of the mouth, where the back wall meets the floor, there begins a tube, the trachea or windpipe, which being composed of alternate rings of soft tissue and cartilage, is at once most firm and most elastic, capable of expanding and narrowing, of lengthening and shortening, to suit the requirements of its functions. As it descends deeper and deeper and reaches the lungs, it enters them through an open door. Along with it there are admitted its faithful companions: the pulmonary artery, bringing the dark blood for aeration; the veins taking the purified blood to the heart; the nerves, to energize every part and guide every movement. The tube splits up into two branches, one going to the right lung, the other to the left. Each branch divides into many limbs, the limbs sub-divide into hundreds of twigs, each twig branches off into thousands of twiglets, each twiglet leads into a narrow court into which numerous little chambers—the air cells—open. Between the exceedingly thin walls, which separate and unite neighboring air cells, there spreads a bewildering network of tiny rills and lakelets of dark blood. About twenty times every minute a current of air rushes in through the wide corridor of the trachea, enters every passage, penetrates to every court, and fills every air chamber. The inflated lungs expand, the elastic ribs fly apart to make room, the diaphragm descends, giving way below. Meanwhile one of nature's great miracles takes place. The air and the blood meet in the air chambers, separated like lovers by a thin partition wall. The air gives off its precious gift of oxygen, which passes through the wall to mingle with the blood. The blood again willingly yields up its poisonous carbonic acid to the air. As soon as this office of mutual love is performed the lungs contract, and the poison-bearing air is forced to go forth and build up the substance of the plants.

But wise nature, or rather the divine wisdom indwelling nature, has used the wind-pipe, or trachea, for a still higher purpose. At the uppermost part of the wind-pipe, just below the cave of the mouth, nature has built a musical instrument called the larynx, which possesses excellencies of the very highest order. Though this musical instrument has but two chords, the two vocal chords, it has an astonishing range of note, an almost boundless power of modulation, a magic faculty of making the air vibrate with soul-bewitching song. By means of it and the other, secondary organs of speech, the infinite Spirit of All has enabled the finite spirit of man to create language, to translate into articulate sound all the phenomena of the universe, and the innermost causes which bind all the realms of nature together, to make manifest through the instrumentality of words the most impetuous as well as the gentlest stirrings of the emotions, and to communicate from mind to mind the inexhaustible wealth of the growing reason. What an immense progress from the howling of the wolf, the roaring of the lion, the bleating of the sheep, the bellowing of the ox, and the chattering of the ape, to the voice of man, to the entrancing song of a Patti, the stirring declamation of a Booth, and the majestic oratory of a Webster or Gladstone! But the evolution of the voice from uttering bestial sounds to being the perfect organ of the soul, is due to the beautiful mechanism of the human larynx, which, when once understood, fills the student with a sense of worshiping admiration for the living Purpose which shapes means to ever higher ends.

And as the divine creative Will and Reason have evolved, in man a magnificent organ of sound, to bring forth the witchery of song and to reveal the inner life of the soul, so He has formed a wondrous organ of hearing, to receive an almost boundless variety of sounds from nature and man, and transmit them as integral parts of experience to the seat of consciousness, where they are organized together with various elements of impression received through the other senses, into the living unity of thought. Who can fathom the world's mystery of mysteries, which weaves itself in nature's secret sanctuary into the purposeful forms of a life to come? In the breathless and silent night of budding existence organs of speech and hearing are fashioned, which perform their office only in the vibrating waves of the circumambient air. Him that planted the ear we can not but adore as supreme intelligence. For wonders of wisdom without number are wrought into the structure of the ear. Of three chambers the Master of life builded the echoing palace of sounds. The first chamber is open to the outer world and the atmosphere. It is closed toward the inner chamber by a membranous curtain, the ear-drum. At the entrance there oozes a fluid, to catch and hold fast intruding insects. The inner chamber is filled with air flowing in through a long channel whose open end is to be seen in the ceiling of the mouth. It is separated from the innermost chamber by a thin wall, in which there is a round window for communication. A trembling bridge made of three little bones, the hammer, the anvil, and the stirrup, is stretched through the length of the chamber from wall to wall, the stirrup resting in and filling up the opening of the round window. The innermost chamber, the labyrinth, is filled with water, which flows around magic vessels containing water. In and around the magic vessels, in the midst of the mysterious waters, there are myriads of musical strings, or keys, made up of the hair-like terminations of the auditory nerve. Wherever the ocean of air without is stirred into waves, the sonorous waves transplant themselves through the other chamber to the ear-drum, and cause it to vibrate. The shock is imparted to the anvil, the anvil moves the hammer, the hammer makes the stirrup quiver. Through the round window the quivering stirrup transfers its own undulating motion to the water within the innermost chamber. A moving shiver runs through the water. The wavelets touch the nerve strings and play upon them as on the keys of a musical instrument. The sound vibrations then travel upward along the pathway of the auditory nerve until the seat of consciousness, where they are translated into feelings, and formed into harmony and thought.

I will not attempt to expatiate on the stupendous wonders which the most perfect of all organs, the most important of the senses—the eye—displays, both in its general and minute structure. It would require a special lecture, replete with the most difficult anatomical and microscopic facts, to bring into view the divine logic incarnate in the organ of vision. Suffice it to say, that when I came to master the plan on which the human eye is constructed, I felt overwhelmed by a feeling of religious awe. Unforgettable as moments of deep religious experience will forever abide with me, the memory of those hours, when the study of the human eye forced upon me the conviction that an inscrutable reason dwells embodied in nature, and reveals itself in the ascending forms of unfolding animate life. The Infinite Self formed the eye to be a window to the soul of man, through which it shall look out upon the phenomena of the universe, receiving impressions of light and color, with all their modifications of intensity and combinations, and thereby acquiring the principal ideas of form, space, and movement.

XVIII

ADOLPH MOSES

Losing God and Finding God (1900)
A Day of Atonement Sermon

> "Seek ye the Lord while He may be found, call ye upon Him while He is near. Let the wicked forsake his way, and the man of sin his thoughts. Let him return to God who will have mercy on him, and to our Lord who will abundantly pardon."
>
> *(Isaiah, lv, 6–7.)*

God may be found, declares the prophet, at certain times favorable to spiritual insight and moral elevation. He is nigh unto us on sundry occasions, when the external and internal conditions awaken in us a quenchless longing to approach the source of all existence and the fountain of our own being. Since, then, God may be found by us at certain auspicious times, it follows that we may lose God under adverse outward and inward circumstances, which dull the organ of spirituality and divorce our soul from communion with the universal Power. Verily, one may lose his God. It sounds paradoxical enough, yet it is one of the most far-reaching and saddest truths. The fact is, our highest possessions are most easily lost. The noblest qualities of our humanity, the finest tendencies of our nature, the loftiest beliefs of the aspiring soul readily depart from us if we make no efforts to preserve and cultivate and develop them. The holiest spiritual wants of our soul are the first to disappear, when moral degeneration sets in. Our lowest qualities and passions, those which we have in common with animals or savages, will stay with us to the end. One may lose the love of knowledge; one may lose reverence for truth and the sense of abhorrence for falsehoods and calumnies; one may lose the love of justice,

192

the love of right and equity; one may lose the love of human brotherhood and the love of benevolence; one may lose the love of the beautiful and the sublime. With the loss of any of these qualities we lose
God in proportion. For they are the manifestations of the divine in
man. With their disappearance God fades out of our life. For God is
not a mere theory. The belief in God is not a philosophical truth which
we infer from given premises. God is not an object of knowledge like
any other knowledge to be stored up in our mind among the thousand
and one facts of observation and reasoning. God to us, in the deepest
and widest sense, is life, ever growing and rising life. God is universal
creative energy in nature; He is moral energy in man. The more truth,
the more God! The more justice, the more religion! The more love, the
more divinity in our soul! The more we break away from selfishness,
the more surely do we find God.

The idea of God and self-centered egotism form irreconcilable
contrasts. True religion and selfishness exclude and repel each other.
He that walks in the way of self-seeking can not find God. Narrow,
hard-hearted selfishness is the root of all sin and godlessness. Genuine
atheism never springs from philosophical reasoning, is never the result
of any theory of the world and man. Even those philosophers who deny
God with their lips have Him in their heart. They deny names, traditions, dogmas. But underneath their very unbelief there is stirring the
spirit of faith in the universal, divine unity, faith in the kinship of all
minds and the brotherhood of all men, faith in supreme and eternal
principles of goodness uniting all mortals and binding upon all souls.
Their denial and unbelief invariably lead to God along new pathways
of loftier thought. But true atheism or godlessness is always of a practical nature. It is the selfish life, as opposed to the life with God and
humanity. The real atheist is the individual who imprisons himself
within his own narrow self, shuts out all common and higher interests, separates himself from the joys and sorrows and burdens of the
world, is indifferent to all aims and relations which do not promise personal utility. This selfish isolation and blind self-love is atheism in its
essence and manifestation.

For the soul of all religion, theoretical and practical, is unity. Religion is the belief in the unity of all things, of nature and mankind, in
one eternal Being; the unity of all the works and the thoughts of man
in his long career on earth, the unity of all star systems and of the whole
drama of humanity's life, in one supreme all-wise Power. The truly

religious man feels and knows that he is a part, though an infinitesimal part, of the universal and eternal Unity. The fruit of that knowledge is humility. We stand in awe and meekness in the presence of the Infinite, with whom we are bound up together in every fibre of our being, in every thought and motion, in all our faculties and works. We find God the very moment we realize that we can not for one single instant break away from our relations to God as revealed in nature and humanity, as manifested in eternal laws governing the external world and determining every movement of the inner world. We feel our individual insignificance, because our eyes are ever straining to gaze upon the countenance of the divine unity and life. We feel our infinite dignity, because we know that we are a revelation of the Eternal. We break down all fences and walls which separate us from God in nature and humanity. Love draws us towards the center of existence, from which we have radiated. We try to complete our poor individual life by assimilating to ourselves the glory and beauty and wisdom and power of God unfolded in the endless evolution of His infinite life. We yearn after the parent cause of our being, and find God along the path of the knowledge of His ways. As soon as we strive to grow beyond the limits of our fragmentary, narrow self, we find ourselves standing before the majesty of the Divine and Eternal and Infinite, and in steady stream His light pours upon the soul which yearns to be at one with the universal mind. This is the reward of humility; the individual finds God near him, because he seeks Him in the universal life.

The footsteps of the Deity can be discerned along the highways of knowledge. The more knowledge we find, the more truly do we find God. Every truth we discover brings us nearer to Him, of whom all things are but signs and symbols. Knowledge growing from more to more is the progressive translation of the mind and life of the Infinite into the mind and life of man. For all nature is the incarnated thought and will of God.

The universe is the volume in which are writ the self-revelations of the Eternal. History is the record of the manifestations of His wisdom, of His attributes, of His all-wise laws, through the minds of superior men, who have felt after Him and longed after communion with His ways. Through knowledge the currents of the universal Mind flow into our individual mind. To use an expression of the Talmud, we are like the blessed in paradise. We sit rejoicing in the effulgence and glory of the Shechina, the divine Spirit diffusing itself through nature and humanity. This truth forms one of the central ideas of Judaism. Religion is called the knowledge of God and His ways. Again and again the injunction is laid upon Israel to know God and the books of revelation. "One of the chiefest crowns of our humanity is the crown of learning." He that despises knowledge turns away from God. "Because thou hast despised knowledge," says the prophet Hosea to the priesthood of his time, "He has rejected thee to be His priest." The love of His knowledge has been ever regarded by Judaism as the love of God. To pursue wisdom means to the true son of Israel to search after God.

Those of you who have lost the love of knowledge, the distinctive characteristic of Israel, have necessarily lost God. If a man shuts himself up forever in a room, closing all windows and doors, stopping up every keyhole and chink, he certainly can not know and judge the world without. He may see, by means of some rushlight or a few stray rays penetrating through some cracks, the few objects within his narrow prison. But all the beauty and glory and richness and joy in the world without will remain hidden from him, and his former knowledge thereof will soon fade out of his mind. If you are indifferent to the knowledge of nature and humanity, you willfully and permanently shut yourself up in the prison of your narrow self. You take note only of the few things which concern your own self, your personal wants and cares. But the great world without you, the majestic world of nature and the still more glorious world of mankind do not exist for you. Such men can not find God, because they have abandoned the way of knowledge, along which alone He can be found. Those who complain that they have lost God, that He is far from their mind and heart, ought to remember that this fatal condition is due to their own narrow materialistic selfishness. Those who have become all earthly have lost the mental organ by which to apprehend spiritual facts. Those who are wholly absorbed in things material, those whose faculties are entirely used up in the service of selfish gain and pleasure, have no means of entering the Temple of Truth, in whose holy of holies dwells enthroned the supreme idea, the idea of God. If you tie up the wings of your spirit so that they lose from want of use the power of upwards flight, how can you hope to rise into the pure and spiritual air of the ideal? If there is no spirit in you, how can you expect to approach in prayer, meditation, and aspiring knowledge the Spirit of all spirits? If you habitually refuse to seek a home for your mind in the world of ideas, it is impossible that you should feel yourself nigh unto Him who is the all-embracing, all-creative idea, the absolute and universal intelligence.

All men can not be searchers after truth, all men can not devote their best energies to the pursuit of knowledge in the field of nature and humanity, but all of us can bask in the light of truth, kindled by illumined minds. All of us may sit down as invited guests at the banquet of wisdom, prepared by innumerable men, who were rich in original insight, who hungered and thirsted after the knowledge of God.

Those who refuse to put themselves into close touch with the searchers after God, with the searchers after truth, simply bar their way to the blissful belief in an all-wise, all-penetrating, all-loving, divine Presence. For He has not left Himself without witnesses. He has spoken to us, and continually speaks to us, through the soul and with the voice of the path-finders of humanity, who have sought Him, His light and His truth, His laws of righteousness and love, with all their heart. The immortal lovers of God and man, the seers of the world, ascended to the summits of thought, which touch the very heavens, and brought down the light of God, the law of life, the treasures of wisdom more precious than all gold and all material pleasures. How can you hope to find God, if you refuse to follow the lead of the men of supreme genius who sought Him and His light all their life, who found Him along the path of knowledge and goodness? The Bibles of humanity lie open before us inviting us to take hold of the spiritual experience of the world's best and most original minds. If you refuse to read the pages written with the heart's blood of the wisest and noblest of the children of men, it is natural that your spiritual life should be pitiably poor. Many have lost God because in the pursuit of material interests they have lost the love of knowledge. Those who keep away from the house of God, who have suppressed within themselves the desire to listen to words of instruction, should not marvel that they can not find God in their hearts when they seek Him on rare occasions, such as this day. Those that habitually despise knowledge can not feel themselves priests of God when some strange mood or accident or a holiday moves them to approach Him. Let them resolve to abandon their ways of wilful ignorance. For callous indifference to knowledge is atheism. It leads to the death of the soul. Let them return to God and worship Him, as the all-sustaining, all-determining and creative Unity of all things. Let them find His ways by the light of knowledge.

Rising to still higher religious thought, we worship God, the universal Spirit, as the Unity of all spirits. As it is said: "He is the God of the spirits of all flesh." All minds are one in the Eternal Mind. All minds have their center and the cause of their unfolding faculties in God. He is the central sun of reason, and all minds revolve around Him, forming the living harmony of humanity in its relation to the parent source of all intelligence. Under this aspect, religion means to feel the kinship of all souls in God, to realize the brotherhood of all men by virtue of their spiritual unity in the Eternal. The more closely men unite themselves in social, religious, moral, and philanthropic relations, the more truly do they find God. For in this unity among men does God reveal Himself. Do we not read in the Sayings of the Father: "Whenever ten or even three men meet together and busy themselves with things spiritual, with matters concerning the laws of God and general welfare, the divine Spirit is among them"?

The first holy circle of divine unity amongst men is the unity between husband and wife. Husband and wife who love each other fervently and faithfully, who with each succeeding year of their wedded life grow more and more into one being, one soul and one heart, find God by this their love. He is with them in their mutual tenderness and self-sacrificing devotion. As far as they have conquered selfishness and become one through love, God is nigh unto them in their very heart and soul. But if husband and wife move through life without love, if their union is but that of prisoners for life, chained together by law, they surely can not find God, even though they may observe all outward forms of religious devotion. Those whose selfishness expels love from their marital relations, banish God, who is the fountain of all love and union, from their heart and home. To return to God, therefore, means first of all that the hearts of husband and wife should purge themselves of every taint of selfishness and blend together in love. By so doing they will find God.

Where mutual love, mutual respect and helpfulness bind together parents and children, brothers and sisters, all the members of such a household form a true family. Theirs is a spiritual unity which renews itself every day in their hearts and actions and words, and grows holier, stronger, and more beautiful with the advancing years of the parents and the unfolding of the children's bodies and minds. The spiritual unity of such a family is in very truth a revelation of the Lord of all spirits. Such parents and such children can not lose God, because He is stirring as love, as duty and devotion at the core of their hearts. The parents represent the mercy and wisdom of God and the spiritual growth of humanity to their children. The children represent the chain of spiritual unity with which the universal mind knits together all generations. A happy home is the first temple of God. The table at which father and mother and children sit together in joy and contentment is the true altar of the God of love. The unity of such a family, the unity in thought and feeling, in sympathy and co-operation, is the type and fountain-head of all forms of unity among men. It is the result and symbol of the unity subsisting between our common Father and all His children.

Those families in which parental ignorance and rudeness, filial ingratitude, disobedience, and hardness of heart keep father and mother and children estranged from one another, those families in which selfishness, envy, and mutual ill-will sway brothers and sisters, are a parody on the idea of God dwelling with the children of men and causing kindred beings to make one music of feeling, thought, and action. Such families are a travesty upon the belief that human love is a reflection of divine love. The fountains of faith, hope, and trust dry up in them. There may be daily prayers, religious ceremonies and observances, they may have God on their lips, but He is absent from their hearts. If we are to find God this day or any other day, we must turn our heart in love and faithfulness to our kindred. If thus we forsake the way of selfishness, God will have mercy on us and reveal Himself as union and love and kindness in the family circle.

That the family is the nursery and home of all true religion, was clearly perceived and beautifully stated by the seers of Israel. The chosen people, the people destined to bring the blessings of the belief in, and the worship of, one only God, the Maker of heaven and earth, the Father of all mankind, to all the races of the earth, is said to have taken rise in one family, the family of Abraham. The light of that faith was transmitted and increased through three successive generations of families. At last it became the heritage of a whole people, and that people was chosen to become a blessing and the means of union to all the families of the earth. This is an intimation of profound significance. Family union and family love must be enlarged in our sympathies to a union of the whole people, to a union of our whole religious community. Our heart and mind must at last embrace the whole human family within the circle of our highest interests. Our spirit must go forth in kindness towards all men and form a unity with all spirits. By such feelings of compassion for all, by such thoughts of all-embracing harmony to which actions must correspond, our life comes to be identified with the universal life of humanity. We make ourselves the center of mankind's ever-growing divine life. Our soul reflects the unity of all men in God. Our sympathy with their sorrows and joys is a direct revelation of the love of God for all His children. We find God in our heart and soul and action.

Let us all, however, take warning: Family love and unity may be hardened into family selfishness and godlessness. Many men make their home the prison of their soul. All love, all tenderness, all care and labor for their family alone, but callousness, utter indifference to the welfare of those standing without the pale of their family! The world at large has no existence to the hearts of such men, except as it may be exploited for their own families. The happiness of other families, the education and honor of other men's children are matters of indifference, if not of envy, to them. The cry of human suffering touches no chord of their hearts. The works of charity in which they share are not the results of genuine sympathy, but are due to social compulsion. Whatever good they may do to others, does not flow from love for their fellow-men, but from calculation or from an irksome sense of the impossibility to escape such deeds. Whatever pecuniary sacrifices they may occasionally make for philanthropic institutions, for congregational purposes, they regard as acts of robbery against their families. Their hearts do not beat in sympathy with the deathless life of their nation. They do not identify themselves with the eternal intellectual, moral and social interests of the people. Their narrow sympathies keep them outside the mighty currents of divine life manifested in the literature and the moral aspirations of their time and generation. They do not place themselves within earshot of the voice of the universal Spirit, speaking through His chosen instruments in art, philosophy, history, and all other utterances of the Divine in humanity. They refuse to take part in the sorrows and hopes, in the repentance and exultation of the human race. The word "humanity" is an empty sound to them. The ideals of humanity are regarded by them as the foolish day-dreams of visionaries. Living thus wilfully away from God who reveals Himself in the secular life of humanity, they naturally can not find Him. When their heart cries, Where is God? no divine voice answers from the heights of Sinai: "Here I am! The place whereon thou standest is holy ground, the sacred ground of humanity's spiritual growth through perennial communion with the Infinite."

All those that have lost God through narrowness and hardness of heart, all those from whom God is far, because they live in egotistical self-isolation, will find Him by renewing in contrition the covenant of brotherhood with their fellow-men, the covenant of active sympathy with humanity's life. God is the pre-established harmony of the spirits of all beings. By identifying ourselves with the personality, with the moral and intellectual interests and highest aspirations of our fellow-men, by forming a spiritual union, starting with the family and embracing ever larger and larger circles of humanity, we re-establish within us that divine harmony which had been overthrown or hidden by our selfishness. By abandoning the ways of self-seeking and returning to our fellow-men, we return to God. He is again found by us in our heart and soul. As we feel our oneness with the children of God in the spirit of love and faithful co-operation, we experience the presence of the Eternal, who is the cause and end of the unity of mankind.

"Love thy neighbor as thyself" and "Love the Lord, thy God, with all thy heart, with all thy soul, and with all thy might," of old have been declared to be the fundamental principles of Judaism. They cohere as the two sides of one idea. They are one creative truth, uttering itself forth in two strains. The love of man and the love of God spring from the belief in the unity of mankind embraced in the unity of God. He that loves his neighbor loves God, the Father of all men. He that loves God, in the true spirit of Israel and not according to ancient or modern paganism, can not help loving his fellow-men, because they are manifestations and symbols of the Divine.

Rising to the highest religious ideas of Israel, we worship God as absolute justice, infinite love, the parent source of all finite goodness, the prototype of all human love. We adore Him as the realized ideal of moral perfection. He is all-just, all-merciful, and holy. As it is said, "The Rock, all His doings are perfect, for all His ways are justice. He is a God of faithfulness without any evil. Just and upright is He. The Eternal is merciful and gracious, abundant in mercy and truth." The attributes of God well up from the soul of man as moral ideas. His ways are revealed as the ways of eternal life to individuals and nations. His being is the universal law; the qualities of His holy will manifest themselves as moral laws in the consciousness of those that seek Him. To love God means to walk in His ways. The destiny of man, individual and collective, is to become an image, however faint, of divine perfection. The highest aim of man is to grow steadily in the elements of justice and mercy and truth. This is the highest end of human life, both of the individual and of humanity. The moral good is our ultimate good. All other ends are but means to that supreme end. The noblest of all ambitions is to strive to be godlike in doing justice, in loving mercy, and walking humbly in the ways of God. A man may obtain the most coveted objects of all forms of ambition, and yet, if he misses that one ambition, if he fails to develop a character swayed in all its movements by the moral laws, his whole life is worthless and a striving after the wind. A good man needs not to ask, Where is God? For He is ever nigh unto him. If you love justice and do battle for it, you have found God, for He is justice. If you have compassion on the poor, succor the needy, clothe the naked, lift up the fallen, and dry the tears of the widow and the orphan, you are realizing the will of the living God. The God of love is with you, revealing Himself in the beauty and holiness of your charitable works. A just and merciful man shares in the life of God. He co-operates with the plans of Providence and helps to work out the salvation of the race. He is the instrument of God in uprooting evil and planting good, in fighting the powers of hatred and malice. He is spreading the reign of universal love.

But he who is not fired with the ambition to grow in the qualities of goodness, necessarily loses God. The individual or the nation that rebels against justice, that tramples underfoot the rights of the weak and the stranger, can not approach God. He that gathers riches by fraud and violence, he who builds his house by injustice, can not find God in his heart nor in the bosom of his family. God and wickedness can not dwell together. If you take no delight in doing works of charity, if you do not seek happiness in making your fellow-men happy, how can you hope to find God, who is the Father of love and the Giver of all good? Selfishness is the root of sin. The sins of injustice and cruelty of every kind banish us from the presence of God. "Your sins," says the prophet, "have separated you and Me, your Lord." Immorality in feeling, thought, and action is true atheism, practical atheism, which is an abomination to God and the soul of humanity. The prayers of the unjust, the uncharitable, and the false are blasphemies. Their temples are dens of moral vileness. The religion of persecutors, the worship of race-proud maligners, is hateful to the Father of mankind. Says the prophet Isaiah: "When ye come to appear before Me, who hath required this at your hands, to tread My courts? Your appointed feasts My soul hateth. And when ye spread forth your hands, I will hide Mine eyes from you. Yea, when ye make many prayers, I will not hear; your hands are full of blood. Wash ye, make you clean; put away the evil of your doings from before Mine eyes; cease to do evil; learn to do well; seek judgment, relieve the oppressed, judge the fatherless, plead for the widow. Then, though your sins by as scarlet, they shall be as white as snow; through they be red like crimson, they shall be as wool." The monition also comes to us from the heart of infinite goodness; the same promise of divine presence and grace addresses itself to us on this great Day of Atonement. The genius of Israel cries aloud: "Seek ye the Lord, while He may be found. Call upon Him, while He is near. Let the wicked forsake his way, and the man of sin his thoughts." Those who have lost God, who is the realized ideal of perfection and the fountain of all goodness, will find Him, if they make man's highest good, the moral ideal, the chief theme of their thoughts and the leading motive of all their actions. Those who complain that God is far from them will soon feel the breath of His presence, if they forsake the ways of pitiless selfishness and strive to make themselves a blessing to their fellow-men. Let but the unrighteous man prostrate himself in humility before the throne of Justice, let the uncharitable open his hand and heart to the poor and needy, and lo and behold, the certainty of divine mercy and compassion will come to him with healing on its wings.

If you strive steadily to stamp your character with the likeness of divine qualities, if you make it the highest ambition of your existence to be fellow-worker with God in establishing justice and mercy and truth on earth, He will be nigh unto you, and you will feel in your heart the uplifting influence of His spirit. You will understand in your soul the beneficent purposes of His providence, and through wisdom and sacrifices endeavor to carry His will into execution. Your sorrows and your joys, your sufferings and hopes will help you to realize that you are not alone and forsaken, but that He is with you, even in the night of your affliction, disciplining you to the service of suffering humanity. If you break away from selfishness, your very griefs and pains will prove spiritual blessings to you. They will open your heart to sympathize with the sufferings of your fellow-men. They will cause you to thrill with godlike compassion for the afflicted children of men. They will cause you to go forth as a messenger of God's mercy, to heal wounds and dry tears, to turn sadness into joy and despair into hope. By such growth in the beauty and holiness of saving compassion you will fulfill the highest aims of religion. For every man is destined to be a watchman and tiller in this garden planted by God, a sower of good and uprooter of evil. We are all called to co-operate with God in making human life ever better, ever more spiritual and beautiful.

We can not understand the mystery of evil, but this much we know, that it is to be made, by works of love and by submission, a means of salvation and moral growth. The world, alas, is full of evils, physical and mental. There are the innumerable ills which flesh is heir to. There are the diseases which gnaw at the vitals, consume the marrow of our bones, float as poison in our blood, rack our nerves, and torture our brain. There are the terrors of imagination, worse than all real evils. There are the evils born of folly and sin, which have come down with us from the years bygone, dogging our steps, harrowing our conscience, and meting out a hundredfold retribution for past transgressions. There are the evils born of the wickedness and brutality of men, the evils of hatred and prejudice, of bloodthirsty religious or racial fanaticism. There are the evils of willful [wilful] falsehood and treacherous calumny. All these demons of evil plague the human race, and who of us has not his share of them?

Some men find God through sorrow and suffering, far more lose Him through pain and distress. The selfish man, when he is in tribulation, physical or mental, cries in the agony of his soul that he can find God nowhere, neither in the world without nor within his own soul. In prosperity and health he lives in egotistical self-isolation, far from his fellow-men and far from God. In sorrow and sickness also he dwells alone or in the narrow prison of his poor self. Woe to the selfish man, when he is beset with evils! Woe to him when nature assails him, with her poisoned arrows, when she takes pitiless vengeance on him for transgressions committed wittingly or unwittingly! Whither shall he flee for refuge from himself? In what thought can egotism offer him a means of self-delivery? He has cared for the world only as far as it supplied him with his wants. He has interested himself in the life of his fellow-men only as far as he could use them for his own interests. To him the idea of God is that of a purveyor of the necessaries and pleasure of his life. God is to him a mighty Being that is invoked for assistance in times of distress and is dismissed and forgotten when no longer needed. He has never identified himself with God and His eternal laws, ruling nature and mankind. He has never identified himself with the deathless sorrows and joys, with the struggles and defeats and victories of humanity. Therefore he is left alone with his troubles. He has infinite pity and hot tears for himself in his misery, but he has no heart-sprung tears and no genuine compassion for others. For this reason he is shut up in darkness with himself. Let his wretched god of self rise up and help him. He may multiply prayers, but all his prayers are but empty words. He has worshiped and served only self; therefore, there is no response from the universal Soul to his dwarfed soul. There is no way of leading from his fenced-in self to Him who is infinite Love, the Father and Saviour of all the children of men. Thus it is that many men lose God through sorrow and suffering, and cry out in their heart, "There is no God."

Yet seasons of distress teach nobler natures to find God more than ever. They learn to know and value the ministry of sorrow and suffering as a crown of glory, as a means of salvation to themselves and others. They realize more vividly than ever the fact that they are a part, though most insignificant part, of the universal order of things. They feel they are an integral part, living members, of the immortal being called humanity. In humility and submission they return to God, who is the unity of nature and mankind, and whose love they recognize in their sufferings. They take up the will of God into their own will. Lovingly they embrace the laws of God in nature as the laws of their own being. They pray with the seers and the martyrs of Israel: "Thy will be done, O God, in heaven and on earth." They recognize that sorrow and suffering are blessings in disguise, that they have been the means of tearing down the walls of self and making man a citizen of the universe. They recognize that sufferings and trials have been and are the means used by Providence to awaken the human mind from its slumber, to compel the spirit of man to find the ways of the Eternal and through the works of reason to bring a thousandfold good out of evil.

We shall find God, if we come to be thankful for our very sufferings and trials, using them as means of moral discipline and spiritual growth. He will be nigh unto us, if we accept in grateful meekness the painful consequences of our sins, regarding them as manifestations of divine justice, indwelling the constitution of things. We shall no longer cry, "Where is God?" if our sorrows tend to emancipate us from the bondage of selfishness, if they cause our hearts to sympathize with the woes of our fellow-men, impelling us to hasten to the rescue of those in danger, to lift up the fallen, to dry the tears of the poor and oppressed. Doing the work of divine mercy to the best of our ability, we shall experience the grace of Heaven, rising as from a living spring from our soul. As the fruit springs from the blossom, so will atonement be the issue of our own merciful feelings and actions. Let us be grateful for our sufferings and sorrows, and regard them not only as a proof of divine retribution, but also as signs of divine love toward us. For there are sufferings of love, according to the wise men of Israel. God intends to try us, and to bring into play all the hidden possibilities of our nature.

Such is the disposition which religion should produce. Such the attitude of mind and heart, which the Day of Atonement is to bring about. Let us, therefore, return to God, to humanity, and our own higher self by dint of our sorrows and tribulations. Let us willingly fall heir to the virtues and the experiences of Israel. For suffering ever was and still is the badge of the Chosen People. It was through infinite suffering that they have been chosen from among all nations to give birth to the religion of humanity. Israel's endless sorrows have been the means of abounding grace, of the gospel of mercy and holiness to the families of the earth. On this Day of Atonement we offer thanks unto the God of Love, that He has made Israel his suffering servant through whom Justice is to be established on earth. Let us take to heart the saying of the rabbis, "Suffering is a blessing to Israel," and let us add, the martyrdom of Israel has been and still is a blessing to the world. The whole Bible is the passion flower which has grown out of the bleeding heart of Israel. Let us fall heir to the great principle, realized by Israel, that knowledge is worship and wilful ignorance a denial of God. Let us bear the truth in our hearts, that an ignorant Jew, one who refuses to make use of the means of wisdom and culture offered to him, is a godless Jew, a shame to the name and conduct of his forefathers. On this great Day of Atonement let us atone for our shortcomings and sins by resolving to make the moral life the highest purpose of our existence. Let us fall heir to the belief of Israel, that it is man's mission to grow Godward in the divine qualities of justice, mercy, and truth. Let us fall heir to the belief of Israel that God is the living, intelligent Unity of nature and humanity.

Let us try to realize the awful idea of that Unity, by making our will move in harmony with His will, by identifying ourselves with the highest interests of humanity. Let religion do a great and noble work for every one of us. Religion should so educate us that our individual life and being shall be, through love, a center of the life of God in man. Religion is the idea of the Universal Unity, the synagogue is the symbol of that idea, worship is its realization. Today we are nearer that realization than on other days, mostly given to personal, material interests or pleasures. Today we are forming a spiritual union in this House of God, rising from grade to grade in dignity and universality. Today each family is united before God, its love being consecrated by the presence of Divine Love. Today we represent the spiritual union of all Israel, past, present, and future. As the people of humanity we give testimony to our faith in the indestructible spiritual unity of all nations of the earth. Today we pray for the peace and moral advancement and happiness of all the peoples, even those that torment and persecute the children of Israel. Today we rise on the wings of meditation and prayer to the firm belief that Yahve, our God, is One, the Law-giver, the King, the Father of all men, that in due time He will establish the kingdom of righteousness on earth. Today we seek Him and find Him. Today we are blessed in knowing that He is nigh unto us, when we call unto Him. Today let each and every one of us abandon the way of self-seeking and forsake the path of sin. Today let us return to God, for He is full of compassion, and to our Lord, who will abundantly pardon. Amen!

Index